THE
INVESTIGATION
OF
RALPH NADER

THE INVESTIGATION OF RALPH NADER

GENERAL MOTORS VS. ONE DETERMINED MAN

by THOMAS WHITESIDE

 **ARBOR HOUSE** NEW YORK

Contents

PART ONE

PART TWO

PART THREE

TO MARIE

PART ONE

1

"A Kind of Uneasy Feeling"

IT WAS DURING the second week of January, 1966, in the Kirkwood Hotel in Des Moines, Iowa, that Ralph Nader first developed the feeling that someone was keeping him under
surveillance. Nader had gone to Des Moines at the invitation
of the Iowa State Attorney General, Lawrence F. Scalise, to
testify during a series of hearings in the state capitol on automobile safety. The previous November, a book by Nader, "Unsafe at Any Speed," had come on the market; its severe criticisms of the automobile manufacturing industry had been
stirring up considerable attention in the press and other media;
and Attorney General Scalise expected that Nader's testimony
before his state committee would be both provocative and
valuable. However, the publicity about "Unsafe at Any Speed"
was not the only reason that Scalise had invited Nader to Des
Moines; Scalise had met Nader the previous year at a seminar
in Washington, D.C., conducted by the American Trial Lawyers
Association, of which both men were members, and Scalise
had been highly impressed with Nader's views on the design
and manufacture of automobiles and product liability, and,
beyond that, on broad questions involving the interrelationship
of large corporations, the law, and the public interest. Scalise
had also been impressed with Nader's unusually determined
concern in the field of consumer protection.

At the time of his appearance in Des Moines, Nader was

nearly thirty-two years old; he was a tall, intense-mannered, dark-complexioned, and very thin man, his black, curly hair cut high around his ears. Nader had been born in Winsted, Connecticut, of parents who originated in Lebanon. He had gone through high school in his home town, after which, at the age of seventeen, he had gone on to Princeton, from which he had graduated *magna cum laude* in 1955, having studied at the Woodrow Wilson School of Public and International Affairs. In 1955, he had entered the Harvard Law School, where he became editor of the Law *Record,* a publication that he attempted, against considerable opposition, to turn into a journal of social significance. Nader was already very much involved in such social issues as the rights of American Indians. At the Harvard Law School, Nader had found prevalent an air of elitism distasteful to him; he saw the school as being more concerned with the training of a generation of corporation lawyer-technicians rather than a generation of young men interested in the law, as he was, as an instrument of social change. Nader's own interests at law school became focussed on such legal issues as what he considered a most serious lack of proper accountability on the part of large corporations to the legislative and regulatory arms of government, and, above all, to the public itself.

In pursuing this theme, Nader, during his final year, had written a long legal term paper on automobile design and product liability. The theme of the paper was that lack of proper corporate accountability to the public interest was responsible, in the automobile manufacturing industry, for a pattern of design defects in cars that was contributing heavily to the annual number of deaths in traffic accidents. The further Nader had gone into this particular subject, the more deeply he had become convinced that the problem of design defects in cars was one of overwhelming national urgency; and this conviction was hardly dissipated by Nader's having witnessed, while hitchhiking around the country as a student, several serious traffic accidents.

In 1960, having graduated from law school and served a

six-month tour of active duty in the Army Reserve at Fort Dix, Nader had entered private practice in Hartford. After four years of this, he had left commercial law and had gone to Washington to pursue the cause of what he liked to call "public interest law," and in particular to pursue the cause of auto safety. He managed to support himself, on a bare subsistence basis, by means of occasional lectures and articles that he wrote, mostly on auto safety, for the *New Republic* and *The Nation.*

During 1963 and part of 1964, Nader did freelance writing on auto safety for the *Christian Science Monitor,* and worked, on a consultancy basis, as a writer and researcher for Daniel P. Moynihan, then the Assistant Secretary of Labor. For Moynihan, Nader prepared position papers concerning the direction that the Administration might take on automobile safety legislation. Moynihan himself had been deeply concerned since the fifties about the relationship between automobile design and highway safety, and had written knowledgeably on the subject in the late fifties, when he had been an aide to Governor Averell Harriman in Albany.

At the end of 1964, and after Nader had finished his assignments for Moynihan, Senator Abraham A. Ribicoff of Connecticut—who, during his terms as Governor of Connecticut, had introduced and enforced with unusual strictness new traffic safety regulations—was considering what legislative measures in traffic safety he might effect on a federal level. In doing so, Ribicoff was considerably influenced by a major work involving auto safety published during 1964—"Accident Research," by William Haddon, Jr., Edward A. Suchman, and David Klein. This book, a compendium of articles on accident research, considered the problem of traffic safety as a problem of public health. One of its chapters dealt in general with the consequences of the crashworthiness of vehicles, and discussed in some detail the toll of the so-called "second collision," after the initial impact in a car accident, between the occupants and the car itself, or their ejection from it. Senator Ribicoff decided, as head of the Senate Subcommittee on Executive Reorganization (essentially, a subcommittee on oversight in governmental functions), to hold public hearings on how the government was organized to deal with traffic safety. His intention was that the role of the automobile as well as of the driver in car accidents should be explored for purposes of drawing up traffic safety legislation. The members of the subcommittee included Senator Fred Harris and Senator Robert F. Kennedy. Just before the end of 1964, the Ribicoff subcommittee's chief counsel, Jerome Sonosky, heard that Nader was a man extremely well informed on auto safety and auto design hazards. Sonosky and Nader got together at the subcommittee's office in the Old Senate Office Building for a long talk on auto safety. The result of this talk and others was that Nader became a voluntary, unpaid adviser to the subcommittee staff during the preparation for the forthcoming safety hearings. These hearings began in March, 1965, and were resumed in July. At the July hearings, the chief executives of General Motors, including Frederic G. Donner, chairman of the board, and James M. Roche, the president of the corporation, testified and were questioned about their role in auto safety. Members of the committee seemed rather unimpressed with the forthrightness of the company's witnesses. Senator Kennedy, in particular, showed some impatience over what he plainly considered a low priority assigned to crash safety research by General Motors, and by the imprecision or apparent forgetfulness of the men in charge of the corporation, as indicated in this exchange:

> *Senator Kennedy:* What was the profit of General Motors last year?
> *Mr. Roche:* I don't think that has anything to do—
> *Senator Kennedy:* I would like to have that answer if I may. I think I am entitled to know that figure. I think it has been published. You spend a million and a quarter dollars, as I understand it, on this aspect of safety. I would like to know what the profit is.
> *Mr. Donner:* The one aspect we are talking about is safety.
> *Senator Kennedy:* What was the profit of General Motors last year?

Mr. Donner: I will have to ask one of my associates.

Senator Kennedy: Could you, please?

Mr. Roche: $1,700,000,000.

Senator Kennedy: . . . You made $1.7 billion last year?

Mr. Donner: That is correct.

Senator Kennedy: And you spent $1 million on [safety research]?

Mr. Donner: In this particular facet we are talking about . . .

Senator Kennedy: If you just gave 1 percent of your profits, that is $17 million.

Between these hearings, Nader was busying himself intermittently with notes for another writing project that he hadn't got very far with. In the summer of 1964, Richard Grossman, a maverick book publisher who ran what amounted to a one-man organization in New York, had become interested in auto safety, and had started to look around for a likely author to prepare a competent book on the subject. Grossman approached James Ridgeway, a young investigative reporter who was then working on an article for the *New Republic* about the unusual number and types of serious accidents associated with the sporty new rear-engined Corvair compact car that General Motors had introduced into the auto market in the model year of 1960, and asked Ridgeway if he had time to write such a book. Ridgeway said that he hadn't, but he suggested that Grossman get in touch with Nader, whose knowledgeability on the subject of auto safety and auto defects he said he had relied on in writing the article about the Corvair. Grossman then approached Nader, who agreed to the project and in September, 1964, signed a contract with Grossman for "an untitled book on auto safety." The result was "Unsafe at Any Speed."

In his book, Nader presented a heavily documented indictment of the automobile industry and the existing traffic safety establishment for massive failures in protecting the public from hazardously designed automobiles, and of the government itself for its failure to set adequate safety standards for the manufacture of cars. And he did so within a wide framework of criticism of the existing social and economic structure. "A great problem of contemporary life is how to control the power of economic interests which ignore the harmful effects of their applied science and technology," he wrote. "The automobile tragedy is one of the most serious of these man-made assaults on the human body. . . . Our society's obligation to protect the 'body rights' of its citizens . . . requires the . . . front-rank support which is being devoted to civil rights."

Then Nader spelled out the dimensions of the tragedy— 45,000 deaths on the highway each year, a million people injured, and an estimated direct cost each year to the country of $8.3 billion in property damage, medical expenses, lost wages, and insurance overhead expenses, and an equal sum in indirect cost that totalled something like two percent of the gross national product. The theme of Nader's book was that the "traffic safety establishment," consisting of private organizations like the National Safety Council and governmental organizations dealing with highway safety like the Department of Commerce and its Bureau of Public Roads, was so heavily influenced by the huge commercial force of individual automobile manufacturers and their trade and lobbying associations, such as the Automobile Manufacturers Association, that its members were being systematically deluded as to a prime cause of the death and destruction on the highways and streets. This systematic delusion, Nader wrote, was the skillful fostering and perpetuation of a myth that was passively accepted by the press and public—the myth that traffic deaths were essentially due to careless driving—to what automobile industry spokesmen kept referring to as "the nut behind the wheel." What Nader had to say, in great detail, was that the existing design of automobiles prevented drivers from using their full capacities to prevent crashes. He pointed out that for the driver the second line of defense in a crash should be the car itself, and that a properly designed car had the potential to prevent or alleviate many of the serious consequences of a crash. Nader's thesis was that a vast number of the annual deaths on the highway were in fact due to unsafe car design and faulty manufacture, and that the automobile industry had been systematically leaving at hazard the lives of passengers by deliberately neglecting design for safety —energy-absorbing bumpers and steering columns, padded dashboards, and passive restraints to protect passengers in a second collision—in favor of flashy styling and car-salesroom gimmickry. What had happened, Nader declared, was that in the rush for profits, the automobile industry was transferring hidden costs, represented by the built-in hazards of the uncrashworthy cars they produced, to the consumer; that substantial parts of the manufacturing costs of cars that should have been going into safety features had been poured, instead, into jukebox dashboards, wildly stamped metal parts such as flaring tailfins, and all sorts of other gewgaws that the sales managers of the auto companies, the Madison Avenue ad men, and the car salesmen could promote as part of what certain Detroit executives proudly called "creative obsolescence." The financial cost to the buyer of a car as the result of the tyranny of the annual styling changes of automobiles came to something like seven hundred dollars a year, Nader charged, but the cost in human suffering that resulted from an industry practice of consistently putting styling, sales, and increased profits ahead of safety he regarded as almost beyond contemplation. Nader's book was dedicated to Frederick Hughes Condon, a classmate and friend of Nader's at Harvard Law School who had become seriously crippled as a result of an automobile accident.

Nader's thesis was not a new one, in the sense that a very small number of people outside the automobile industry, who included Haddon and Moynihan, had already been writing, in scientific vein, about the scope and nature of the tragedy brought about by the modern automobile. As far back as 1959, for example, Moynihan had written, in *The Reporter* magazine, a very prescient article presenting his and Dr. Haddon's views on the problem of traffic safety—that this was a problem of health to be approached by the discipline of epidemiology rather than merely by the discipline of law enforcement. But what Nader did, in "Unsafe at Any Speed," was successfully to convey to the reader, in a sharp, vigorous, adversary style, a sense of the leadership of an entire industrial complex in collusion—in collusion with itself and with legislative and regulatory bodies over which it exerted a most powerful influence—to deprive the public not only of the safely designed vehicles to which it was entitled but also of basic information concerning the vast number of defective cars capable of causing death and destruction on the highways on a massive and continuing scale.

In the course of doing so, Nader focussed his attack on what he declared to be lethal deficiencies of design in one particular car—the 1960 through 1963 models of the General Motors Corvair.

The Corvair had been conceived by the engineering staff of General Motors Chevrolet Division, and in particular by Edward N. Cole, then the head of that division, as an engineering breakthrough—the first American automobile to be built with a swing-axle independent rear suspension and with an aluminum, air-cooled engine mounted in the rear. The Corvair was supposed to incorporate the very latest knowledge and deepest experience in rear-engine car design, and this design was supposed to provide the occupants of the car with a pleasing combination of a stable vehicle, a good ride, and easy handling characteristics. The car was in the compact class, yet it was supposed to carry six people comfortably, and it was made with a sporty look. In the four model years from 1960 through 1963, General Motors dealers sold approximately a million and a quarter Corvairs to the driving public. In "Unsafe at Any Speed," Nader's thesis was that the Corvair, in its 1960-63 model form, was a lethally unstable car; that, in designing it, the General Motors people had ignored warnings in the early fifties from Maurice Olley, one of G.M.'s own most creative engineers, in a technical paper concerning inherent hazards of this type of rear-engined automobile; that the Corvair had a fatal tendency to go out of control and to roll over, especially in cornering under certain conditions; that many of these accidents were associated with a dangerous tendency of one or another rear wheel to "tuck under" the chassis under these conditions; that many deaths and injuries (some horrifying examples of which Nader cited from more than 100 product liability lawsuits brought against General Motors on behalf of people or the estates of people killed or injured in accidents involving Corvair cars of the 1960-63 vintage) had resulted from these alleged design defects; that the principal officers of General Motors could hardly but be aware of the existence of these defects; that the company nonetheless had concealed essential facts about the stability of the Corvair from the public and had neglected to take appropriate steps to minimize these defects until the 1964 model year.

"Unsafe at Any Speed" was published on November 1, 1965, and the charges that Nader had made in it, particularly those concerning the Corvair, got considerable attention in the press; Nader himself was interviewed by a number of reporters, and he put in several appearances on television interview programs to talk about automobile safety.

On January 6, 1966, Nader held a press conference at the Sheraton Cadillac Hotel in Detroit to discuss automobile safety and the criticism of the automobile manufacturers that he had made in "Unsafe at Any Speed," and he had sent an open invitation to each of the four big automobile companies to send representatives to debate him at the same press conference. The invitation was either ignored or declined by the companies. General Motors, through Louis Goad, a General Motors executive vice-president and assistant to James M. Roche, president of General Motors, issued a statement saying, "We do not agree with the conclusions drawn by Mr. Nader and can see no point in engaging in a discussion with him concerning these conclusions at a press conference." However, the G.M. statement invited Nader, in turn, "to discuss these important matters" with engineers of the company at the General Motors Technical Center at Warren, Michigan. When a reporter asked Nader at his press conference at the Sheraton Cadillac about the G.M. offer, Nader said that he had already visited the G.M. Technical Center several times. "You always get the standard tour," he told the reporter. "They [G.M. officials] won't talk specifics; they brush off questions with the reply that the information is 'proprietary.'" However, after the press conference, Nader said that he would try again at the G.M. Technical Center, in the hope that this time his visit would produce some frank discussion of issues he had raised in his book, and he notified G.M. that he would accept the invitation to visit it.

On January 7, Nader went on to Des Moines to participate in the series of hearings that State Attorney General Lawrence Scalise had scheduled there. Scalise himself already had had, for some time, a deep interest in the automobile safety issue and in the general area of consumer protection. As Attorney General of Iowa, Scalise had managed to get a state consumer protection law put on the books. The state law allowed the State Attorney General to hold hearings on all subjects involving defects in merchandise sold to the public. (At that time, Iowa and Illinois were the only states in the Union that made such official public hearings legally feasible.) It was this authority that enabled Scalise to convene the January hearings on auto safety.

Besides Nader, Scalise had invited a number of other specialists in automobile safety problems. They included Jeffrey O'Connell, a professor of law at the University of Illinois and the co-author of "Safety Last," another well-documented book on auto safety that had been published around the same time as "Unsafe at Any Speed"; Dr. Paul Gikas, a pathologist at the University of Michigan who had been studying—very often at first hand, by hurrying to the scene of automobile accidents that had just occurred—the types and extent of injuries suffered by the victims of auto crashes and their relationship to design components of the cars involved in these crashes; and Dr. Thomas Manos, a former principal design engineer for the Ford Motor Company and now an associate professor of mechanical engineering at the University of Detroit, where he specialized in motor vehicle safety design and crash research. Scalise also invited the heads of each of the American automobile manufacturing companies to testify, or to send company representatives to do so. But each of the companies declined. When the hearings started, a number of automobile industry people were on hand to witness the proceedings, but the only representative of the automobile business to testify was Karl M. Richards, of the Automobile Manufacturers Association, the principal trade association and lobbying arm of the industry, and he was not an engineer.

In his testimony, Nader called the refusal of individual automobile companies to have their own people appear a "shocking display of contempt" for the people of Iowa. He asked, indignantly, "What reasons could there be for auto makers, who have taken literally billions of dollars out of the State of Iowa through the sales of their trucks and automobiles, not to ... appear in person and answer questions pertaining to the hundreds of deaths and thousands of injuries which occur yearly in this state involving the operation of those products which they sell?" He went on, "There is quite an enormity to this arrogance, I think."

Nader pointed out that, unlike any other transportation vehicle—the airplane for example—the automobile did not have to meet meaningful pre-production public safety standards, that its role in causing accidents and injuries was still virtually uninvestigated, and that the auto manufacturer, unlike the driver, was under the restraint of no criminal sanctions if he built lethal defects into his car. What the industry needed, he said, was to be brought within a "responsible rule of law" in the interests of public safety. "Power is the only language the industry understands," he said, "as befits any Goliath ranking so high on the corporate brutality index for so long with so little challenge."

And Nader went on to enumerate a series of regulatory steps that he believed Iowa could enact to protect the consumer from unsafe automotive design. They included mandatory filing by automobile companies of all service bulletins; a requirement that all motor vehicles purchased by the state be required to meet standards beyond those currently established by the General Services Administration for purchases of automobiles by the U.S. Government; and the establishment of fully equipped and properly qualified teams of state inspectors to investigate automobile accidents occurring in the state. If such investigating teams already existed, he said, "the Corvair problem would have been uncovered within the first year of that automobile's macabre performance on the highways of Iowa and the other states."

Shortly after Nader finished testifying, Richards, of the Automobile Manufacturers Association, gave the committee a glowing account of the progress of automotive safety in this country and the interest of the automobile manufacturing industry in promoting it further, particularly in the area of driver improvement, which, following the industry line, he called "our greatest hope" for traffic safety improvement in the future. "Gentlemen, we have done a magnificent job in the United States, if you look at it," he told the committee. "I certainly feel . . . that we have been able to do a great job in maintaining a working uniformity of the [highway safety programs of the] states and I attribute this to the fine and intelligent cooperation of the public officials in the states and legislatures. . . . It couldn't have been achieved otherwise and I think sometimes you underestimate the intelligence of these people. They are not going to be carried away by half-thought-out ideas of inexperienced people."

Later on in the proceedings that day, Nader put a series of sharp questions to Richards concerning the publication by automobile manufacturers of data on the crashworthiness of their vehicles. Richards said that before he answered Nader's questions, he had some of his own. "I am rather curious to know what your connection is here," he said. "You are not a citizen of Iowa. Who pays your expenses out here?"

Nader replied that, like other witnesses who had testified on automobile safety, he had been paid nothing except out-of-pocket expenses, and that these were reimbursed by the State of Iowa. Richards then gave Nader some generalized answers.

It was in the period preceding and following his appearance before the Scalise committee that Nader began to feel other signs of curiosity about his presence in Des Moines. Several times and in several places in the Kirkwood Hotel during his stay he noticed a man hovering in his vicinity— he remembers seeing him twice on the first floor and once outside his room on an upstairs floor—and something about the man's demeanor as well as his repeated presence gave Nader what he has described as "a kind of uneasy feeling" that the man was there to keep an eye on his movements.

The feeling was strong enough to cause Nader, toward the end of the hearings, to inform Scalise of his developing suspicions. Scalise became sufficiently concerned about what he thought might be a possible case of harassment of a witness before his committee that he ordered the state Bureau of Criminal Investigation to look into the matter. But, Scalise has recalled, by the time the state investigation really got under way the safety hearings were over, the state investigators were unable to turn up any useful leads concerning the source of Nader's uneasiness, and the matter was dropped.

2

"Why Don't You Go Back to Connecticut, Buddy Boy?"

ON JANUARY 14, a day after the hearings in Des Moines ended, Nader, accepting the invitation that General Motors had extended to him earlier, went by appointment to the General Motors Technical Center at Warren, Michigan. With him he took Dr. Gikas, the pathologist and automobile-crash investigator. The two men were shown into the office of Edward Cole, who was then an executive vice-president of General Motors and who is now president of the corporation. There, with Cole, were three other high General Motors executives—executive vice-president Louis Goad, Harry F. Barr, vice president in charge of engineering, and Lawrence R. Hafstad, vice-president in charge of research. There was also present a man some of whose activities Nader was to learn more about during the next three months—Louis H. Bridenstine, the assistant general counsel of General Motors. "At the time when General Motors invited me out, I was under the rather naïve impression that their chief purpose was to have a frank exchange of views," Nader said later on. He found Bridenstine friendly enough. He was holding in one hand a copy of "Unsafe at Any Speed," and Nader noticed that the top edge of the volume was "just bristling" with paper clips, presumably as page markers. "Bridenstine said that they had spent six weeks with the book," Nader has said. "They'd obviously checked *everything*. The only thing they seemed to have come up with was that I had put two quotes together, as one, without any dots to indicate that words had been omitted. That happened to have been a typo."

Nader was told that he would be shown a presentation in a nearby conference room that dealt with the design and handling characteristics of the Corvair. Before he was taken to the conference room, Nader was asked by Bridenstine, in a manner that Nader took to be a request for a clarification before Nader actually saw the presentation, whether Nader represented any clients in Corvair cases. Nader says that Bridenstine then added a few words to indicate that he didn't believe Nader did represent such clients. Nader has said that he told Bridenstine "very clearly" that he did not.

Nader remembers the general atmosphere of this encounter with the top management level at General Motors as being marked by a certain attitude of bonhomie—"they quickly insisted that everything be on a first-name basis"—and an air that, despite their differences, they were really all in the same cause together, and could even pursue that cause with mutual profit.

According to Nader, "Three times during my visit Ed Cole made the hint—trying to size me up—that I might turn out to be more effective putting my ideas to work from the inside rather than from the outside. 'Why don't you come over and join us—put your ideas to work here?'—that was the gist of it." Nader says he ignored such remarks. During his visit Nader was shown, as part of the presentation on the Corvair, films of the Corvair in action, films that the General Motors people indicated to him showed the Corvair to be a stable car under various driving conditions. He was also taken on a tour of the G.M. proving grounds. Nader left the G.M. Technical Center with the feeling that his arguments on behalf of auto safety had made no real impression on his audience, and that he had been made the object of a not-so-subtle exercise to see if he couldn't be bought off and shut up by being put on the G.M. payroll. His conception of the monolithic structure of the automobile manufacturing business was markedly reinforced. As for the Corvair and the G.M. presentation he had seen concerning its characteristics, he considered the car to be as unsafe as he ever had.

January 14, the day on which Nader made his visit to the G.M. Technical Center, also happened to be the day on which, in Washington, Senator Ribicoff's office let out to the press advance information of an official announcement to be made by the Senator on January 17 that the Senate Subcommittee on Executive Reorganization would resume its hearings on automobile safety in the beginning of February, and that Ralph Nader would be a principal witness at those hearings.

Subsequently, the exact date for Nader to deliver his testimony before the subcommittee was settled on as February 10. For several days before the date of his appearance, Nader began to receive, at the rooming house where he lived in northwest Washington, some unusual telephone calls from several anonymous males. Nader had no private telephone in his room and no telephone number listed under his name in the Washington telephone book. He took his calls from a pay phone that hung on the wall of his landlady's ground-floor hallway. The calls became increasingly annoying.

Typically, a male voice would say, "Mr. Nader?"

"Yes," Nader would say.

Then the connection would be broken.

As the date for Nader's testimony before the Senate sub-committee drew closer, the number of strange calls increased. Most of them were made after 7 P.M. Some contained words of advice. "Why don't you change your field of interest?" one caller asked. Another call had suggested, in a menacing manner, "You are fighting a losing battle, friend. You can't win. You can only lose."

On the night of Wednesday, February 9, Nader was pre-paring the statement that he was to present to the Ribicoff subcommittee the next morning. He was interrupted by at least half a dozen calls like these:

"Mr. Nader, this is Pan American."

"Yes?"

The caller hung up.

"Mr. Nader?"

"Yes?"

"Please pick up the parcel at Railway Express."

Again, the caller hung up.

The last call came at four o'clock in the morning: "Why don't you go back to Connecticut, buddy boy?" The line went dead.

The next morning, Nader read a long and detailed prepared statement on automobile safety before the Ribicoff subcommittee. In it he called for federal legislation to establish a series of meaningful public safety standards for automobile crashworthiness; for the creation of a federal facility for research into automobile design safety, including the production of prototype safe vehicles; for the creation of an extensive federal program of statistical compilation on automobile crashes, injuries, and deaths; and for federal financial assistance to the states for accident-injury investigation teams and federal pressure on the states for more explicit and uniform highway safety standards.

As Nader began to read his statement, he was repeatedly interrupted and hectored by one of the subcommittee members, Senator Carl T. Curtis of Nebraska, a senator known to be friendly to the automobile industry. Curtis kept pretending that he couldn't understand Nader's language, then went on to question Nader about the consultative work he had carried out for the Department of Labor, about how he had been paid, about when he had begun to volunteer his advice and services to the Ribicoff subcommittee, and about the relationship between his work on "Unsafe at Any Speed" and his work as a paid or unpaid government consultant. The implication was that there was something fishy about Nader's help to the government and that he had been using his services to the government and the Senate subcommittee as a vehicle or cover for commercial exploitation of his book.

"When did you do the work on this book?" Senator Curtis demanded of Nader.

"That book, Senator, had its gestation almost a decade ago, when I saw a little girl decapitated when a glove compartment door opened in a car that collided at fifteen miles an hour," Nader replied, referring to one of the accidents he had witnessed in his student-hitchhiker days.

Eventually, Senator Robert Kennedy broke in to observe, with some heat, that "as I hear the questioning of Mr. Nader, it sounds like he is a criminal of some sort or is guilty of some crime. I think he should be allowed to be permitted to go on with [his] statement." He added sharply that "there seems to be a concerted effort to prevent Mr. Nader from reading [his] statement."

Even then, Senator Curtis persisted. He openly called Nader's connection with the Ribicoff subcommittee "a book-selling proposition," and he accused Nader of making distorted statements in the book about the automobile industry.

"I welcome criticism of all kinds, and I want to reply to it," Nader told the senator calmly. "In fact, I have consistently tried to have the auto industry appear in public and discuss these issues on a serious basis, and many radio and TV stations have tried to get the auto industry to discuss this. And they have uniformly failed. The industry does not want to discuss this . . . in the public domain. They don't want to join the issue. They don't want to respond. They want to keep this private and secret. And I think this is a laceration of the basic principles of corporate citizenship, and I think it is a very, very sad thing that is happening."

The following morning, Sonosky, the Ribicoff subcommittee chief counsel, telephoned Nader and told him that the typed transcript of his testimony was ready for him to look over. Sonosky was carrying out a routine practice in the handling of testimony given before congressional committees: before such testimony is sent to the Government Printing Office to be incorporated into the formal printed records of the hearings involved, witnesses are given the courtesy of making minor corrections—of misspelled names, for example, or of grammatical slips made in oral testimony. Nader told Sonosky that he would be coming to Capitol Hill later on that day, and that he'd try to drop by and pick up the transcript.

Sonosky recently recalled what subsequently happened. "Later that afternoon, about four o'clock, a young Capitol policeman came into my office. He was from Connecticut and was on Senator Ribicoff's patronage list. He'd done some clerical work for me on the subcommittee before we got him his policeman's job. He'd seen Nader around, and knew him to say hello to. Well, he told me he wanted me to know he'd heard that Nader had come into the New Senate Office Building a while before—he'd gone to a room next to the press room on the ground level for a television interview by the N.B.C. newspeople—and that, just after Nader had come into the building and gone to the press room, two men came in and asked a building guard where this fellow—they described Nader's appearance—had gone in the building. The guard apparently became suspicious of the way the two men were behaving and eventually called in a Capitol police lieutenant, who asked the two men to leave the building."

Sonosky had reacted with a keen political reflex. "When I heard that I picked up the phone," he says, "and called Senator Ribicoff. I said, 'Senator, I think a strong auto safety bill has been passed.' The senator asked me what I meant by that. I said, 'They've followed Ralph Nader into the New Senate Office Building!' Ribicoff just laughed, in a manner of, 'I'll be damned.' Who 'they' were we didn't know. But we did know that the Administration's auto safety bill, which had existed since August and which we hadn't yet had presented to us, would need strengthening, because in our view nobody in the

Executive Branch knew how to write a strong auto bill. This incident looked like something that would give us help in strengthening it."

Two days later, the Sunday edition of the Washington *Post* ran a short item, or what Sonosky called "a little blip," on an inside page, headed, "Car Safety Critic Nader Reports Being 'Tailed.' " The item read, in part:

> Two men believed to be private detectives "tailed" Ralph Nader, author of a controversial book on auto safety, in the New Senate Office Building on Friday and were told to leave by Capitol police.
>
> This was disclosed by Nader yesterday and supported by Bryce Nelson, a Washington Post reporter who inadvertently became involved in the bizarre episode when he was mistaken for Nader.
>
> Nader, who wrote "Unsafe at Any Speed," had gone to the Senate Office Building for a television interview.
>
> When he left the recording studio, he said, he was told by Building Guard Marshall Speake that two men, said to be in their late 30s and of medium height, had been following him.
>
> A lieutenant was summoned who told the men that such activity was not allowed and asked them to get out. Capitol police declined comment since no arrest had been made.
>
> Nader said that he had had suspicions that he was under surveillance, but had never had any clear evidence until the Friday incident. He said that because his book deals harshly with the auto industry he suspects the men were employed by a car manufacturer.
>
> Reporter Nelson said he was mistaken for Nader yesterday by a guard, apparently Speake, who said he looked like Nader's "identical twin" and mentioned the incident.

The article, which was unsigned, had been written by Morton Mintz, a reporter for the *Post* who was also the author of "The Therapeutic Nightmare," a book that had been published around the same time as "Unsafe at Any Speed" was and that dealt with abusive practices of the drug industry and associated regulatory failures within the federal government.

On Saturday afternoon, Nader had gone into the editorial offices of the *Post* and told Mintz about being followed into the New Senate Office Building. Mintz thought it had the makings of a good news story but felt that he needed some sort of independent confirmation before the *Post* used it. He told Laurence Stern, then the national editor of the *Post,* about Nader's tale and told him he wished he could confirm the story. Stern said that it was a funny thing, because Bryce Nelson had just been telling him a strange tale involving Nelson, Nader, and detectives in the New Senate Office Building. Nelson, who was sitting nearby at his desk in the *Post* news room, then gave Mintz the confirmation he needed.

Five years later, the details of the incident as it affected Nelson are still fresh in Nelson's mind. "I remember coming out of the press room of the New Senate Office Building that Friday when one of the Capitol policemen told me that a couple of people were tailing me," he has recalled. "The policeman said, 'I thought you'd be interested.'"

"I thought that was pretty ridiculous. I was on my way to the Old Senate Office Building and I carried right on in that direction. Then I turned around, went back to the guard, and said, 'What do you *mean* two people tailing me? What's this all about?'"

"The guard said, 'Well, didn't you come out of that room?' —pointing to the door next to the press room. I told him that I hadn't been in that particular room. Then the guard said, 'Well, you look like the exact double of someone else. There were a couple of detectives who were tailing a guy who's been writing about auto safety.' I don't know the guard's name. I asked him several days later, but he wouldn't tell me. He seemed to feel that he probably shouldn't have told me about the incident in the first place. He had just been trying to do me a favor, I guess."

3

"We Never Reveal Our Client's Identity"

IN THE DAYS FOLLOWING his appearance before the Ribicoff subcommittee, Nader received a number of congratulatory calls and letters, but not all of them had to do with his Senate testimony. For example, one day when Nader talked over the telephone to Professor Harold Berman, under whom he had worked at the Harvard Law School in 1959, Professor Berman began the conversation with a greeting that went something like, "Congratulations. I understand that you are being considered for a job." He said that a man had visited him to inquire into Nader's background, with the explanation that Nader was being considered for some kind of well-paying research position, although by what employer was not made clear. Nader told Professor Berman that he hadn't applied for any kind of job.

Then Nader got a warm, handwritten note from Thomas F. Lambert, Jr., the editor-in-chief of the American Trial Lawyers Association *Journal,* a publication for which Nader had frequently written. Lambert wanted to let Nader know that he had been interviewed by a man who said his name was "Mr. Dwyer," who worked for an organization the name of which Lambert remembered as "Management Consultants" or "Management Associates," at 53 State Street in Boston. Mr. Dwyer, whom Lambert described to Nader as "an Ivy League type," had said that he represented a prosperous client, whom he did not name, who was interested in employing Nader. He wanted to know, among other things, how capable Nader was in his grasp of technical matters, particularly in the area of automobile safety. The Ivy League interviewer was also interested in Nader's drinking habits. Lambert wrote that he had recommended Nader without reservation and had assured Mr. Dwyer of Nader's industry and sobriety. And Lambert ended his note by warmly wishing Nader success in whatever job it was that he was being considered for.

Nader was now pretty thoroughly on the alert. Although, as he subsequently remarked before Senator Ribicoff's subcommittee, "In order to preserve my own equanimity I don't generally look around, turn my [head] back when I am walking," he couldn't help but be sensitive to the presence of unwanted company while he was moving from place to place.

On Wednesday, February 16, Nader flew from Washington to Philadelphia to make an appearance on the Mike Douglas television show. On the program he spoke about the designed-in hazards of automobiles and the "brainwashing" of the public by the advertising and public-relations campaigns of the automobile industry and its allied organization, and he advocated new and strict federal and state standards providing for safe automobile design and for a break in what he said was a front of corporate secrecy concerning defects and accident statistics of particular car models.

After his appearance at the studio where the Mike Douglas show was being taped, Nader headed for the Philadelphia airport. He had a reservation for a United Air Lines flight to Washington that left at 3:30 P.M. Nader was barely in time for the flight, and by the time he arrived at the departure gate the other passengers had boarded the airplane. As he hurried through the gate he became aware that two men who had been sitting on a bench nearby quickly got up, went through the gate just after him, boarded the plane, and took seats in the economy section close to where he sat down. After the flight arrived at Washington National Airport, at about 4:15 P.M., and the passengers were getting off, Nader went down the ramp quickly and inside the terminal building, and ducked through various areas and doors to shake off the two men, who, he was convinced, were following him.

The following Sunday evening, in Washington, Nader dropped in at a drugstore a couple of blocks from his rooming house. He went over to the magazine rack and was leafing through an automobile magazine when a young and attractive girl, a brunette in her twenties whom he'd never seen before, came up to him. She said, "Pardon me, I know this sounds a little forward. I hope you don't mind, but can I talk to you?" She said that she and a group of friends met from time to time to "discuss foreign affairs," and she invited Nader to join them. Nader was taken aback, but in a polite way he attempted to put the girl off by saying that he was from out of town. But the girl was insistent. She said there happened to be a meeting that same night, and she invited him again. When the girl became persistent, Nader said he wasn't interested and turned away. The girl walked out of the drugstore.

On Wednesday, February 23, Nader had another interesting experience while shopping. This time he was in a Safeway supermarket near his rooming house, and he was just picking out a package of cookies for himself when he was approached by yet another attractive girl in her twenties, a blonde wearing slacks. Excusing herself for approaching Nader, she told him that she needed some help in moving "something heavy" into her apartment nearby, and that "there's no one to help me." She said it wouldn't take long. When she repeated her plea, Nader said that he was sorry but he had a meeting to attend and was late. There were a number of other unaccompanied men in the store, but, Nader noticed, the girl didn't ask any of them for help. She walked right out of the supermarket. The air of these encounters, which were unique in Nader's experience, made Nader feel reasonably sure, especially considering all the other unusual events happening around him, that the girls must have been employed to lure him into some compromising situation.

Later on in the same day as the approach by the blonde in the supermarket, Nader learned from Richard Grossman, his publisher, that Dexter Masters, the editor of *Consumer Reports,* had had, in midafternoon, a telephone call about Nader from an individual Masters described as "a smooth-talking fellow." In a front-page review of "Unsafe at Any Speed" in the January 23 issue of *Book Week,* Masters had called it a "straight-out indictment" of the automobile industry for its "subordination of transportation values and simple safety to its pattern of styling for sales." He had concluded that "it will be a hard book for the industry to ignore, and it just might be something more than that. There are some signs that the safety issue is beginning to burst the bonds in which it has been wrapped for so long."

According to Masters, the call from the "smooth-talking fellow" had been made to Masters' apartment in New York. The caller said he understood that Masters had reviewed "Unsafe at Any Speed" and asked if Masters could tell him anything about Nader. Masters' response to this, as later quoted in the *New Republic,* was that "I didn't know him, and what did he want to know for. The man said he represented the 'Gillian' Agency or something that sounded like that. . . . They were investigating for a client who was interested in hiring Nader to write some articles. Did I think it ["Unsafe at Any Speed"] really was a good book? I said I thought it was an excellent book. . . ." The caller thanked Masters and the conversation ended, whereupon Masters, who didn't think the call represented a very brilliant piece of investigation, called Grossman to tell him about it.

By the time Nader heard about the call to Dexter Masters, the name of a " 'Gillian' Agency or something that sounded like that" was no longer altogether new to him.

On the late evening of Monday, February 21, he had had a telegram from his old Harvard classmate, Frederick Hughes Condon, the friend to whom "Unsafe at Any Speed" was dedicated, asking him to call Condon at his home in Concord, New

Hampshire. Condon was now assistant counsel to the United Life and Accident Insurance Company, in Concord. Nader called Condon at about one o'clock in the morning, and Condon told him how he had been approached and interviewed by an investigator in his office on Monday about Nader. Condon, who very quickly had become suspicious of the *bona fides* of the investigator, had had the presence of mind to write an account of the interview right after it had ended.

According to Condon, it was about 12:30 P.M. on February 21 that he was first approached about Nader. The approach was made in the form of a telephone call from a man who introduced himself as "Mr. Warren." Mr. Warren said that he would like to see Condon at Condon's office at three o'clock that afternoon to speak to him about a friend of Condon's:

> He identified this friend as Ralph Nader, and stated that Ralph had written a book which is dedicated to me, and that Mr. Warren has a client who is very much interested in hiring Ralph to do some research and writing and Mr. Warren is doing an investigation into Ralph's background to make sure that there aren't any left-wing activites, sexual problems, or that Ralph isn't an odd-ball or anything of that nature. He also stated that they wanted to be sure that Ralph was capable of doing work in other fields, and that they wanted to be sure that he wasn't just stuck on this subject of car design, and intent on pursuing this subject alone to the exclusion of all others. I asked who his client was. He stated, "Well, we never reveal our client's identity."
> . . . I asked [Mr. Warren] if he was associated with an attorney and he said yes, a Mr. Gillen of New York City. He gave me to believe that Mr. Gillen's office specialized in investigations . . .

Condon told Mr. Warren that he couldn't see him at three o'clock, but that he might be able to see him half an hour after that, depending on whether a meeting Condon had to attend ended by that time. Mr. Warren said that would be quite all right; he didn't mind waiting.

The meeting that Condon attended went on for some time past 3:30 P.M. At 3:40 the office receptionist came around to the room where the meeting was held, obviously looking for Condon. Condon was too intent on the business at hand to be interrupted, but he assumed that Mr. Warren had arrived. The meeting broke up about 4:20, and Condon, upon returning to his office, found a note from the receptionist saying that "I have a Mr. Gillen waiting for you in the lobby." Condon, wondering what had happened to Mr. Warren, had the receptionist show Mr. Gillen into his office.

He found his visitor to be a neatly dressed man of about forty-five or fifty, of medium height and build, "but with a peculiar barrel-chested quality." He was wearing a finely patterned sports coat, and glasses with heavy black frames.

> I think his eyes were blue, and his hair was kinky-curly, combed straight back neatly, and steel gray in color. He had a peculiar voice, probably baritone, and a hesitant way of speaking which I cannot put into words, but which I would recognize at once. I was sure from his voice that he was the same person who had spoken to me on the phone, although his name had changed in the interim.

Condon apologized for having kept his visitor waiting for so long. Mr. Gillen, without mentioning the absent Mr. Warren, did not seem at all disturbed that he'd had to wait for an hour. He said that was okay. Gillen repeated, in pretty much the same words, and indeed in pretty much the same voice, what Warren had said his interest was in Ralph Nader. Gillen began to talk of "Unsafe at Any Speed." He asked if Condon had read the book—Condon said yes, he had—and Gillen said he had read "parts" of it and "felt like staying in bed" and was afraid to drive a car. Condon let him know that he was in complete agreement with what Nader had written in "Unsafe at Any Speed."

Gillen had lots of questions to ask. Throughout the interview he remained seated, and in doing so he kept on his lap a

tan attaché case he had brought with him. The attaché case was
unlatched, but the top of the case was kept down. Condon
wondered whether it contained a tape recorder. Throughout the
interview he made scrawled notations on blue-lined notepaper,
but in Condon's judgment, not enough to make any report
from: "He was either relying on his memory, or was taping
the conversation." Condon noted that his interviewer "had a
restless way of glancing about him whenever he was going to ask
a question which he considered important."

According to Condon, Gillen repeatedly asked, perhaps
three or four times, whether Nader drove a car or not and
whether he had a driver's license. Condon said he didn't remember—he explained he hadn't seen Nader for three years
or so. Gillen, persisting, wanted to know what kind of car
Nader had driven in previous periods. Did he have a car at
Harvard? What make? Had he ever been involved in any automobile accidents? Why was Nader so interested in the subject
of unsafe design of cars? Condon told him of Nader's interest
as it developed from the senior year paper he had written at
the Harvard Law School. But that didn't seem enough for
Gillen. He wondered why this technical subject interested
Nader so much when he had no apparent background in engineering matters. He wanted to know where Nader had roomed
while at law school, and wanted to know if he had any left-
wing activities or affiliations at Harvard. Condon told him that
the only organizational connections he knew Nader to have
had consisted of his membership on the Harvard Law *Record*
and of his being Phi Beta Kappa at Princeton.

Gillen then went on to ask—and this was the sort of question that caused Condon to refer to his visitor's "restless way
of glancing about him"—if there was any reason why Nader
was not married.

At first, Condon pretended not to understand the significance of this question. Eventually, he said to Gillen, "Are you
asking me if he's a homosexual?"

According to Condon, the answer was, "Well, we have to

inquire about these things. I've seen him on TV, and he certainly doesn't look like . . . but we have to be sure." Condon assured him there were no grounds for concern in such an area.

The interview then veered onto Nader's ethnic background. He said he understood that Nader was of "Syrian" ancestry. Condon corrected him and said that Nader's ancestry was Lebanese. Gillen's response, as Condon remembered it, was "Well, it's about the same thing. We just want to know if there is any anti-Semitic feeling there."

After about twenty minutes, Gillen stood up and chatted casually for a few moments, and mentioned that "he didn't know what kind of offer his client was going to make to Nader, but he was sure it would be a good one." Then he asked when Nader had met Senator Ribicoff; he wanted to know if Nader had met the Senator right after Nader had finished law school and had returned to Connecticut to practice. Condon indicated he couldn't be of much help there.

> I said I didn't know that Ralph even knew Senator Ribicoff, although I had supposed that he probably did now, after having testified before his committee. He seemed quite disappointed that I did not know when Ralph had met Senator Ribicoff, and pursued the question from several different angles before dropping it. I got the idea that the circumstances of Ralph's acquaintance with Senator Ribicoff was quite important to him for some reason. His disappointment that I had no knowledge on the subject was written all over his face.

Only at the end of the interview did Condon's visitor touch on the subject of the absent Mr. Warren. According to Condon, "He mentioned that at first Mr. Warren was going to come up and see me, but he figured he would come himself, since he was in Cambridge anyway visiting his son." Then the visitor left, tan attaché case and all.

4

"What a Blunder It Would Be If a Company Were Caught"

NADER NOW HAD VERY LITTLE DOUBT about the origin of the investigation of him, which, he decided, was continuing in spite of the appearance of the Washington *Post* item about his having been tailed into the New Senate Office Building. Nader's response to the continuation of the investigation was to seek further exposure of it in the press, and he turned to one of his closest friends in the Washington press corps, James Ridgeway, the investigative reporter for the *New Republic* whose article entitled "Car Design and Public Safety," which had appeared in that magazine in September, 1964, had been drawn in great part from information supplied by Nader.

Together with David Sanford, then a staff writer and now managing editor of the *New Republic,* Ridgeway did some further digging on the subject of the still continuing investigation of Nader, and the result was the appearance in the March 12, 1966, *New Republic* of an article entitled "The Dick." The article, which was written by Ridgeway, gave the first clear chronological account of the details of the investigation as they had come to Nader's attention. Ridgeway and Sanford put in calls to different detective firms, including Management Consultants in Boston, the organization mentioned by the investigator who had approached Thomas Lambert. According to the Ridgeway article, at Management Consultants, of 53 State Street, a man who identified himself as John Dwyer would say only, "I am not at liberty to discuss any of these matters."

However, David Sanford managed to have better luck when he put in a long-distance call to a detective firm called Vincent Gillen Associates, of Garden City, New York. He spoke to a man who identified himself as Vincent Gillen himself. And, according to the *New Republic* account:

> Mr. Gillen seemed flustered. "We've made inquiries about Nader," he said. "I spoke with Condon myself; another of our men contacted Masters." Gillen said he could not disclose the name of his client, but said, "A lot of people were mentioned adversely in that book." Recovering his composure, he told the reporter: "I am a private investigator. We have hundreds of clients; we write thousands of reports, primarily on employment matters. I was asked by a client to make an investigation of Ralph Nader. I understand that he is an intelligent, articulate fellow. And my client told me he was considering him for an important job, to do research on something, I don't know what."
>
> "I knew Nader was a writer," Gillen said, "and I went out and bought 'Unsafe at Any Speed.'" Gillen read the book and "felt like staying in bed. I was afraid to drive a car," he said. "I thought at the time, he'd better know what he's talking about or somebody might yell."
>
> "Is somebody yelling?" the reporter asked. There was a pause before Gillen said once more that Nader was being considered for a job. The investigation was not yet complete, the detective said, and then added, "All I can say is, it is good for Nader."

Although the issue of the *New Republic* in which the Ridgeway article appeared was dated March 12, it actually went on the newsstands on March 4, and its publication seems to have stimulated a number of other reporting pieces in newspapers dealing with the investigation of Nader. On March 6, the New York *Times* ran a long article under a Detroit dateline headed "Critic of Auto Industry's Safety Standards Says He Was Trailed and Harassed; Charges Called Absurd." The article recapitulated the principal investigatory incidents of which Nader was aware, and it told of his belief that women had tried to lure him into compromising situations. The article said that Nader "has put the blame on the industry for the inquiry," and it reported him as believing that the purpose of the investigation was to harass or discredit him in advance as a potential witness before a congressional committee.

The *Times* article quoted Gillen as saying in a telephone interview that he had investigated Nader on behalf of an employment agency, the name of which he declined to reveal. Gillen was quoted as saying, "I've had reason to believe from what we saw and what we heard that other people were investigating Nader." He didn't indicate who these other people might be, and what their interest in Nader was likely to be based on, but he let the *Times* reporter know that he had finished his own inquiry.

The *Times* article dealt with Nader's campaign for auto safety and his authorship of "Unsafe at Any Speed," and it gave a brief biographical sketch of Nader. "Most of Mr. Nader's friends pictured him as a rather austere man who leads a Spartan life and spends most of his time working on various problems that interest him," it said. The article also said that so far as his work on auto safety was concerned Nader "shows no signs of slackening off on what he considers a crusade."

According to the *Times* dispatch, "Spokesmen for the major manufacturers in Detroit dismissed Mr. Nader's charge [of being investigated, trailed, and harassed] as ridiculous. Several indicated a belief that the investigation wouldn't be worth the trouble." And the article quoted unnamed "industry sources" as explaining why.

> The industry sources doubted a company would be responsible for the investigation of Mr. Nader, for several reasons.
> They all regarded its potential as limited. Also, one informant pointed out, "Think what a blunder it would be if a company were caught at it."
> But the main point, in some instances expressed rather

indignantly, was that the investigation of Mr. Nader appeared aimless and somewhat clumsily handled.

"You can bet that if one of us was doing it it would be a lot smoother," one source said. "If we were checking up on Nader he'd never know about it."

On March 6, the *Herald Tribune* also ran a story on Nader and the investigation. The article quoted Nader as saying, "It's funny, but at the same time they're tailing me . . . I keep getting invitations to go out to Detroit and look at the industry and at their executive suites."

The statement from Detroit that the very visibility and imperfection of the investigation guaranteed that the automobile industry wasn't responsible for it was an intriguing piece of reasoning. But it did not satisfy Senator Ribicoff, who was now becoming very aroused about the whole matter. On March 8, on the floor of the Senate, he referred to current articles in the press "which state that Mr. Nader has been the subject of intensive investigation by detective agencies hired by unknown persons [and] that he has been followed and subjected to harassing telephone calls." He said that the implication in these press stories that there was some connection between Nader's testimony before the subcommittee and the alleged harassment was "an extremely serious matter," and he observed that since federal law made it a crime for anyone to intimidate or impede a witness before a congressional committee, he was asking the Department of Justice to investigate.

On the Senate floor, Senator Ribicoff was joined in this request by Senator Gaylord Nelson of Wisconsin, who called the reported investigation "a filthy business." Senator Nelson also declared—somewhat inaccurately, if he had in mind the insurance company with which Frederick Condon was associated —that "an officer of a firm for which Nader worked was questioned at great length by a flashily dressed private detective who conducted a scandalous quest for possibly lurid material."

On March 9, in Detroit, spokesmen for the automobile

companies were having a hard time with members of the press, who were hounding them with questions. John S. Bugas, vice-president of the Ford Motor Company, released a statement declaring flatly that "Ford Motor Co. has not been, nor is it now, directly or indirectly involved in any alleged investigation or harassment of Mr. Nader." With this statement in hand, reporters pressed executives of each of the three other big auto companies for similar assurances. "They received firm denials at the Chrysler Corporation and the American Motors Corporation," the *Times* reported. The *Times* added, "General Motors declined comment."

Shortly after eleven o'clock on the night of March 9, after the first editions of most morning newspapers were already off the press, a General Motors public relations man delivered a statement to the Detroit offices of a number of newspapers. The statement said that "following the publication of Mr. Ralph Nader's criticisms of the Corvair in writings and public appearances in support of his book 'Unsafe at Any Speed,' the office of [G.M.'s] general counsel initiated a routine investigation through a reputable law firm to determine whether Ralph Nader was acting on behalf of litigants or their attorneys in Corvair design cases pending against General Motors."

It continued, "The investigation was prompted by Mr. Nader's extreme criticism of the Corvair in his writings, press conferences, TV and other public appearances. . . . Mr. Nader's statements coincided with similar publicity by some attorneys handling such litigation. It is a well known and accepted practice in the legal profession to investigate claims and persons making claims in the product liability field, such as in the pending Corvair design cases."

The statement declared that the investigation of Nader "was limited only to Mr. Nader's qualifications, background, expertise and association with such attorneys" and that "it did not include any of the alleged harassment or intimidation recently reported in the press. If Mr. Nader has been subjected to any of the incidents and harassment mentioned by him in newspaper stories, such incidents were in no way associated with General Motors' legitimate investigation of his interest in pending litigation."

Then the statement dealt with Nader's visit to the G.M. Technical Center at Warren in January and his subsequent activities:

> He was shown a number of engineering and research testing and development programs in the field of automotive safety. A number of the accusations in his book were discussed at length, and a presentation was made of the evidence used in the successful defense of the only two Corvair lawsuits tried.
>
> Mr. Nader expressed appreciation for the courtesy in providing him with detailed information, but he nevertheless continued the same line of attack on the design of the Corvair in a number of subsequent press conferences, TV and other appearances. This behavior lends support to General Motors' belief that there is a connection between Mr. Nader and plaintiffs' counsel in pending Corvair design litigation.

The General Motors statement made front-page news throughout the country and was given prominent treatment in television network news shows. "G.M. Acknowledges Investigating Critic," the headline in the New York *Times* went. "GM Concedes It Ordered an Investigation of Car-Safety Critic: Denies 'Harassment' " went that in the Washington *Post*. "GM Admits 'Routine' Quiz on Safety Critic," the Detroit *News* headline read, more conservatively. A report in the New York *Times* on March 11 said, "The General Motors statement came as a sharp surprise to the rest of the industry." It continued, "Mr. Nader angrily denied that he represented any of the plaintiffs in the Corvair suits and said he had suspended his law practice during his crusade for greater auto safety." However, the same article noted that "General Motors officials hinted that they could 'prove our case' on Mr. Nader's connection with lawyers handling Corvair suits against the company."

The same article in the *Times* said that a General Motors

spokesman, asked about the "reputable law firm" in Washington employed in the company's inquiry into Nader, identified it as Alvord & Alvord. "A partner [of Alvord & Alvord], named by General Motors, Richard G. Danner, declined comment last night. His Washington office reported this afternoon that Mr. Danner had left the city," the *Times* said.

On March 10, on the Senate floor, Senator Ribicoff announced that his subcommittee would hold hearings on March 22 on the Nader-G.M. affair. He said that "the parties in this matter should come before the subcommittee to present their views." He added that he expected General Motors to back up its charges concerning Nader's connection with pending Corvair litigation, and that "I also expect a public explanation of the alleged harassment of a Senate committee witness." Senator Ribicoff said that he was inviting Nader, representatives of detective agencies involved in the investigation of Nader, and the president of General Motors himself to appear as witnesses. Senator Robert F. Kennedy took the floor briefly after Ribicoff's announcement and there followed an exchange that apparently made the terms of the witnesses' appearance clear:

> *Mr. Kennedy:* Could we also request that [the president of General Motors] bring all of his records in connection with this [detective] agency?
> *Mr. Ribicoff:* That request will be made concerning the records of the detective agency and the investigation.
> *Mr. Kennedy:* Could we also have the detective agency bring all its records in connection with this matter?
> *Mr. Ribicoff:* I think the request is a proper one, and that request will be made of the detective agency.
> *Mr. Kennedy:* Could we also ask General Motors Corp. to have available in the room any individuals from General Motors who have detailed knowledge of these transactions with the detective agency?
> *Mr. Ribicoff:* The request will be relayed to the president of General Motors.

On the following day the U.S. Department of Justice announced that in response to Senator Ribicoff's request it would investigate Nader's allegations, and that the F.B.I. was entering the case.

Within a few days General Motors let it be known that it had hired, as special counsel for the company where the forthcoming Senate hearing was concerned, Theodore C. Sorensen, the former special adviser to the late President John F. Kennedy and now a partner in the New York law firm of Paul Weiss, Rifkind, Wharton & Garrison.

5

"I Want to Apologize Here and Now"

THE MARCH 22 HEARING was held in the Senate Caucus Room
—the big, high-ceilinged, chandelier-hung room that had been
the scene of many famous hearings. It was packed with the
public, the press, and the radio and television people and their
equipment.

Senator Ribicoff opened the proceedings with some remarks
on the efforts of the subcommittee during the previous year to
deal with the "controversial topic" of the federal role in traffic
safety, and the progress it had made in adding safety features to
the design of new automobiles and to a national highway safety
bill lately forwarded to Congress by the President. He noted that
much of the subcommittee's success so far had resulted from
"the willingness of experts in this important field to express
their views vigorously and frankly." He emphasized the importance of "this right to testify freely without fear or intimidation." And he said that at this session the committee would
look into "the circumstances surrounding what appeared to be
an attempt by General Motors to discredit Mr. Ralph Nader, a
recent witness before the subcommittee."

The first witness to be called was Nader. But Nader wasn't in
the room. The subcommittee went into recess for fifteen minutes, and when Nader hadn't shown up by that time Senator
Ribicoff asked James M. Roche, the president of General
Motors, to go ahead with his prepared statement. Before Roche

did so, Senator Ribicoff asked Roche, "as a matter of formality," to give his testimony under oath. Roche thereupon was sworn. (So were all the subsequent witnesses who testified that day.)

Roche, a tall man in his sixties with white streaked hair and a solemn appearance, began by saying that when Senator Ribicoff had issued the invitation to him to testify concerning "this corporation's responsibility for a private investigation of Mr. Ralph Nader, a witness before this subcommittee who has been critical of the automobile industry's efforts on traffic safety and particularly the GM Corvair," Roche had "immediately stated our intention to cooperate with this subcommittee in every possible way."

Roche then went on to offer, on behalf of General Motors, a broad apology to Nader: "Let me make clear at the outset that I deplore the kind of harassment to which Mr. Nader has apparently been subjected," Roche declared. "I am just as shocked and outraged by some of the incidents which Mr. Nader has reported as the members of this subcommittee."

He said that "as president of General Motors, I hold myself fully responsible for any action authorized or initiated by any officer of the corporation which may have had any bearing on the incidents related to our investigation of Mr. Nader." He added that he did not know of the investigation when it was initiated and that he did not approve it.

"While there can be no disagreement over General Motors' legal right to ascertain necessary facts preparatory to litigation," he said, "I am not here to excuse, condone, or justify in any way our investigating Mr. Nader. To the extent that General Motors bears responsibility, I want to apologize here and now to the members of this subcommittee and Mr. Nader. I sincerely hope that these apologies will be accepted. Certainly I bear Mr. Nader no ill will."

Having made this considerable admission before the Senate subcommittee, the assembled press, and all the television cameramen, the president of General Motors then went on to make certain disclaimers. He said that to the best of his knowledge—

and he said he had "made every effort to obtain all the facts" since learning of the matter two weeks previously—"the investigation initiated by General Motors, contrary to some speculation, did *not* employ girls as sex lures, did *not* employ detectives giving false names . . . did *not* use recording devices during interviews, did *not* follow Mr. Nader in Iowa and Pennsylvania, did *not* have him under surveillance during the day he testified before this subcommittee, did *not* follow him in any private place, and did *not* constantly ring his private telephone number late at night with false statements or anonymous warnings."

Roche indicated that the investigation of Nader had been started in November. He said that at that time Nader's book had not yet been published. Further, he said, at that time Nader neither had appeared nor was scheduled to appear as a witness before the Ribicoff subcommittee, and Nader was not regarded by anyone at G.M. as a consultant to the subcommittee. In short, the investigation was "wholly unrelated" to the proceedings of the subcommittee and Nader's connections with them.

And, Roche insisted, "There has been no attempt by, and it has at no time been the intention of, General Motors Corp., or any of its officers or employees to invade his privacy, to defame his character, or to hinder, impugn, coerce, or prevent his testimony before this or any other legislative body." As for Nader's political and religious beliefs and attitudes, his credit rating, "or his personal habits regarding sex, alcohol, or any other subject," Roche said he had no personal interest whatever in these matters. "While I do not personally know Mr. Nader," Roche said, "I am informed that he is an articulate attorney and citizen who is deeply interested in traffic safety and has written and spoken extensively on the subject." He added, "We in General Motors certainly would not want any private citizen to think for one moment that he was not free to criticize our corporation or products, before this subcommittee or anyone else, without fear of retaliation or harassment of any kind. While we do not agree with many of the opinions and allegations Mr. Nader has put forward, General Motors has responded to his public criticisms not by responding in kind or ignoring the problems but by inviting him to meet with us to discuss those questions of safety which concern us all. Mr. Nader spent a day at the G.M. Technical Center . . . early in January visiting with G.M. executives and engineers. We hope we will have the opportunity to meet with him again in the future."

It all sounded reasonable, even friendly. Roche then told the subcommittee that he owed it an explanation of "exactly what happened, as best as I have been able to ascertain." He touched on the number of lawsuits that General Motors had been facing relating to the design of the Corvair and observed that "the general counsel of our corporation has responsibility to the stockholders to defend all such suits with all his strength and ability and with every proper method and measure." He said that both state and federal courts had consistently recognized that product liability cases of this kind "necessarily and customarily require considerable investigation," including investigation of the qualifications of experts involved in such cases. The general counsel of G.M. had become "troubled," he said, by what appeared to be a "concerted effort" of several trial attorneys handling most of the Corvair cases "to stimulate cases and the kind of sensationally adverse publicity that might influence juries against the Corvair." He wanted to know whether the activities of some attorneys, including Nader, violated bar association rules concerning the discussion of pending or anticipated litigation; whether they—if their writings might be introduced in evidence in court—were entitled to the legal definition of "expert"; and whether they could properly be cross-examined in any trial in which they might appear as an expert witness, for the purpose of showing any possible "bias, lack of reliability or credibility, if it were a fact that they had a self-interest in the litigation or had been attempting deliberately to influence public opinion."

As a consequence, Roche said, the general counsel felt "in Mr. Nader's case, and only in Mr. Nader's case, that he could not get the answer to these questions that troubled him "without using a private investigating agency to check on Mr. Nader's credibility, reliability and qualifications as an expert witness and his ties, if any, with these attorneys."

A "brief inquiry" in Nader's home town in Connecticut "revealed nothing," he said. Nader had given a Washington address on a legal paper filed in a federal court case, but, since he "could not be found in any Washington telephone or legal directory, the general counsel had asked a Washington attorney, Mr. Richard Danner, to secure an investigation of the facts needed." And Roche emphasized that at that time it had not been announced that Nader would be a witness before the subcommittee. He said that the general counsel, treating the investigation of Nader "like all other investigations of fact relating solely to pending and anticipated litigation," did not consider it necessary to inform the other officers of General Motors about it. In fact, Roche said, "this investigation was initiated, conducted, and completed without my knowledge or consent, and without the knowledge or consent of any member of our governing committees." He said that he had not been informed of the "preemployment investigative methods which would be employed by Mr. Gillen and his associates" and that the information gathered in this effort, which had been terminated the preceding month, "was, not surprisingly, irrelevant for the very narrow purposes which our general counsel had originally intended."

When Roche had finished, Senator Ribicoff commended him for what the Senator called his "forthright statement." So did Senator Milward L. Simpson of Wyoming, who called his statement "very forthright and helpful." So did Senator Kennedy, who called it "a most forthright statement."

> *Senator Kennedy:* It is very helpful to the committee. I am sure it was difficult to make, and therefore all the more commendable.
> *Mr. Roche:* Thank you, sir.
> *Senator Kennedy:* I extend my appreciation to you for

your efforts to come before the committee and give us all of the facts in connection with this matter, and I commend your candor and your honesty in doing so.

Mr. Roche: Thank you, sir.

It had indeed been a difficult statement for Roche to make: here was the president of the largest corporation in the world, the employer of more than half a million people in this country alone, sitting in a blaze of floodlights reading sentences about detectives and telephone calls and apologizing before the whole world to a young man who lived in a Washington rooming house for that giant corporation's behavior toward him.

But how much had Roche really apologized for? The statement had undoubtedly been very carefully drawn up, with the collaboration of General Motors' most skilful counsel, and it had had put into it, no expense spared, the literary talents and keen political intuition of Sorensen, the former presidential assistant and major speech writer and adviser to the Kennedy family, now hired as special counsel to General Motors. On behalf of General Motors, Roche had apologized to Nader—who, by the time Roche finished his statement, was in the room—but he had apologized to him only "to the extent that General Motors bears responsibility" for the investigation—the aim of which, Roche had insisted, was legally and ethically proper.

Sorensen was sitting to Roche's right during the hearings. He did not address the subcommittee, and, apparently, said nothing to Roche during the proceedings except at one point, after Roche had finished his statement and was awaiting questioning by members of the subcommittee. What Sorensen said to Roche then was spoken in a low voice, but a voice loud enough, it seems, for his words to be overheard by a reporter for a news service who had written several articles on auto safety and who was sitting nearby. "I remember what Sorensen had to say. In fact, I can hardly forget it," this man has told the author. "There was the master of all that reverse English leaning over with a hand cupped to one side of his mouth and saying to the president of General Motors, 'Deny the girls.'"

6

"That Statement Really . . . Is Not Accurate"

HAVING COMMENDED ROCHE on his statement, Senator Kennedy said that there were "a few questions" that he would like to ask the witness, and the first of them proved to be somewhat awkward for Roche to answer. Senator Kennedy wanted to know whether Roche agreed that the statement that General Motors had put out in reaction to the press reports on the tailing of Nader—the statement of March 9 declaring that General Motors had undertaken a "routine" investigation of Nader "limited only to Mr. Nader's qualifications, background, expertise and association with [Corvair case] attorneys"—was a misleading one. Roche wouldn't say that the G.M. statement was misleading, although he said that had he known all the facts that he now possessed, "I suspect that the wording of the statement might have been somewhat different." However, he said, the G.M. statement "represented the general intent of the investigation at that time." Since then, he said, he had learned that "in the approach to the investigation, there had to be some basis [by this Roche seems to have meant an ostensible basis] for making the investigation." Consequently, "It was the judgment of the people who were arranging for the investigation that a preemployment type investigation would be made, and that is [what] was undertaken. In the course of that investigation, apparently some areas were probed in a very unfortunate way as it turns out."

"Would you say now that this was a routine investigation to determine whether Mr. Nader was acting on behalf of litigants or their attorneys?" Senator Kennedy asked.

"I would say, Senator Kennedy, that it is not a routine investigation insofar as General Motors is concerned, but it is my understanding that this is considered a routine investigation of potential witnesses in connection with litigation that may be of interest to a defendant," Roche said.

Senator Kennedy then read over the sentence in the G.M. statement declaring that the investigation was limited only to Nader's qualifications, background, expertise and association with attorneys litigating with G.M. "That statement really, as it turns out, is not accurate," he said to Roche.

"That was the intent of the statement, and the entire intent of the investigation," Roche said.

Senator Kennedy, pressing on, read the part of the G.M. statement stating that if Nader had been subjected to "the incidents and harassment mentioned by him in newspaper stories," such incidents were "in no way associated with General Motors' legitimate investigation of his interest in pending litigation."

"That . . . is also not accurate, is it?" he asked Roche.

"Well, I think it depends on the interpretation of acts of harassment, Senator Kennedy," Roche replied. He added, "I think what we meant by that statement was that certainly we had been assured that our investigation had not had anything to do with the harassing telephone calls."

Senator Kennedy wanted to know whether it was true that Nader had received calls from people investigating him.

Roche said that Nader had been called "twice to my knowledge."

"Isn't it correct that he was followed?" Kennedy asked.

"He was under surveillance in Washington for a period of about one week; yes, sir."

Kennedy once more read that part of the G.M. statement denying that the incidents of harassment mentioned by Nader in newspaper stories were connected with the G.M. investigation.

"That statement, really, Mr. Roche, as it is being developed before the committee, is not accurate," Kennedy said again.

Roche seemed unwilling to concede this. "Well, again I think, Senator, that it gets back to what is an element of harassment," he said.

Kennedy said, somewhat sharply, "Maybe I will take back what I said about your statement. I thought your statement indicated that you thought there had been harassment."

"I think that there has been some harassment," Roche said, at last. He went on to tell Senator Kennedy that "Perhaps our initial release was too broad," but he said that the intent of the G.M. statement, when it denied any connection with "the incidents and harassment" mentioned by Nader in newspaper stories, had been to deny "the use of girls accosting Mr. Nader, the employment of detectives who were giving false names, and the constant ringing of his telephone at night." And in that sense, Roche insisted, G.M. had not conducted "any of these items of harassment." However, the president of General Motors then conceded that "to the extent that this went into private affairs and other questions, which is regrettable, that those are acts of harassment, and I believe that they are, then to that extent the statement is not clear."

"I think that is a mild way of putting it, if I may say so, Mr. Roche," Senator Kennedy said. "I commended you on your statement, and I commended it because I thought it was frank and honest, and I think that it *is* frank and honest. But as I gather from your statement today, you said that there had been acts of harassment by representatives of those who were associated with the General Motors Corporation and you apologized for it. This statement of March 9 quite clearly indicated that no such events or incidents ever occurred. My point was that the statement of March 9 . . . is inaccurate, not because of statements that are made by Mr. Nader, but because of your own statement here."

Senator Harris of Oklahoma then took over the questioning of Roche. He wanted to know whether Roche had felt no responsibility to delve further into the facts about the investigation before approving the press release saying that the investigation only concerned Nader's possible connection with pending lawsuits. Roche replied that "I thought . . . that our first obligation was to admit our responsibility in connection with the investigation." He said he had been assured by the G.M. legal staff that the investigation had been made solely for the purpose of determining Nader's connection with Corvair litigation. Asked who in particular had given him this assurance, Roche said that it had come from Louis H. Bridenstine, G.M.'s assistant general counsel, "who was working on the problem at the time."

"He assured you of something . . . that was not in fact true, then?" Senator Harris asked.

"Well, it was not true at the time; yes, sir," Roche said, and he went on to explain:

> Well, I think that our people were not aware of all the things that had happened, and I think maybe there was some misunderstanding between a preemployment investigation and what might be considered to be a routine investigation. I have been told . . . that it is quite common practice in making preemployment investigation—and this was a preemployment investigation pretext that was used—that questions of background and questions of this kind with respect to the drinking and the moral habits of an individual are part of that kind of an investigation.

"You are saying then that your own legal staff—no one in G.M. to your knowledge knew in advance that this investigation would go into facts that were not required to prepare the lawsuit; is that what you say?" Senator Harris asked.

"To my knowledge I don't think that was contemplated; no, sir," Roche said.

"Then who did make that decision? Who made the decision that extraneous matters would be investigated?" Senator Harris said.

"I think that the decision was made by the people who were conducting the investigation," Roche said.

"They, just on their own, decided to do more than was required?" Senator Harris said.

"I have been informed that the preemployment pretext, as it has been referred to, was decided to be the basis for the investigation, and that decision, insofar as I know, was made by the investigating agency," Roche said.

"And no one else knew about that before they did it on their own," Senator Harris said.

"Not to my knowledge; no, sir," Roche said.

"Nobody within G.M.?"

"Not to my knowledge."

"Nobody within your general counsel's office?"

"Not to my knowledge."

Senator Kennedy interrupted this exchange to say that he had been reading an advance copy of the statement that was to be read by Richard Danner, the attorney in the Washington law firm of Alvord & Alvord. Senator Kennedy said that the Danner statement gave some information concerning the beginning of the investigation, "and he talks about a Miss Murphy who I understand is in the legal department of General Motors Corporation." Senator Kennedy read a portion of Danner's statement referring to a discussion that Miss Murphy had had with Danner concerning "the type of information needed" in the Nader investigation, including "the date and type of government employment, sources of income, type and locale of law practice, if any, business associates, movement, and, in short, a complete background investigation of Mr. Nader's activities."

In response to other questions by Senator Harris, Roche said that he was aware of this discussion of "a complete background investigation" of Nader, but he didn't construe this as indicating that extraneous matters were called for in the investigation. "I think that what we were interested in, Senator, what our general counsel's office was interested in, was some knowledge of Mr. Nader's background, expertise in the area of automotive design, his background as an attorney, and his possible interest in Corvair litigation," Roche insisted, "and those were the only areas that were of any interest to us . . . neither I personally nor General Motors has any other possible interest in Mr. Nader."

Senator Harris wanted to know whether Roche was aware of the nature of "Miss Murphy's instructions about how the investigation was to be conducted" at the time that he approved the G.M. press release; Roche said that he wasn't; he had been given to understand that a routine investigation was involved. Senator Harris suggested that Roche was, perhaps, "rather upset" with Miss Murphy because she had "let you go ahead and issue a press release which didn't state the whole facts." Roche said that he was upset about the whole affair.

"Let's not focus on Miss Murphy, whoever she is," Senator Kennedy said.

"Miss Murphy is a very capable young lady and a member of our legal staff," Roche said.

Senator Ribicoff then spoke. He told Roche that there was no question in his mind but that Roche was an honorable man. But he said he thought that what the committee had to deal with was a question of policy concerning large corporations, and the responsibility of their leaders to preserve the individual's right of privacy. He said the subcommittee had obtained the detective reports that had been sent to General Motors in the Nader case. And Senator Ribicoff said he was particularly struck by one thing about the contents. "The detective who was following Mr. Nader reported very frequently," he said to Roche. "This is a very thick book with daily reports. It runs to many pages. It is apparent, as you thumb through and read this report, that practically none of the investigation had anything to do with what you contended your investigation was for in your news release of March 9. Practically no questions were asked of other litigants or attorneys involved in litigation concerning the Corvair. There was very little inquiry concerning Mr. Nader's legal activities."

Senator Ribicoff remarked that he knew Winsted, Nader's home town, and he drew a picture of the probable effect of the investigation in such a place:

> Detectives invade this small town. They go to the high school principal and start making personal inquiries about a young man of the town who went to high school [there].
>
> They ask questions of private citizens. They go to his boyhood friends. . . . They . . . ask questions whether a man like Ralph Nader was anti-Semitic. They ask questions about his sex habits. They go into questions about his employment, who his friends were, why isn't a man like this at his age married? What grades did he get? Would you hire him? Now it doesn't take very long for people to start repeating that. Before you know it, you have a man who has led a private and honorable life having reflections cast upon his entire character, and that of his family, because of these questions . . . and this must be happening all over America with many other Ralph Naders.

And then, after it was announced that the subcommittee would resume its hearings on the federal role in traffic safety and that Nader would be one of the witnesses,

> the detective agency employed by General Motors placed Mr. Nader under constant surveillance. . . . When he went into a restaurant to eat, detectives saw who he was eating with and what he ordered for lunch. They got the [numbers] of the taxicabs he was riding in. They followed him when he went into a bank to make a deposit or make a withdrawal. They tried to determine what hours he kept in the roominghouse where he lived.

Senator Ribicoff asked if Mr. Roche didn't think that all this activity on behalf of American business was, to say the least, most unworthy?

"Yes, I would agree with you, Senator," Roche said.

Then Senator Kennedy, reverting to the question of the veracity of the March 9 press release put out by General Motors, wanted to know whether the general counsel of G.M. had approved this release. Roche replied that he hadn't approved it —"It was read to him over the telephone. He was not in [Detroit] at the time." But did the general counsel make any objections to the fact that it wasn't completely accurate, Senator Kennedy wanted to know. No, he did not, Roche said.

"Was he aware—he must have been aware of these investigative reports that he had, since he had ordered these investigations," Kennedy said.

"He was aware of the reports and the investigation, yes, sir," Roche said.

"Have you found any explanation as to why, therefore, he did not make any effort to give the accurate and complete story to the public?" Kennedy asked.

"I think that the only explanation . . . again gets back to the preemployment type of investigation, and whether or not questions of this kind are considered to be commonplace in that type of investigation," Roche said.

Senator Kennedy once more read to Roche from Danner's prepared statement, in order, he said, to "give you what, according to Mr. Danner's testimony, he said, talking again of poor old Miss Murphy." The burden of what Senator Kennedy read out was that it was Miss Murphy who had requested on behalf of General Motors "a complete background investigation of Mr. Nader's activities." Senator Kennedy then repeated his contention that the General Motors statement of March 9 had been misleading and in respects false. In his response to Senator Kennedy, Roche again declared that there had been no improper intent involved in the original investigation or the General Motors statement. And he said that while the investigation "may have strayed from the path," he was satisfied "in all honesty and good faith" that "our right to investigate in connection with litigation in the protection of the good name of our product" was the sole motivation in "attempting to find out something about Mr. Nader's interest in the Corvair cases."

7

"I Am Not Proud of That Particular Part of It"

THE NEXT WITNESS WAS Aloysius F. Power, the general counsel for G.M. He was a stockily built man wearing glasses with a heavy frame across the top. First, he read a prepared statement saying that the investigation of Nader was undertaken by him "in the discharge of my responsibilities as general counsel" for the automobile company. He said the investigation was undertaken "as a prudent and appropriate measure in the preparation of the defense of a series of major lawsuits then pending against General Motors." He declared that it was not undertaken for the purpose of harassing or intimidating a witness before any congressional committee. He explained that at the time the investigation was ordered the design of the Corvair was under concerted attack in a hundred and six lawsuits pending in twenty-three states. He then gave a long list of legal citations in support of what he said he considered a proper line of inquiry to determine the possible bias or self-interest of an attorney writing for publication on a matter that was the subject of pending or anticipated litigation. He submitted, for the record, copies of a number of articles Nader had written in legal publications and in magazines—the magazine articles included excerpts from "Unsafe at Any Speed"—critical of the design of the Corvair and of General Motors. And he cited references to Nader's name in publications and a circular letter issued by the American Trial Lawyers Association. Some members of this professional association were keeping in touch with one another concerning Corvair litigation they were engaged in, through the ATLA and ATLA literature, and in one letter from the ATLA. Nader was described as "a lawyer who has developed expertise in the area of automobile manufacturer liability" and a person who had "a substantial amount of information on the Corvair."

Power said this prompted him to ask: Who was Ralph Nader? Was he, as a lawyer, possibly violating Canon 20 of the Canons of Professional Ethics of the American Bar Association by publicly discussing pending or anticipated litigation in the outcome of which he might have an interest? Were his writings "part of an organized nationwide publicity campaign to pretry the Corvair cases by television, newspaper, and magazine, and to precondition prospective jurors in the cases still to be tried throughout the United States?" As a result, said Power, on November 18, 1965, "at my suggestion, an attorney on the legal staff telephoned the Royal-Globe Insurance Company, the General Motors product liability insurer, to inquire whether it had used an investigator in Connecticut who might be able to obtain information about Mr. Nader.

"We were advised that Mr. William F. O'Neill, 16 Prospect Street, East Hartford, Connecticut, had in the past made several investigations for the Royal Indemnity Company," he told the subcommittee. "Mr. George Leafort of Royal Indemnity was requested to ask Mr. O'Neill to make a check on Mr. Nader to obtain whatever information he could with respect to his qualifications, and whether or not he was a trial lawyer in Winsted, Connecticut."

As a result, he said, O'Neill sent a report dated November 21, 1965, to General Motors. He said his report indicated that Nader had never practiced law in Winsted, although he had practiced briefly in Hartford after graduating from law school. He said O'Neill "advised" that Nader apparently was not living in Winsted, although his parents and a brother lived there, and that he probably could be located in Washington, D.C. Power added that "although the [O'Neill] report indicated that Mr. Nader was regarded as having considerable intellectual ability, it failed to disclose any technical background or experience which would qualify him as an automotive expert."

The next development was, Power said, that Nader's book "Unsafe at Any Speed" came on the market in November, and "was extensively reviewed and attracted widespread attention." Power noted that the entire first chapter of the book "was devoted to a criticism of the Corvair, including a rehash of the Pierini [a Corvair case] settlement."

Against this background, he said, "it became increasingly important to learn who Mr. Nader was and what were his connections, if any, with the litigants or attorneys in the Corvair design cases." These were the principal considerations, he said:

1. It was possible that Mr. Nader was seeking to build a reputation and become an expert witness in pending Corvair litigation. If so, a detailed knowledge of his background and training would be necessary.

2. Our self-imposed silence on the merits of the issues involved in this Corvair design litigation in order to remain in compliance with the Canon of Ethics was being misconstrued as an admission that this adverse publicity was true. This could affect not only pending litigation, but the reactions and attitudes of potential jurors and our many customers and stockholders. Definite evidence that Mr. Nader was financially interested could be used to counter his attack.

3. If Mr. Nader was financially interested in this litigation as an attorney, or if he was receiving pay or financial assistance from these litigants or their attorneys, then we could consider bringing this extensive and distorted publicity on pending litigation to the attention of the appropriate people having jurisdiction over violations of the Canons of Ethics. Practically all of the material he was using in his writings to attack the Corvair appeared to come from material collected or obtained by plaintiff's counsel in pending Corvair litigation. ATLA publications were calling attention to his writings and to Mr. Nader as a source of information and material for design and particularly Corvair design litigation.

Definite evidence that Mr. Nader was financially interested could be used to counter his attack.

As Power put them, these considerations certainly sounded like plausible legal reasons for making some sort of check, however reluctantly, on the *bona fides* of a member of the bar with whom General Motors might expect to contend directly in court as an expert witness in Corvair cases. Power gave the subcommittee his account of what then happened. He said that "in a discussion of a proposed investigation of Mr. Nader between members of the [G.M.] legal staff handling Corvair matters of possible sources for developing information on Mr. Nader, Miss Eileen Murphy, a member of the General Motors legal staff who is responsible for our law library, stated that she could ascertain from persons in Washington, whom she knew during the several years that she had served as law librarian for the Civil Division of the Department of Justice, a recommendation or recommendations as to who in Washington might be best qualified to handle such an investigation."

As a result, he said, Miss Murphy telephoned Richard Danner of the Washington law firm of Alvord & Alvord on December 22, 1965. "She pointed out that Mr. Nader's book . . . had been published on November 30, which not only criticized the Corvair automobile, but characterized it as unsafe. Mr. Danner was told that I felt it necessary in order to properly defend the pending lawsuits, to attempt to find out if Mr. Nader was associated with litigants or attorneys for litigants in the pending Corvair cases, and if he had any qualifications as a potential expert witness in these cases."

He said that Danner asked Miss Murphy to get in touch with him after the Christmas holidays. They were to have a conference shortly after the holidays, but it was delayed until January 11. On that date, he said, Miss Murphy had a meeting with Danner at his office in Washington. At this meeting, she gave him "biographical data concerning Mr. Nader" and a copy of the O'Neill report. Then, Power said, she told

Danner that the General Motors people thought the investigation should cover these general areas:

> Where does Mr. Nader live and where does he practice law if he is practicing? Had he been employed by the federal government? What other employment? Where is the source of his income? What were the details of his background that might affect his writings? Especially does he have any engineering background, since some of his writings indicate some tendency to espouse causes, what facts as to his background and personality might indicate whether his writings were for the purpose of furthering another cause?
>
> What would account for the absence of objectivity unusual in a lawyer in writing about the Corvair? Does he have any connection at all with ATLA or ATLA attorneys? Are there any indications that he might be working as a consultant to lawyers handling Corvair cases against General Motors?

Power said that at the conclusion of the discussion on Nader, Danner said that he could undertake the assignment. Miss Murphy said she would return to Detroit and telephone Danner after discussing Danner's fee with the general counsel of General Motors. On January 13, Miss Murphy called Danner and confirmed the assignment.

(In reciting this chronological sequence of events to the subcommittee, Power neglected to mention—perhaps because he did not consider it relevant—that January 13 was the eve of Nader's visit, at the invitation of General Motors, to the G.M. Technical Center.)

Power confirmed that Danner employed Vincent Gillen to do the actual investigation of Nader. He said that Danner was instructed on February 14 to cease surveillance of Nader, but that the General Motors legal staff was informed that surveillance had already been stopped, on February 11. He said that on February 28 Danner was told to end the entire investigation.

As to the contents of the reports received by General

Motors from Danner concerning Nader—these reports covered the period between February 9 and March 14—Power said that these "did not contain any statements detrimental to Mr. Nader's character." He remarked that "there understandably was some information on unrelated matters which was of little or no value for the purposes for which the investigation was intended." However, he said, the reports did indicate that Nader had no educational background or work experience in motor vehicle engineering or technical research; "that he did not appear to have the background to qualify as an expert witness in Corvair design cases; and that he was reported to have had very little trial experience as an attorney." Furthermore, he said, the report disclosed that according to Thomas Lambert, the editor-in-chief of the American Trial Lawyers Association publications, Nader "had in fact done consulting work for lawyers who represent litigants in Corvair design cases against General Motors."

When Power had finished his prepared statement, Senator Ribicoff asked whether Nader had, as a matter of fact, actually represented any litigants in any Corvair case.

"As far as I know, I would say he hasn't represented any litigant as such, as an attorney," Power conceded.

Senator Ribicoff noted "the large number of individual reports" in the Gillen file concerning Nader, and he said the index of the reports indicated that between fifty and sixty people had been interviewed about Nader.

"Now, in the course of questioning, the most intimate questions were asked concerning Nader; isn't that correct?" he asked Power.

"Now, on that I want to first point out," Power replied, "that from the reports that we got and the understanding of the man who was engaged by Royal up in Connecticut, he did not present any questions, as I understood, along those lines."

And then Power went on, helpfully, "The point was made by different people that were talked to—'Now, remember this fellow is not like his brother and his father,' and then they commented that they were anti-Semitic. That is what started some of this. And that report, as you must remember, was turned over by us, as we stated before, to Mr. Danner, and . . . I'm sure he showed it or discussed it—he can tell you that himself—with Mr. Gillen. But that is where some of this was generated."

Senator Ribicoff made it clear that he was talking about the investigation of Nader as a whole, rather than one phase or another of it. "You talked to his associates on the faculty at the University of Hartford," he told Power. "You tried to get hold of the tax collector. You talked to his friends. You talked to his business associates. You talked to all these people, yet the only conversation that the detectives [had] that apparently had any association at all with the Corvair was with this man Lambert, is that right?"

Power agreed that this was so. However, he pointed out, "Oftentimes you make an investigation to find out something specific, and you will end up with a great many statements that don't amount to anything for what you want. But it is the normal course of the investigation."

Ribicoff was not impressed, and he pointed out with some warmth that "a week before [Nader] was to appear before the committee and the day after he appeared before the committee, he was under constant surveillance . . . to determine where he went, who he associated with, what restaurants he ate in, what he ate, who he talked with, what time he got home, when he went to the bank." And he wanted to know, "What did that have to do with the litigation on the Corvair?"

"As far as I am concerned, nothing," Power replied.

"Then why was he placed under this type of surveillance?" Ribicoff asked.

"I don't know," Power said. "It was considered to be the appropriate way to go by the people who were investigating him."

"Let me ask you this, Mr. Power," Senator Ribicoff said.

"Suppose for no apparent reason you were under constant surveillance for a period of a few weeks. Everything about you was checked. Where you went, whether you were home, whom you associated with ... would you consider yourself harassed, if you were under that type of surveillance for two weeks?"

"Well, yes. It would depend on the extent to which I was; yes," Power said.

"Would you feel, too, that if you were aware ... that you were being followed around by people and you didn't know why, that there was a sense of intimidation involved?" Senator Ribicoff asked.

"I might have drawn that conclusion," Power replied. He added, carefully, "I don't think it is a necessary conclusion."

"Do you think that this helps or hurts a man's character to have detectives asking these most intimate questions?" Senator Ribicoff asked.

"Well, I don't think it is very good. I don't think it is helpful," Power said.

"And yet basically you were the one, the general counsel of probably the largest corporation in the world, responsible for putting into motion this type of activity against a young man who you said you didn't even know anything about," Ribicoff said.

"That is right, yes," Power said.

"And I don't imagine today, looking at it, you are very proud of your activities," Ribicoff said.

"No, I am not proud of that particular part of it," Power said. But he went on, "I think one thing must be borne in mind. That this man has written a book in which he charges that we were sacrificing safety for profits, and he alleges that the car, the design of the car, is unsafe. We have a few hundred thousand out there, and we certainly wanted to see what proof he had. We have had this issue litigated in two cases in court, and it will be litigated in others in the future. And when a person puts out a book like that, I have never heard of such a thing . . . it is unusual, that is all, and that is why we checked into it."

In ending his questioning of Power, Senator Ribicoff observed that Nader had come to the subcommittee with some information about basic defects of automobiles, and that members of the subcommittee felt he had something to say. He pointed out that such a man, when he appeared before a committee, was subject to examination and cross-examination, and that "whoever wants to answer [the witness's charges] does have a right to answer." He added, "But in a society as complex as ours, certainly a man with a story to tell, a man with a complaint, a man carrying a banner . . . a man who feels that there is a wrong in our society that he would like to correct—shouldn't that man . . . be able to come, to be able to tell his story . . . without having the largest corporation in America hire a series of detectives to follow him around day and night?"

And turning to where Nader was sitting in the audience, Senator Ribicoff concluded by declaring, "And may I say to you, Mr. Nader, that I have read these [detective] reports very carefully, and you and your family can be proud, because they put you through the mill, and they haven't found a damn thing out against you."

8

*"The Investigation Went Beyond . . .
Its Intention"*

THE NEXT WITNESS WAS Louis H. Bridenstine, the assistant general counsel of General Motors, and it seems that Senator Kennedy had to work to come to grips with him on the subject of the investigation of Nader. When the G.M. statement of March 9 was drawn up, was Bridenstine aware of the fact that "the investigation had gone beyond the question of routine investigation?" the Senator wanted to know.

"I only knew what was in the [Gillen] report, in looking at the copies that had come in," Bridenstine said.

"That indicated, did it not, that there had been a surveillance?" Kennedy asked.

"I knew that there was a surveillance because there was an indication that there had been a surveillance; yes, sir," Bridenstine said.

"If you could just answer the question," Senator Kennedy said acidly. "You [and Mr. Power] are both lawyers. Just say yes or no."

"Yes," Bridenstine said.

"You knew it?"

"Yes, I knew it."

"And then did you know that they had inquired into Mr. Nader's sex life?"

"No, I did not."

"Did you read the reports?"

"Yes, sir."

"But you didn't see anything about that?"

"I didn't know anything about the questions. I read the report. I still don't know what they asked," Bridenstine said.

"Let me rephrase it," Senator Kennedy said. "Do you know there had been things in the reports regarding Mr. Nader's sex life?"

"The only thing I read in the report was good about Mr. Nader," Bridenstine said.

"Now, now, now, now, I am not questioning that Mr. Nader's sex life wasn't good. Can we start again then," Senator Kennedy said, unrelentingly. "Did you see anything in the report regarding Mr. Nader's sex life. Now you remember that?"

"I saw statements that Mr. Nader was manly. Is that what you have in mind, sir?" Bridenstine asked.

This didn't go down very well with Senator Kennedy. "Well, let me just say—you know what I am talking about and you know what we are driving at. Did you find anything in the report that indicated anything about his sex life or the fact that he was normal or abnormal?" He added, sarcastically, "Did you answer questions like that to Mr. Roche of the General Motors Corporation?"

"Senator, I don't—"

"Let's get along with it. You know it was in the report."

"I don't want to be facetious, but Mr. Roche doesn't ask me these kinds of questions either," Bridenstine said to Kennedy.

"It might have helped General Motors if he had?" Kennedy said.

"Yes," Bridenstine said.

"You know what I am talking about now," Kennedy said. "There were things in the report, were there not, that were other than inquiries into his relationship with Corvair?"

"There are other matters reported; yes, sir."

"This information was available to you when you were drawing up the [March 9 G.M.] statement," Kennedy observed.

"Yes, sir."

"Why did you then put that it was a routine investigation initiated through a reputable law firm 'to determine whether Mr. Nader was acting on behalf of litigants or their attorneys on Corvair' and later on say 'it was a limited investigation'?" Kennedy asked.

"That was the purpose of it, sir."

"But that in fact was not the investigation, was it?"

"Yes, sir; that was the purpose of the investigation."

"I understand maybe you say that was the purpose, but the fact is the investigation went far beyond that; did it not?"

"The investigation included matters other than this; yes, sir," Bridenstine said.

"Then why didn't you inform the Senate ... and the American public that the investigation went in fact far beyond this?" Kennedy asked.

To this, Bridenstine replied that he would have to give "the background" concerning the question. He indicated that he had been called into Roche's office on March 9 and was told by Roche that "there is an investigation going on" concerning Nader. He said he had replied, "I heard it myself. I will check into it immediately."

"I wanted to find out the purpose of the investigation, and this, of course [presumably, a "limited investigation"], was the purpose."

"But you already knew about the investigation," Kennedy said.

"I knew an investigation was going on, but I hadn't followed it all, sir," Bridenstine explained.

"You were aware, then?"

"It was in the office; yes, sir."

"And you had seen some of the reports."

"I saw the reports that day. Went through them."

"You had not before that?" Kennedy asked.

"I may have looked at one earlier if it crossed my desk. I don't recall, sir," the assistant general counsel said.

"If you will just be completely candid as Mr. Roche was before the committee, if you will just be completely candid with us, then we can move along," Kennedy said sharply.

"All right, sir."

"The fact is, you didn't just learn about the investigation," Kennedy went on relentlessly. "At that moment you knew the investigation was going on."

"That is correct," Bridenstine said.

"You read a number of reports and you were called in to report further on it," Kennedy said.

"That is right, sir," Bridenstine said. "I was called in and asked about it by Mr. Roche. I checked with the people in the office, and I said, 'Here, Mr. Roche, is what happened.' We had initiated . . . an investigation. It was for the purpose of finding out Ralph Nader's association . . . with the Corvair design cases, if he were associated with them. 'And what did the investigation cover?' I inquired [presumably of "the people in the office"]. 'It covered his qualifications and covered his background . . . his education, his expertise, and his association with these lawyers.' And [for the G.M. statement of March 9] I wrote the words just that way, sir."

> They [presumably Bridenstine's superiors] said, "What about these alleged harassment things that are appearing in the newspaper?" So I inquired then, although I had read some myself in the Detroit papers, about them, and went through every one. I had our people call Mr. Danner, to find out if any of this [alleged harassment] was involved, and they said no, on the newspaper reports, and that is why I told Mr. Roche that this is not true.

In answer to further questions, Bridenstine conceded that he "did discuss the surveillance" of Nader with Roche, "because the surveillance was mentioned in Philadelphia and I believe in the Senate Office Buildings in the articles in the newspapers." But he said he had made no mention of the surveillance of Nader undertaken on behalf of General Motors because he didn't consider that "that was the harassment that Mr. Nader had been complaining about in the newspaper. The harassment was these other items ... harassment on a plane from Philadelphia . . . harassment in Iowa."

"Did the newspaper articles include harassment at the time of surveillance?" Kennedy asked.

"Is surveillance harassment, sir?" Bridenstine asked, and he went on, "I didn't include surveillance as harassment." He insisted again that the investigation of Nader was intended to be a limited one, relating only to Nader's qualifications, background, expertise, and association with Corvair litigation attorneys. But Senator Kennedy kept at him.

"You don't say [in the G.M. statement] the investigation was 'intended,'" Kennedy pointed out. "You state categorically that it was ... a limited investigation." Eventually, he got Bridenstine to go so far as to say that "if it will help us any, I will agree that it was misleading, but I will say that it wasn't intended as such."

At this point Senator Harris attempted to establish just how much Bridenstine did know about the contents of the detective reports on Nader before the G.M. statement of March 9 was issued. Referring to the first of these detective reports, which was dated January 13, 1966, he asked Bridenstine when General Motors had received it. Bridenstine said that it had been received on February 7, and he said, under questioning, that he had "probably" read the first group of reports around the time of receipt and that he had also "hurriedly" gone through the reports as a whole on March 9, prior to the press release. Then Senator Harris, reading from the second page—the first page except for the title page—of the very first detective report on Nader that was received by General Motors, quoted a passage saying that "Nader definitely never manifested anti-Semitic tendencies." Senator Harris observed that the same subject recurred in other interviews by detectives "all the way through this particular report." Referring to page 13 of the same first report by the Gillen investigating agency, he read this passage:

> We had a lengthy discussion with Athanson [George A. Athanson, with whose Hartford law firm Nader had been associated after his graduation from law school; Athanson is now Mayor of Hartford] about Nader's personality, why he was not married, any possibility that he drank to excess or had any vice. Athanson said definitely Nader did not drink, have any known vice, and said he was the type who did not "have time for girls," no effeminate tendencies, and in fact was "on the manly side."

Therefore, Senator Harris told Bridenstine, "you obviously knew that when the report was first received in your office, and you obviously knew that again just prior to the March 9 press release. And do you now still say that ... this was a limited investigation? And if so, what would you call an unlimited investigation?"

"The investigation went beyond, I assume, based on this, its intention," Bridenstine said.

9

"This Unequal Contest Between the Individual and Any Complex Organization"

AFTER A LUNCH RECESS, Nader appeared before the subcommittee. He apologized for putting in a late appearance at the beginning of the hearings. He explained that "I usually take no more than twelve minutes to come down from my residence to the Capitol by cab. In this instance I gave myself twenty minutes. And I waited and waited and waited and waited to get a cab, and as my frustration mounted, I almost felt like going out and buying a Chevrolet."

Nader then made his statement. He said that this was "not the first, nor the last, time when issues transcending in importance the particular individual find a focus for serious treatment and resolution through an individual case." He recalled that during the course of his research for "Unsafe at Any Speed," he had continually encountered "a profound reluctance, in not a few cases it could be called fear, to speak out publicly" on the part of people who were aware of neglect, indifference, and suppression of engineering innovation concerning the design of safer automobiles. He said that in his experience this reluctance was not confined to people who worked for the automobile business directly but was also to be found among people in related industries, in universities, and in government service. "I soon realized," he told the senators, "that the stifling of candid expression embracing dissent from the suffocating orthodoxy of the times was the key reason why auto design safety took until 1965–66 to receive public attention and the serious concern of government, instead of 1936 or 1946 or 1956. The price paid for an environment that requires an act of courage for a statement of truth has been needless death, needless injury, and inestimable sorrow."

One of the factors that had seriously contributed to this atmosphere, he said, was "the absence of adequate insulation or protection for individuals against corporate transgressions into their privacy and personal status." He spoke of the "elaborate arrangements" that often had to be made in order for him to make contact with people who had information to give him, of his "initial incredulity" at hearing descriptions of a "farflung apparatus" of detectives and security agents deployed by the automobile manufacturing companies in fields far removed from the protection of design and trade secrets, and of his growing realization of the extent to which, by the use of such apparatus, human frailties could be exploited to silence criticism and dissent.

He said that while the trademark of modern society might be the organization, its "inspiring and elevating contributions" still flowed from individual initiatives, and he said that unless these initiatives were kept open in society, the "creative and humanizing infusions" of a people's energies would atrophy.

"Yet in a confrontation between an individual and a corporate organization, between myself and General Motors if you will, the systematic immunities accrue to the corporation which has outstripped the law that created it," he said. "I am responsible for my actions, but who is responsible for those of General Motors? An individual's capital is basically his integrity. He can lose only once. A corporation can lose many times and not be affected. This unequal contest between the individual and any complex organization . . . is something which bears the closest scrutiny in order to try to protect the individual from such invasions."

As for the invasion of privacy, he said, he didn't care for

the word privacy—"I would rather call it the invasion of the self rather than invasion of privacy."

He said that "any critic must expect a focused interest in his doings," but "there should be, in all decency, an economy to be observed in the exercise of such corporate curiosity," and in his case, "Surely the questioning by private detectives of people who know and have worked with me (including the crippled and pained person to whom my book is dedicated) . . . in an attempt to obtain lurid details and grist for . . . slurs and slanders goes well beyond affront and becomes . . . an encroachment upon a more public interest."

Then Nader went on to make several comments on the General Motors contentions, in the March 9 statement, about the nature of his activities. He declared that "there is nothing more legitimate and honorable in the practice of law" than the representation of clients in product liability cases. He stated categorically that he did not represent any clients or act on behalf of any of their attorneys in Corvair litigation. He said he wanted to "correct a misleading impression" in the G.M. statement about his reaction to their Corvair presentation during his visit to the G.M. Technical Center at Warren, and that in fact he had been "singularly unimpressed" with it.

"If General Motors wishes to know why I spent an inordinate amount of time on the Corvair," Nader told the subcommittee, "it is because the Corvair is an inordinately dangerous vehicle." He declared that the design of the Corvair "provides a spacious and instructive case study of the subordination of safety considerations to the tyranny of the cost accountants and the creative lethality of the stylists."

Nader then went into considerable detail concerning what he said were the defects in the design of the Corvair and the hazards of the car to the safety of people who rode in it: in particular the relationship he said existed between the simple swing-axle rear suspension system of the 1960–63 Corvairs and vehicle instability characterized by "tuck under" of the rear wheels and rear-end breakaway frequently leading to rollover.

What he was trying to show by all this, he said, was that "a civilized society will not tell the victims of automobiles that it is up to them to prove that the automobile is defective" even though "the difficulty of that proof staggers the imagination." He said that although in court a plaintiff must prove his case, "I think beyond that that we should have standards and legislative frameworks by government that will in effect make sure that the automobile manufacturer has to prove that his vehicle is safe before he puts it on the market.... The curious immunity from legislative investigation which has clothed specific car makes and models ... must be terminated."

Before finishing his statement, Nader said that he wanted to reply to several of the points brought up in testimony of the General Motors executives that might have cast some adverse reflection on him. As to his "material motive," he said that he had been out of his law practice for two years, during which time he had been primarily engaged in trying to further a campaign for the legislation of safety standards for automobiles, and that in this period he had repeatedly turned down invitations to handle cases. He said that royalties on his book, "although I have not yet received the first installment," comprised his prime source of income, and he said that these royalties would be devoted to the cause of auto safety. He said that he received no fee for providing information to attorneys handling Corvair litigation. He said that he had once acted as a consultant to the plaintiff's attorneys on a case dealing with a 1960 Chevrolet, after the case had been tried and lost. He said that about two or three months after he began advising the attorneys they received a verdict of $225,000 against General Motors, and that his entire reimbursement for that, including expenses, had been $475. And he said of the mention in the American Trial Lawyers Association newsletter that he had information on the Corvair, "The reason why Professor Lambert placed that bit of information in the newsletter is because he knew that I would provide such information without a fee. He has a very fine sense of legal ethics in this matter and it was only on this basis that he did this."

Nader then wound up his statement by referring to what he said was "a particularly sensitive matter" with him—the effect of the General Motors investigation of him upon his family, and he touched upon the testimony of the general counsel of General Motors in this respect. "The statement by Mr. Power trying to distinguish between members of my family by repeating a bit of scurrilous gossip . . . and in effect leaving an implication on my brother and my father is very unfortunate. I think . . . that had nothing to do with the particular inquiry on hand, and I resent it deeply as I am sure my parents and my brothers and sisters resent it as well," he told the subcommittee.

Senator Ribicoff told Nader once more what he had said after Power's testimony, that from the investigation he had emerged with a completely clean bill of health and character. "While you have suffered as a result of this, for whatever it is worth," he remarked, "you do have the satisfaction of knowing that the detective agencies, at the rate of $6,700 [the fee that the Gillen agency charged General Motors for the investigation], haven't been able to find a thing on you."

"Thank you, Senator. Had they asked me the questions, I could have saved them the trouble and the money before it ever started," Nader said.

Senator Kennedy put several questions to the witness, and then asked him "one final question. Why are you doing all this, Mr. Nader?"

Nader paused briefly before replying. "I think the initial difficulty in answering that question, Senator, can be put in this way," he said. "If I was engaged in activities for the prevention of cruelty to animals, nobody would ever ask me that question. Because I happen to have a scale of my priorities which leads me to engage in activities for the prevention of cruelty to humans, my motivations are constantly inquired into."

Basically, he said, the motivation was this: when he considered the "horrible carnage" involved in the automobile over the years, he had asked himself how human genius could be applied to provide an engineering environment of both highway and vehicle which would protect the occupants of cars from the consequences of the errors and the continuing errors of automotive and highway design. He told Senator Kennedy that as things stood, laws were being written, manipulated, and interpreted so as to focus almost entirely on the driver's role, without taking proper account of the role of the vehicle in automobile accidents.

What had struck him when he had got out of law school and when he looked at the advances made in science and engineering—in space and missile systems, for example—was the tremendous gap between the possible and the actual in society, and he had become "incensed at . . . the tremendous amount of injustice and brutality in an industrialized society without any accountability, without any responsibility . . . that people sitting in executive suites can make . . . decisions which will someday result in tremendous carnage. And because they are remote in time and space between their decision and the consequences of that decision, there is no accountability." In particular, he had been shocked by "the drastic gap between the performance of the U.S. auto industry and its promise," and he said that he would like nothing more than to see the U.S. auto industry offer the world, which was altogether now losing some 175,000 people and witnessing close to 50 million injuries in highway accidents a year, a crashworthy vehicle.

So far as the G.M. investigation of him was concerned, he said that he considered himself harassed by it. He said, "I don't intimidate easily," but he added that he had to confess that at certain times he had not been without second thoughts concerning the penalties and pain of working as a critic in the area of auto safety.

"I think the thing that has persuaded me to continue in this area," Nader told the subcommittee, "is that I cannot accept a climate in this country where one has to have an ascetic existence and steely determination in order to speak truthfully, candidly, and critically of American industry, and the auto industry. I think if it takes that much stamina something is wrong with the enabling climate for expression in our country. . . . This is not an ideological problem. This is a problem of individuals confronting complex organizations."

10

"I Told Miss Murphy That a Suitable Pretext Would Be Used"

THE NEXT WITNESS USED WAS Richard G. Danner, the attorney with the Washington law firm of Alvord & Alvord, through whom, according to General Motors, instructions for the investigation of Nader had been transmitted.

Danner said that on December 22, 1965, he had received a long-distance telephone call from Eileen Murphy of the legal department of General Motors in Detroit. According to Danner, Miss Murphy said that she would like to talk to him "concerning a problem in the legal department" concerning Ralph Nader. She said that, as a result of a preliminary investigation, G.M. had obtained some background information on Nader, but that this investigation covered only his earlier years, and that additional information was necessary to give a complete picture of Nader. And she had asked Danner if additional investigation of Nader was decided upon by G.M., whether Danner could "recommend a competent investigative organization to handle this matter."

Danner said he had told Miss Murphy that he felt certain he could find an investigative agency to do the job, and he suggested that, because of the imminent holidays, they get together sometime after the first of the year. He had then telephoned Vincent Gillen, the head of Vincent Gillen Associates, Inc., an investigating agency in New York—a man whom Danner said he had known for some years, whose services he had used "in interviewing potential witnesses" on one occasion, and whose work he had found to be "competent, businesslike, and ethical." He explained that he asked Gillen over the telephone if he was in a position to handle an investigation that might reach into several states, and he said he had told Gillen that "such investigation would be of the background and activity type concerning an individual." Whereupon, Gillen "did assure me that he was equipped to handle such an investigation and would be pleased to serve us."

Then, on January 11, Miss Murphy had come to Washington and they had a discussion about Nader. "This time," Danner said, "Miss Murphy furnished me all the information which she had concerning Mr. Nader, including a copy of an investigative report covering some activities in Connecticut and some background data that she had apparently compiled from press, magazines and other publications."

Danner said that at this same meeting Miss Murphy then had "related to me other facts and matters for investigation":

> Miss Murphy stated that it was strongly believed by her and the legal department of General Motors that Mr. Nader was in some manner connected with or working for the plaintiffs' attorneys in the Corvair negligence suits against General Motors but that no compelling proof of this had been adduced as yet. A discussion in some depth ensued at which time Miss Murphy went into details as to the type of information needed, including the date and type of government employment, sources of income, type and locale of law practice, if any, business associates, movement, and, in short, a complete background investigation of Mr. Nader's activities. We discussed the difficulties involved in this type of investigation, particularly the strong possibility of Mr. Nader's learning of the investigation from persons interviewed. I told Miss Murphy then that a suitable pretext would be used but this would be left to the investigative agency. All instructions to the investigative agency were to be handled by me, and all reports submitted by the agency were to be sent to me for transmittal to General Motors.

Following that discussion with Miss Murphy in which he received the instructions from G.M., Danner said, he had telephoned Gillen in New York, and Gillen had come to Washington to see him on January 13, when Danner "told Mr. Gillen the purpose of the investigation, and ... discussed in detail the difficulties involved in trying to establish Mr. Nader's connections with plaintiffs' attorneys." He said that Gillen was of the opinion that information about Nader's connections with plaintiffs' attorneys would "most likely be discovered by a regular preemployment type of investigation," and that the two men agreed that such a pretext should be used in carrying out the investigation. He said that the two men discussed the possibility "of having to resort" to surveillance on Nader, and agreed that they would not undertake physical surveillance unless "a determination was made that such was absolutely essential." Gillen then estimated his charges for the investigation on a weekly basis; Miss Murphy, in Detroit, was told about this by telephone; and she called back the same day to say that the investigation had been approved by the general counsel of General Motors and that it should proceed. It formally began that day, January 13, and thereafter, until about March 14, Danner said, he had relayed a series of reports from Gillen on to General Motors in Detroit, for Miss Murphy's attention.

Danner declared that he considered the investigation into the background and connections of Nader "as being perfectly proper, since it had for its purpose to determine what connection, if any, Mr. Nader might have with the plaintiffs' attorneys in the Corvair suits." He said that it was "a routine investigation such as are conducted every day in connection with business, industry, or the practice of law" and that it had never occurred to him that Nader might be called as a witness before a Senate committee. He asserted that "never was there any intention to harass, intimidate, or in any manner embarrass Mr. Nader for any purpose, certainly not to influence his testimony or cause him not to testify."

Danner then dealt with the charges made concerning "questions asked of interviewees pertaining to sex and to religious prejudices of Mr. Nader." He said he could assure the committee that any such questions that "might have been asked" would come about in this way. "You must realize," he said, "that in any preemployment type investigation, designed to develop background information concerning a subject, that statements or references will be made as to the subject's personality, character, attitudes, and a variety of other topics. When a subject matter is raised, it must be pursued to its logical conclusion, and particularly if it is derogatory in nature, the investigator must be extremely careful to continue his inquiry until he has established the statement or has completely dispelled it. This is elementary investigative technique, and I am certain that it would be considered unfair to Mr. Nader to have such questions raised and thereafter not cleared up by further investigation."

Danner ended his statement by denying that General Motors had ever instructed him, or that he had instructed Gillen, concerning the use of girls to entice or entrap Nader, and he also denied receiving or giving instructions to have telephone calls made to Nader.

When Danner had finished making his statement, Senator Ribicoff asked the attorney, "I am just curious: Is this part of your work, hiring detectives and other people?"

"Well, Mr. Chairman, I guess in the law business ... you encounter new phases ... this is the first time I have done this type of thing," Danner replied. He said that he had merely acted to hire the detective agency and to forward its reports to Detroit.

"Is there much of this done to your knowledge generally?" Ribicoff wanted to know.

"Well, not from experience, but from what I read and hear, this is a rather commonplace thing in business, in industry ... investigating the background of people," Danner said. "Usually it is for preemployment or maybe it is the basis for an interview. They want to talk to someone, but they would like to know more about them." He added that he had "read several articles that this is becoming more and more widespread, and even the use of technical equipment."

After asking a couple of other questions, Senator Ribicoff turned over the questioning of Danner to Senator Kennedy, who handled the witness in comparatively perfunctory fashion. "Let me just ask you a few questions," he said to Danner. "First, I understand you have a fine reputation, as does your law firm."

Senator Kennedy wanted to know whether Danner had understood from the discussions he had with the representatives of the General Motors legal department that he was merely to have investigated whatever relationship may have existed between Nader and the Corvair litigation.

"That was the primary purpose. There was no question about that," Danner replied.

Senator Kennedy said that the key question in his mind was whether and to what degree General Motors had asked for detailed information on Nader's background; and what kind of information the company wanted. He remarked that "from the way they [the executives of G.M.] testified before the committee, I would think that there was an impression that this decision was made by the investigative agency and by you." And he put it to Danner: was the whole effort to obtain this background information on Nader, the detail on Nader, "a decision that was made by them or was it a decision made by you or by the investigative agency?"

"I think it is difficult to pin down who made that decision," Danner said. "I can only say that they [the G.M. people] came to me and discussed their problem, the need for a complete investigation. Many things were mentioned in connection with the investigation as to how far it should go, where it had led in this direction, should it be pursued." In answer to other questions, he said that he had given instructions on January 26 to put Nader under surveillance, that the surveillance had lasted for a week, and that G.M. had been informed of the results of it "at some place along the line."

"Who got into the question first about anti-Semitism? Was that raised with you?" Senator Kennedy wanted to know, referring to Danner's meeting with Miss Murphy of the G.M. legal staff.

"That was presented to me. I didn't know Mr. Nader or anything about him," Danner said.

"Who raised the question of looking into his sex life?" Senator Kennedy asked.

"That came about during the discussion," Danner said. "As I recall, in determination of his associations, if he was married, if he was not married, what sort of girl friend did he have."

"How would that be helpful in finding out about the Corvair?" Kennedy asked.

"Well, I think probably none really on the Corvair, but I think it might reflect in some manner on his background," Danner said.

"Did you discuss all these questions with General Motors representatives?" Senator Kennedy asked.

"Not in this detail," Danner said.

"Did you discuss with them that you were going to inquire into his relationships, his personal relationships with other people?"

"In connection with the background investigation, yes," Danner said.

"And did they give their approval to that?"

"Yes."

11

"I Suppose Maybe You Could Start with the Truth"

DANNER WAS EXCUSED, and, surprisingly, the person who had given the instructions to Danner on behalf of G.M. for the investigation of Nader, Eileen Murphy, who was present in the hearing room and who, indeed, had been sworn in earlier along with Power, Bridenstine, and Danner, was not called to testify as to exactly what instructions G.M. had given Danner.

Instead, the next in the cast of characters called was Vincent Gillen. Throughout the hearing, the head of the private detective agency, looking pretty much as Frederick Condon had described him in his memo—about forty-five to fifty years of age, neat, of medium build, but with "a peculiar barrel-chested quality . . . glasses with heavy black frames . . . hair was kinky-curly, combed straight back neatly"—had been sitting in the audience. He was wearing a bluish suit and a red-and-blue striped tie. He seemed altogether unfazed by all the uproar caused by the discovery of the G.M. investigation, and from time to time he had even taken out a pocket-size miniature camera (of the kind familiar from spy films) and without embarrassment photographed the proceedings going on in front of him.

After identifying himself and telling the subcommittee that he welcomed the opportunity "to inform you frankly and fully about the investigation of Ralph Nader," Gillen, in a rather gravelly voice, launched into a glowing review and appraisal of his professional experience and standing—three years as a special agent of the F.B.I. after graduating from law school; seven years of investigative work for Metropolitan Life Insurance Company; another nine years of personnel work with Otis Elevator, Rexall Drug, and Reeves Instrument; and, under license to the State of New York to conduct a private investigative business ("A thorough character investigation . . . is conducted in New York to make sure a license is not issued to anyone not meeting the high standards set by the state"), some eight years as president of Vincent Gillen Associates, of New York City, with offices in Paramus, New Jersey, and Garden City, New York. Almost sixty percent of the work performed by his agency consisted, he said, of "conducting preemployment and background investigations for employers in all facets of our great economy," and the rest of it of "myriad management problems and a few personal."

Gillen denied that he or any of his employees had trailed Nader in Des Moines on January 10. He said that around December 22, 1965, Richard Danner had telephoned him and asked if he was in a position to conduct an investigation in several eastern states. He had told Danner that he was, and on January 13, he and Danner conferred at Danner's office in Washington. At that meeting,

> [Danner] said that he was representing General Motors Corp. and wished to find out something about the background of Ralph Nader, who held himself out as an expert in the safety field. Nader claims not to represent claimants in lawsuits, but the language of Nader's writing and speeches seemed identical with those appearing in papers filed in suits against General Motors. General Motors had made some investigation of Nader but had not found out much. He is not listed in any phone directory in or about Winsted, Conn., his hometown, nor in Washington, D.C. Danner wanted to learn all he could about Nader's background, his expertise in safety, his source of income, and his associates especially in the legal profession.

Gillen went on to say that Danner and he "discussed the fact that people are reluctant to give information about a person . . . when the client is a large corporation," and agreed because of this "to tell no one the name of the client, a standard investigative practice." He explained, "We knew that the information we wanted could be uncovered in a normal, routine preemployment-type investigation. We decided to use that pretext."

Gillen then explained some of the investigatory problems involved—problems concerning the investigators, the interviewees, and the subject of the investigation. "As you gentlemen are aware," he said to the committee, "whenever any investigation is made, people interviewed invariably jump to the conclusion that something is wrong with the person being investigated, especially if no reason for the inquiry is given. On the other hand, if people are told the person is being investigated for a position, no stigma is attached to the inquiry. We do it every day. The principal reason for using the preemployment pretext was to prevent any inference of wrongdoing on the part of Mr. Nader and to prevent any 'character assassination.' "

Gillen then outlined the course of his field investigation of Nader. He said it began in the Winsted-Hartford area on January 25, but that "not a single person we interviewed in Connecticut knew where Nader could be found, except possibly in Washington." In the meantime, he said, he had sent a request for investigation in Washington "to my associate, Mr. D. David Shatraw, former F.B.I. agent, president of the Arundel Investigative Agency, Severna Park, Maryland," with what Gillen said were these "rather prophetic" words:

> We must be careful not to arouse the ire of Nader. Keep in mind that he is a brilliant fellow and a good writer and he could, no matter how unjustly, write something about us which would be rather damaging. Hence it is important that interviews be handled with great discretion and under a suitable pretext.

Simultaneously, he said, he had the investigation pursued in the Boston area through the services of Charles B. Allen, also a former F.B.I. agent, of Management Consultants, Inc. From all of these inquiries, he indicated, little about Nader's sources of income or his activities was established, and so, on January 26, the decision was made to start surveillance of Nader "when we located him." A Washington address had appeared on some legal papers filed many months before, and someone from the Arundel investigating agency called the landlady of the rooming house at that address to find out if anything was known of Nader; "to his surprise", he was told by the landlady that Nader roomed there. The surveillance of Nader began on Friday, February 4, by the Arundel agency, Gillen said, but after two days Arundel told him that due to a heavy workload they were unable to continue it, and Gillen sent two of his own men from New York to continue the surveillance. But he said that on the late afternoon of February 9 full surveillance was discontinued, on Danner's instructions, because, as Gillen said, "it was not being very productive."

He said that Danner had suggested a "spot surveillance" instead of a full surveillance on Nader, and that Danner had suggested that his men might pick Nader up after he had testified before the subcommittee. He said that on February 9 he told one of his agents to call the subcommittee office to find out if and when Nader was scheduled to testify, and that around noon on February 10 one of his agents called the subcommittee office and was informed that Nader was actually testifying at that time and was almost finished.

Thus frustrated, Gillen told his men to start the spot surveillance at around 11 A.M. February 11, and as he described the events that followed, "About 1:30 P.M. . . . one of our men saw Nader enter the New Senate Office Building. He followed." Gillen added, for the benefit of the subcommittee, "The man on the scene makes a quick decision and you have to live with it. That sort of thing can happen in any investigative organization.

I am sure Senator Kennedy knows this from his experience as Attorney General when he was responsible for all government investigative agencies."

"I am glad that you brought me into this," Senator Kennedy observed, smiling.

Gillen went on to deny that his men followed a newspaper reporter in the mistaken notion that he was Nader. "These men had followed Nader several days and knew him well," he said. "They did not tell a guard that they were looking for Nader. . . . One agent did describe Nader to a guard and the guard said a man fitting that description had entered the TV studio. Our agent then phoned his associate to join him. They were both in the corridor, some distance apart, when they were, independently, asked to leave. They left. I sincerely regret this incident and again apologize to the Senate for it."

Gillen also denied that he or any of the former F.B.I. people with whom he worked used any women during the investigation. Then he went on to give his version of his interview with Condon in Concord. He denied that he had used a tape recorder during that interview, and he gave this account of his questioning of Condon concerning Nader's personal life:

> I asked if, at Harvard where they had been law school classmates, they had "double dated." Condon said 'no' and explained that he, Condon, was married then. . . . I asked if he had ever met any of Nader's girl friends or has seen him with a girl. Condon said, "Oh, if you are concerned about that, don't worry about Ralph. He's all right," or words to that effect. I asked no other questions along that line. We then had a casual discussion regarding the difficulty such an intelligent fellow, with a wide range of interests, has to find a suitable girl to marry. It certainly was not my intent in that casual talk to pry any further into that aspect.

"Please keep in mind the pretext, and I urge you so strongly to keep in mind the pretext," Gillen said to the subcommittee. "Any investigator conducting a preemployment background investigation of a mature, healthy, intelligent unmarried man who apparently has sufficient income to support a wife, must ask questions of this nature. They are essential questions in every government background investigation."

At this point Senator Kennedy, who had been riffling through a thick bound volume of typewritten pages that appeared to be the detectives' reports on Nader, interrupted Gillen's statement. "Your testimony, Mr. Gillen, is proceeding on the supposition that this is a preemployment background investigation, isn't it?" he said to the witness. "Were you trying to hire Mr. Nader for something?"

Gillen said he had already made his reasons for the "preemployment pretext" clear in his testimony.

"But then you go ahead and excuse all of the steps that you take thereafter on the basis that this was a regular preemployment investigation or a regular Government background investigation," Senator Kennedy pointed out. He also observed that Gillen had made use of false names and included "all of these personal questions" about Nader on the basis of an alleged preemployment investigation that in fact was not such an investigation, and that none of this had been authorized by Nader.

Gillen's reply to this was that "when you conduct an investigation under a pretext, you have to carry it out completely. . . . You have to ask all questions normally pertinent to that pretext. If you do anything less or inject extraneous matters, you run the risk of losing the pretext."

"But you were lying," Senator Kennedy said. "What you mean [is] that you were conducting an investigation under a lie and that you had to carry the lie out completely."

Gillen didn't seem bothered by this charge at all. "Did you ever have that happen while you were the Attorney General?" he demanded of Senator Kennedy.

"No, I did not, but I am asking *you* the question," Senator Kennedy said.

"Did any of the investigators [in the Department of Justice] ever do it?" Gillen asked, persisting.

"I want to ask *you* the question," Senator Kennedy said.

"You were conducting [the investigation] as a lie, were you not?"

"Well, you get very little investigative material if you conduct it openly on all occasions, sir. You know that," Gillen told Kennedy, unworried.

"I understand that, but what disturbs me—" Senator Kennedy began to say, in reply.

"If you understand it, why don't you let us do it, then?" Gillen demanded quickly.

"Mr. Gillen, because it disturbs me what you were doing. This was a form of harassment. What disturbs me even more is that you don't seem to have realized it," Senator Kennedy said.

But Gillen said he didn't consider that he had used harassment. Continuing with his prepared statement, he said that none of his investigators had asked any embarrassing questions or intimated anything lurid about Nader, while conducting the investigation. "Furthermore, our investigation uncovered absolutely no indication of any abnormality on the part of Ralph Nader. On the contrary, he is obviously an intelligent, personable young man and I join with him in expressing regret that people have seen fit to misconstrue routine inquiries for their own sensational purposes."

Gillen went on, "The same thing applies to the questions regarding anti-Semitism. Virtually everyone we talked with in Winsted cautioned us not to attribute to Ralph the attitude . . . of some members of his family. In fairness to Ralph, we had to ask that question of all those with whom he associated during his adult life. I am happy to state that none of the people we interviewed believes Ralph Nader is anti-Semitic."

Explaining once again that "when you conduct an investigation under a pretext, you have to carry it out completely. You have to ask all questions normally pertinent to that pretext," Gillen said that it was because of this professional consideration that "we could not ask directly about Mr. Nader's association with attorneys or claimants, in Corvair cases." As a result, he said, "We had to wait for the Corvair matter to develop; it did develop. A Boston friend mentioned that Ralph Nader has done much consulting work with several attorneys who happen to represent a number of claimants in Corvair cases. That was a major purpose in our investigation. We achieved that objective. It was accomplished through a routine background type investigation."

And Gillen ended his statement with the declaration that he stood on the quality of his reports and the motto of his company: "There is no substitute for quality and integrity."

Senator Ribicoff then tackled Gillen for a while. "General Motors contends that all they were seeking to discover was whether or not Nader was tied up with Corvair litigation, yet your basic investigation throughout had to do with the personal life and character of Mr. Nader," he told the detective.

"Yes; with the anticipation that somewhere along the line we would get that little bit of information we wanted, sir, and we did," Gillen said. He continued, "We got the lead that these are [the lawyers] that he had been dealing with according to [Thomas] Lambert, who ought to know. Now, you have got to follow that up. Subsequently that could be followed up. I wasn't going to prove it in February or necessarily in March. This is a very delicate investigation. And I never had the slightest dream about the cookies and the girls things coming up. They didn't know he was being investigated. It was one of the strangest coincidences in the world, if you want to look at that frankly and honestly." And Gillen said that both he and Danner had "discussed it—this fellow [Nader] was apparently setting the situation where he will be an expert witness or will be accepted by jurors or judges as an expert witness so let's find out how expert he is and everything about him which may be of value to the trial counsel in subsequent litigations." It was because of this, he said, that he had felt, and Danner had agreed with him, that "we should uncover every aspect of his life which someday may be of value to our client. That is my concept of doing a good job for the client, getting the complete background."

Then Senator Kennedy took over the questioning, and

among the things he wanted to know was whether Gillen ever called Nader himself to tell him that he was conducting an investigation of him.

"What would you suggest I tell him?" Gillen asked the Senator.

"I suppose maybe you could start with the truth," Senator Kennedy said.

Gillen said that, as a matter of fact, he had tried to get in touch with Nader in the first few days of the investigation, through the office of his publisher in New York.

"Were you going to tell him you were going to conduct the investigation?" Senator Kennedy asked.

"Oh, no-o-oo. I was going to try to interview him," the detective said. He added, "I knew very little about him. And I have had great success in investigations, sir, including when I was in the F.B.I., in talking with people under a pretext, and drawing them out and getting their whole life history. People like to talk about themselves. And I had hoped there to get the whole story of what he was doing."

It was an intriguing vision—Gillen drawing out Nader under a pretext of getting his whole life history. Senator Kennedy wanted to know more.

"What were you going to say to him if you got him on the telephone?" he asked.

"I was going to set up an appointment with him," Gillen said.

"And how were you going to describe yourself?" Kennedy asked.

Gillen clasped his hands together over the typescript of his prepared testimony before him on the witness table, and, with a keen glance, gave the question his professional consideration.

"Oh, in some appropriate manner, sir," he said.

"Just give us an example," Kennedy urged.

"Well, what does it matter so long as he believed it?" Gillen said.

"I mean, just give us an example," Senator Kennedy said.

"I would suppose I would say I had a client . . . who had some axe to grind in connection with drugs or some other cause . . . and he was going to write a book and delve into it," Gillen said. "There are a lot of aspects of our economy which if one had the talents of Nader you could write a document about. I would figure out some pretext." But he added that in terms of what actually happened, "I didn't have to think about it much . . . because [Nader] never called me back."

Senator Kennedy attempted once more to get Gillen to see the difference between a preemployment investigation made with the subject's consent and an investigation made with the use of a false pretext and without the consent of the subject. Gillen got very impatient at this. "Oh, Senator, come on, come on," he said. "For goodness sake, where did I learn to do this? In the F.B.I.!"

"Well, maybe Mr. Hoover should come up and testify . . . wherever you learned it, you were proceeding under false pretenses, were you not?"

"Gee, you know, you can get into a lot of semantics here," Gillen said, wonderingly.

Once again Gillen denied any harassment of Nader. "I will just say that . . . if it is a crime, and if I am guilty then I should be indicted and prosecuted," he declared.

"I don't know that there would be a violation of law. I am not suggesting that," Senator Kennedy said.

"What *are* you suggesting? I did something not wrong and you are criticizing me!" Gillen cried.

Senator Kennedy said what he was trying to suggest was that, at any rate, the officers of General Motors apparently "finally were able to see" that there had indeed been harassment of Nader, because they had apologized to Nader.

But Gillen wouldn't budge. "I think there is a misunderstanding of what Mr. Roche said," he told Senator Kennedy. "As I read it, he said, 'if these things happened,' that what Mr. Nader says happened, 'I apologize and I regret it.' He didn't say they *did* happen."

"We can bring Mr. Roche back," Senator Kennedy said, warningly.

"Get the transcript," Gillen told Kennedy.

"I have the testimony. I had understood that Mr. Roche apologized," Senator Kennedy said.

"Well," Gillen said, "Let's read it carefully: 'I deplore the harassment to which Mr. Nader has apparently been subjected.' . . . Let's get this clear, now. Mr. Roche did not apologize for doing it [meaning, presumably, engaging in acts of harassment]. He said if they happened, of course he apologized, but there is no proof they happened and I am telling you they didn't happen."

Senator Kennedy said he would like to ask Roche about that.

"I am glad to have a chance to have it corrected," Gillen said.

At this point Senator Ribicoff intervened, to say that he had the impression from Roche's testimony that Roche was sorry that the investigation had taken place and that he would not undertake such a thing again, and that if he had known about it in the first place no investigation of Nader would have been conducted "as you had conducted it, Mr. Gillen."

Senator Kennedy asked Roche if he would care to stand up and say that the interpretation of Senator Ribicoff and his own concerning harassment of Nader was correct.

"That interpretation is correct, Senator Kennedy," Roche said.

But even then, Gillen would not admit to having harassed Nader. He said that "the client doesn't owe me any great explanation," but that Danner's secretary had called him and said, "Stop the surveillance," after Gillen had read or heard about a news item "concerning these men [Gillen's agents] allegedly following a couple of reporters and all that other nonsense [in the New Senate Office Building]." He declared that "if you don't know you are being followed, where is the harassment? You see. So there was no point in following Nader after it was in the newspaper that he thought he was being followed. You know that, sir. And so far as harassment goes, how about the investigators of our government who follow spies, Red spies all over the country? Are we harassing them? They are not harassed until they know they are being followed."

"Are you putting Nader in the same position as you would a spy you are following around?" Senator Harris asked.

"You know, Senator, that I am not; no, sir," Gillen said.

He went on to say, "I have answered it about twenty times already . . . my assignment was to get the complete life and background of Ralph Nader, and in order to get it, I thought that these things [matters concerning Nader's personal life] would in the normal course of investigation be covered. And if they were not covered, they would be suspect." He said that he had warned Danner at the beginning that Nader might well discover that the investigation was going on, and that he asked Danner, "Are you prepared for what may happen? . . ." And he said that Danner had told him, "Don't worry about it."

Therefore, Gillen said, "I did it as gently and discreetly and fairly to Nader as could possibly be done. And in order to accomplish that objective, we had to ask those [personal] questions or at least have it covered in the course of the investigation." He added, "Incidentally, sir, it was first brought up by the high school, and we had to clear it up. The high school principal said to our investigator—and he showed us the yearbook which said, 'Ralph Nader—woman hater.' He said, 'Now some people get the wrong impression about Ralph and this stuff. Do not pay any attention to it.' There is where it first raised its head and we had to pursue it in fairness to Ralph. I have told you that, and so did Danner."

"What the hell is all this 'fairness to Ralph'? Senator Kennedy said sharply. "You keep proving that he is not anti-Semitic and he is not queer. 'In fairness to Ralph'? Ralph is doing all right. You were just a public-spirited citizen rushing around the country in fairness to Ralph?"

"Well, I did not hear—all right. I was doing a job, and I

still think it was a good one," Gillen said, defiantly, and he went on saying that until he was excused from testifying.

And when Gillen had finished, Roche made a final appearance as a witness, to ask permission, which was granted, to put into the record—"inasmuch as Mr. Nader has commented rather extensively on the Corvair"—a long statement by General Motors made in January, before the Michigan Senate, in defense of the stability of the Corvair. And he also made a brief statement in which he emphasized that "the position of General Motors . . . was contained in my opening statement this morning" and "not accurately set forth in our March 9 statement, which I regret." He said that such errors would not happen again. He declared, on behalf of G.M., "It has not been, and will not be our policy in the future to undertake the surveillance or broad background investigation of those persons who write or speak critically of our corporation and our products." And he said he hoped that his apologies on behalf of himself and General Motors to the committee and to Nader "will be accepted in the spirit in which I offer them."

To this Senator Ribicoff responded warmly. He commended Roche "for your candor, for your sensitive appreciation of what was involved." And he said, "I am sure that your expression will have an influence on many others in the realization, I think the phrase Mr. Nader used himself, of the integrity of an individual, the integrity of a person's self-respect for another person's privacy. I think that this whole thing has been unfortunate."

And Senator Kennedy, too, said that he commended Roche. He said he considered Roche's statement "extremely helpful as far as General Motors is concerned. And General Motors . . . I think stands for something, not only in this country, but around the world."

"Thank you, Senator and Mr. Chairman," Roche said.

And on that conciliatory note, the hearing ended. It had been a historic confrontation between the force of a huge corporation and a single citizen who had criticized that corporation, and the solitary citizen had clearly come out of the confrontation with flying colors. That evening on network television, tens of millions of people were able to see the president of General Motors apologizing to the Ribicoff subcommittee and to Nader for the manner in which Nader had been tailed and investigated, and the next morning they could read about it in detail in the press, under front-page headlines such as that appearing in the New York *Times:* "G.M. Apologizes for Harassment of Critic." It had been a hard day for General Motors, but it seemed that Roche's apology, for which members of the committee had commended him warmly, had done as much as could be done under the circumstances toward redeeming the reputation of the corporation, so injured by what had turned out to be an unseemly excursion into the private life of a critic and writer whose probity, happily, had withstood all the personal inquiries made about him. "By apologizing, Roche became the statesman, and the image of the corporate entity he represented became fused with his," Nader remarked dryly to the author of this book not long after the hearing, speaking of the manner in which G.M. seemed to him to have emerged from it, at least as far as the mass media were concerned. Certainly, in the press, Roche had received high marks for what was considered his candor under difficult circumstances. And, on the whole, the subcommittee seemed to have accepted his position, and even, with reservations, the position of the senior officers of the G.M. legal staff, that the basic intent of the investigation of Nader had been a proper one directed at Nader's potential as an expert witness in Corvair cases and his association, if any, with litigating Corvair case attorneys—an investigation that, if carried out in that spirit, was not inconsistent with accepted legal practice. But, as matters had been presented by General Motors witnesses at the subcommittee hearing, the inference was that the investigation ordered by G.M. had become distorted by the antics of a private detective agency in concentrating on Nader's private and sex life instead of his potential as an expert witness in Corvair cases and his relationship with Corvair attorneys. To judge from the testimony of the G.M. officers, the villain of the piece was Vincent Gillen, who had injured the reputation of General Motors by failure to heed the instructions given him, and had changed a proper investigation into an unwholesome frolic.

And yet Gillen, who could easily have pleaded having misunderstood his client's instructions, had been most obdurate in denying that he had gone astray in this respect. Certainly, he had sworn under oath that the whole object of the investigation revolved around an attempt to discover Nader's connections, whatever they might or might not be, with Corvair case attorneys, and that he had thrown in investigative material on Nader's personal life partly to conceal the basic intent of the investigation and partly just for good measure, so that his client would have a complete background dossier on Nader. But at the same time Gillen had been absolutely unyielding in insisting that the tasks he carried out were in accord with what had been expected of him professionally; and at one point toward the end of his testimony he almost seemed to be challenging the president of General Motors as to what the intent of the investigation had been. And also, toward the end of his testimony, addressing Senator Ribicoff, he had made one peculiar statement about what he had in mind in investigating Nader:

> You see, Senator, one thing here that hasn't been made clear. Mr. Danner and I discussed this, too. He is an attorney, of course, and so am I. I don't know that he discussed it with General Motors, but it was quite evident to us that General Motors would eventually be faced with Ralph Nader quite likely as an expert witness in cases, Corvair cases, and I felt, and Dick Danner went along with me, that we should uncover every aspect of his life which may someday be of value to our client.

No member of the subcommittee remarked on it, but it seemed most strange that Gillen should have said, of the possibility that Ralph Nader might appear as an expert witness in

Corvair cases, that "I don't know that he [Danner] discussed it with General Motors." Why should Gillen have thus detached himself from instructions he must have assumed were given Danner by General Motors? Hadn't a prime purpose of the whole investigation been, according to what both Roche and Power had sworn to the subcommittee it really had been, precisely to determine if Nader were a potential expert witness in Corvair cases? Why the hedging? If this wasn't a prime purpose, what *had* the instructions given Danner by General Motors consisted of? Why was it that the one person who knew what the instructions to Danner actually were—Eileen Murphy—had *not* been called upon to testify as to their nature? Had Gillen made serious misrepresentations to the subcommittee about what he had been instructed to do? Had he been misrepresenting the facts, and the officers of General Motors telling the plain truth? Or vice versa? Or had he *and* witnesses from General Motors been misrepresenting, under oath before a Senate subcommittee, the purpose of the investigation of Nader? As it happened, subsequent developments were to cast interesting light on at least some of these questions, and in a manner unforeseen by Gillen or the representatives of General Motors.

PART TWO

12

"A Routine Investigation"

NADER'S POSITION after the March 22 hearings was that, no matter what sort of bruising General Motors might have taken over the affair, the corporate practices that had been the object of the criticisms made in "Unsafe at Any Speed" remained essentially unchanged. "A statement of contrition is not an act of reform," he told a reporter concerning the apology for which the president of General Motors had been so warmly commended by the senators on the subcommittee.

A short time after the hearing, Nader tried to obtain at least some comprehensive notion of the contents of the actual investigative report, which General Motors had made available to the subcommittee. He wished to look further into what General Motors might have wanted Gillen's investigators to find out about his life and activities. But, he now discovered, the report had magically disappeared—whisked away through the efforts of Theodore Sorensen. The former presidential adviser, in his capacity as special counsel for General Motors, had convinced the subcommittee staff that the detective reports on Nader's private life were private property—G.M.'s private property.

For the rest of that spring, Nader was preoccupied with the business of providing interested senators and congressmen with information and suggested amendments that might become part of the National Traffic and Motor Vehicle Safety Act—the passage of which, thanks to the public attention given the subject of auto safety through the Ribicoff subcommittee hearings, was a foregone conclusion. (The Act was passed by the Senate unanimously on June 23, 1966, and signed into law by President Johnson on September 9 of that year. The Act required the Secretary of Transportation to establish appropriate federal automobile safety standards, and imposed civil sanctions on manufacturers who produced vehicles or parts not meeting those standards. It also required manufacturers who discovered defects in vehicles they produced to notify purchasers of these defects. However, the Act did not provide criminal penalties for serious violations of the Act; nor did it authorize the Department of Transportation to force manufacturers to recall and remedy defects in vehicles at their expense. These are provisions that Nader has consistently fought to have included in federal traffic safety law.)

After some thought, Nader decided not to drop the subject of the intrusions into his private life that had come about as a result of the General Motors investigation. At the annual meeting of the corporation in Detroit on May 20, 1966, Frederic G. Donner, chairman of the board of G.M., assured stockholders that the investigation of Nader had gone "beyond the general counsel's intentions," and that only because of "the ineptitude of an over-zealous gumshoe" [Gillen] had the investigation delved into Nader's personal life.

Nader was by no means convinced that Gillen was the principal culprit. On November 14, 1966, Nader filed suit in New York State Supreme Court against General Motors, charging that the firm had subjected him to "harassment and intimidation, [and] intruded into and invaded his seclusion, solitude and private affairs." Nader further charged that its investigators had interviewed his friends under false pretenses, cast aspersions on his "political, social, economic, racial and religious views, tendencies and possible prejudices," and had brought into question his integrity, "his sexual proclivities and inclinations and his personal habits, such as the use of intoxicants, narcotics and the like." As co-defendants in the suit Nader named Vincent Gillen and his agency, Vincent Gillen Associates. The suit asked for total damages of more than five million dollars. In a separate public statement Nader said that "any money damages obtained as a result of the court's decision will be explicitly devoted to the cause of safety for all." Nader was represented in the suit by the New York law firm of Speiser Shumate Geoghan Krause & Rheingold. General Motors announced that the suit had been referred to former Federal Judge Simon H. Rifkind of the law firm of Paul Weiss, Rifkind, Wharton & Garrison. A General Motors spokesman said that Judge Rifkind "advises us that General Motors has no legal liability to Mr. Nader and that in due course the courts will vindicate our position."

As for Gillen, he told a reporter that Nader's charges were "a lot of nonsense," and that he wasn't concerned about the suit at all. Two days later, Gillen went further. Commenting on the suit, he told a reporter for the Detroit *Free Press,* "He [Nader] claims he was followed in all those places—Detroit, Philadelphia—I would refer him to a psychiatrist. He was followed, but not at the times he claims." Two weeks after the quotation was published in an article by the reporter in the *Free Press* on November 17, Nader brought suit for libel against Gillen for $100,000. Whatever the merits of this suit as such, it represented a fruitful move by Nader's lawyers toward obtaining some sort of cooperation from Gillen concerning the facts of the G.M. investigation of Nader. They assumed, correctly, that relations between General Motors and Gillen had deteriorated considerably since the March hearings. In fact, it appeared that by the time Nader brought his libel suit against Gillen, General Motors had already decided to abandon Gillen and to leave him to his own devices in defending the invasion-of-privacy suit Nader had brought against both parties in November. This turned out to be a considerable mistake on the part of General Motors, for in doing so the firm's attorneys reckoned without the cunning of Gillen. It so happened that, in undertaking the investigation of Nader, Gillen had covered himself, to an extent unknown at the time to the General Motors legal staff, by keeping a great many records of his transactions with General Motors representatives. When Nader's lawyers called upon Gillen to produce his records of the Nader investigation and to submit to pre-trial interrogation under oath in the libel case, they had him pretty much where they wanted him. Gillen began to talk, and a great load of previously unrevealed facts about the General Motors investigation came tumbling out.

Perhaps a convenient starting point in trying to place Gillen's disclosures into the sequence of events during the General Motors investigation of Nader is the latter's visit to the General Motors Technical Center at Warren, Michigan, on January 14, 1966. This was the visit in which, according to the G.M. statement of March 9 telling of the routine and strictly limited nature of the investigation of Nader, "Mr. Nader expressed appreciation for the courtesy in providing him with detailed information" concerning the design and safety of the Corvair—although he nonetheless continued, in later public appearances, to attack the Corvair. It was the same visit that the president of General Motors, testifying before the Ribicoff subcommittee on March 22, referred to in this hospitable tone:

> We in General Motors would not want any private citizen to think for one moment that he was not free to criticize our corporation or products, before this subcommittee or anyone else, without fear of retaliation or harassment of any kind. While we do not agree with many of the opinions and allegations Mr. Nader has put forward, General Motors has responded to his public criticisms not by responding in kind or ignoring the problems but by inviting him to meet with us to discuss those questions of safety which concern us all. Mr. Nader spent a day at the G.M. Technical Center . . . early in January visiting with G.M. executives and engineers. We hope we will have the opportunity to meet with him again in the future.

The General Motors executives with whom Nader met at the Technical Center at Warren included, as has been stated previously, Edward Cole, then an executive vice-president and now the president of the company, who had been the main force behind the development of the Corvair; several other vice-presidents; and Louis Bridenstine, the G.M. assistant general counsel. Also present was Frank Winchell, one of the engineers most intimately connected with the Corvair and the most effective expert witness used by the company to defend the Corvair before juries in Corvair product liability cases. According to what Nader told a reporter not long afterward and to what he has repeated more recently, his visit was marked by several broad hints from Cole that perhaps Nader would be more effective working on behalf of auto safety within the G.M. organization than working as an outside critic. And according to Nader's testimony before the Ribicoff subcommittee, Bridenstine, before taking Nader into a room during his visit to see a prepared presentation concerning the design and performance characteristics of the Corvair, asked him, in roughly these words, "You are not involved—" or "You do not represent clients in any Corvair cases, do you?" and then, according to Nader, "said a few words to indicate that he didn't believe I did"—upon which, Nader asserted, "I clearly told him that I did not."

Bridenstine had not mentioned to Nader that General Motors had launched an investigation into Nader's background the previous month; and that, not finding any particularly revealing information on him, the company, with its general counsel's approval, had put another investigation of him in motion by sending Miss Eileen Murphy of the G.M. legal staff to Washington to retain Danner, who then had hired Gillen.

In having initiated what the G.M. statement of March 9 had called "a routine investigation through a reputable law firm," the people at General Motors knew what they were doing. Alvord & Alvord was, in fact, a well-known law firm in Washington. The use of it was part of the cover under which General Motors was operating in its investigation. Why should G.M.

not have put its own investigators to work on Nader? The company had a large force of its own security agents, some of them, like Gillen, undoubtedly ex-F.B.I. men, capable of doing the job. But operating in this fashion involved an element of danger if something went wrong. By retaining an associate of the firm of Alvord & Alvord, G.M. was hiring, essentially, not legal advice but legal privilege that the courts recognize in the lawyer-client relationship. Danner was a lawyer, it was true, but that was not what he was known best for being. He too was an ex-F.B.I. man, who, according to Gillen, had been the special agent in charge of three regional F.B.I. offices, including, in the forties, the office in Miami. In 1946, Danner had resigned from the F.B.I. and he had become city manager of Miami for a couple of years. In 1950, he became the campaign manager for George Smathers, who was running in the Democratic primary campaign that year against the liberal internationalist Senator Claude Pepper. The campaign was distinguished by Smathers' charges that Pepper was soft on Communism and Communists, and by the publication of photographs and allegations all claiming to show a connection between Pepper and known Communists. The level of the campaign was also indicated by Smathers' repeated declaration, in a sly, accusatory tone before rural Florida audiences, that Pepper's sister in New York was a "well-known thespian." As a result of Smathers' onslaught, Pepper was defeated in the Democratic primary. Pepper, now a Congressman, has no kind words for Danner's part in the 1950 campaign.

Danner did not become a member of the bar until 1961. In 1964 he became associated with Alvord & Alvord, of which a senior partner was George E. Allen, who certainly knew his way around Washington and the White House. (During the Truman Administration, *Life* referred to Allen as a "Truman crony"; in the Eisenhower era, when Allen was still welcomed at the White House, *Time* respectfully referred to him as "adviser to presidents.") Alvord & Alvord presumably felt they had a use for a man of Danner's background. It is certainly clear that G.M., which had many lawyers on its own staff and could have its pick of skilled lawyers in Washington—indeed, its pick of skilled lawyers in the biggest and most powerful law firms in the country—did not hire Danner in the capacity of an experienced attorney. It hired him as an ex-F.B.I. agent-in-charge who knew how such investigations as that G.M. wanted made of Nader were conducted.

According to Danner's testimony before the Ribicoff subcommittee on March 22, he got in touch with Gillen after Eileen Murphy approached him on December 22, 1965, and asked him to find a detective agency to investigate Nader. Danner would have had several reasons for contacting Gillen. Gillen, like Danner, was an ex-F.B.I. man, and Vincent Gillen Associates held the New York franchise of Fidelifacts, Inc., a nationwide private investigative outfit largely run by former F.B.I. men. Danner had not known Gillen in the F.B.I., it seems, but later on, at one point after Danner had left the F.B.I. but before he had joined Alvord & Alvord, he had used Gillen's services "in interviewing potential witnesses," as Danner put it in his testimony before the Ribicoff subcommittee. ("I found Mr. Gillen's services on that occasion to be competent, businesslike, and ethical," he assured the senators.)

The use of Gillen had a further advantage for Danner and his client. Gillen, too, was an attorney, and although his actual practice of law had been slight, Gillen, the private eye in the service of Danner, could throw off his investigator's guise and put on his attorney's hat when the occasion suited. The prospective working relationship between Danner and Gillen, and between Gillen, his employees and the former F.B.I. men whose investigative services Gillen might call upon throughout the country during the investigation, could also be construed as coming within the privileged sanctuary of professional legal practice. From the point of view of the General Motors people, this was a promising situation for such a touchy job, since it provided yet further strata of legal immunity for the intensified investigation of the young critic of the corporation—which Danner could assure the senators under oath on March 22 was merely "a routine investigation such as are conducted every day in connection with business, industry, or the practice of law . . ."

13

"Wow, This Is Dynamite that Might Blow"

WHAT DANNER AND THE PEOPLE at General Motors did not know was that Gillen, when he was receiving his instructions, secretly switched on a miniature recorder that he carried on his person, and put the instructions on tape, which he took the precaution of hanging on to, just in case.

It was from this tape that Gillen, in his pre-trial examination under oath by Stuart M. Speiser, Nader's lawyer, in the Nader-Gillen libel suit, offered a partial transcript that he had made of the instructions he swore he said he had received from Danner. And the purpose of the General Motors investigation, as indicated from the contents of this partial transcript, hardly accorded with the descriptions of the purpose of the investigation that had been given under oath to the Ribicoff subcommittee by the president, the general counsel, and the assistant general counsel of General Motors, or with the account of the associate of the "reputable law firm" who had been retained by General Motors, or with the purpose as described by Gillen himself before the subcommittee under oath.

[Danner]: This is a new client . . . could be a very important one. They came to me and I'm anxious to do a good job because they have had trouble getting investigators . . . they want me to work with someone I trust . . . It concerns this fellow who wrote this book. [Here, Danner appears to have produced a copy of "Unsafe at Any Speed."] They have not found out much about him. His stuff there is pretty damaging to the auto industry . . . What are his motives? Is he really interested in safety? Who are his backers, supporters? Some left wing groups try to run down all industry . . . How does he support himself? Who is paying him, if anyone, for this stuff? How did he get all this confidential information from government reports or committees? . . . Was he put in there deliberately?

[Gillen]: Is he an engineer?

[Danner]: No evidence of it; he went to Harvard Law . . . They made some half-baked investigation in Connecticut . . . He is not there and apparently is or has been in Washington . . . I don't know where he is . . . strange, but he doesn't show anywhere in any directory . . . Here is what they gave me on him . . . You take this with you and a copy of the book and take over from here . . .

[Gillen]: This is dynamite. I remember reading a review of three books on this stuff [auto safety] in the New York *Times* recently . . . This book got the biggest play.

[Danner]: Yeah, that's why they are interested . . . apparently he's in his early 30's and unmarried . . . interesting angle there . . . They said, "Who is he laying? If it's girls, who are they? If not girls, maybe boys, who?" They want to know.

[Gillen]: Wow, this is dynamite that might blow, Dick, you know that.

[Danner]: Yeah, he seems to be a bit of a nut or some kind of screwball . . . Well, they want to know, no matter what. They want to get something, somewhere, on this guy to get him out of their hair, and to shut him up. I know it is a tricky one . . . that's why I called you . . . I told them [I] thought you could do this . . . You're a lawyer, as I recall . . .

Gillen's transcription continues this way:

[Danner]: How do you think you will approach this?

[Gillen]: I have been trying to figure that out because you know we will have to get close to him to get what they [the clients] want . . . You know . . . are they prepared for the worst? The subject is certain to learn of the investigation.

[Danner]: Yeah . . . that's why I told them I would know just how you plan to go about it and I want your ideas to see if they fit in with my ideas . . .

[Gillen]: I think the answer will be found in a thorough preemployment investigation. We make hundreds of them every week.

[Danner]: That's a good idea . . . about the safest . . . I go along with that . . . Excellent . . .

[Gillen]: But, Dick, somebody must be in a position to say they authorized you to ask for it . . . If it blows . . . who will be there to say he is interested in hiring him? . . . A lot of organizations would be glad to have this fellow with his research and writing ability, from what I see in the book ["Unsafe at Any Speed"] right now.

[Danner]: I'll take care of that.

[Gillen]: You'd better give me an idea of who . . . because I may be forced to identify my client . . . suspicion is bound to [fall] on the auto industry. I'm a lawyer . . .

[Danner]: Why don't you be co-counsel with me and hire your organization [Vincent Gillen Associates] to do the job?

[Gillen]: I've done that. Good, but I believe as a private investigator in New York I would have to identify my client . . . I'm not sure as a lawyer I would, but I would just say that I am co-counsel with you . . . What is it here in D.C.?

[Danner]: I'm not sure, but I will take care of that and this idea will add an extra layer . . . so we'll be that much safer. Don't worry about it. . . .

[Danner]: . . . If you can't readily determine who [Nader's] supporters are, who he is dealing with, his sources of income, we may have to put a tail on him . . . Don't do it without my O.K. . . . I think a tail will show who he is contacting . . . His language in articles and the book is appearing in lawsuits in several parts of the country . . . I'll tell you in the strictest confidence, to be revealed to no one, even in your own organization . . . General Motors . . . If we handle this right, both of us will get a lot of business from them.

The conversation then reverted to the subject of finding an organization that could be persuaded to make a declaration, if the Nader investigation "blew," that it had been a prospective employer of Nader and as such had been responsible for the investigation:

[Gillen]: They [the G.M. people] must have membership in many organizations . . . support them well . . . Many of

those groups could actually use a fellow with Nader's ability
. . . It won't have to be directly connected with the automotive
business, the further the better . . . That's the answer.

[Danner]: He's Syrian, or something, and maybe you will
find an anti-Semitic angle which is mentioned in [G.M.'s existing investigation] reports . . . that will be interesting to Ribicoff.

The significance of this observation lies, of course, in the
fact that Senator Ribicoff is Jewish and that Danner, in giving
instructions to Gillen on behalf of General Motors, was already
well aware of Nader's relationship with the Ribicoff subcommittee. He had to be perfectly well aware of it if only because
the very dust jacket of the copy of "Unsafe at Any Speed" that
he handed to Gillen during this interview described Nader as
"an attorney who was an adviser to the Senate subcommittee
investigating automobile hazards . . . a consultant to government agencies, legislative committees and . . . the author of
articles and lectures that have alerted the legal profession to
the need for preventive action to bring automobile safety under
a more comprehensive rule of law."

Besides the copy of "Unsafe at Any Speed," Danner handed
Gillen two other documents, the detective later said. One was a
copy of an original investigation into Nader's background that
Aloysius F. Power, the general counsel of General Motors, had
ordered made on November 18, 1965, and that had been
carried out by William F. O'Neill, the private investigator of
East Hartford. The result of this was a seven-page report by
O'Neill, dated November 21, 1965. This was the report that
Danner seems to have been referring to when he told Gillen
that General Motors had "made some half-baked investigation
in Connecticut." The report was not detailed. It dealt principally
with Nader's background in Winsted, his home town, and it
was padded with a list of headings of magazine articles that
Nader had written, mostly on auto safety. It said that Nader was
not practicing law in Winsted. It contained not a word about
Corvair litigation, and it did not address itself to the question of

any connections that Nader might have with lawyers bringing Corvair product liability suits.

The other document that Danner handed to Gillen was seven pages long and on plain paper, as was the O'Neill report. It bore no initials. It had been passed on to Danner by Eileen Murphy. Power, in his testimony before the Ribicoff subcommittee on March 22, described it only as "biographical data concerning Mr. Nader," and this document was not otherwise discussed at the hearing, nor was it produced there, although later evidence indicates that it could have been. Some of its contents were most interesting. The contents of the "biographical data concerning Mr. Nader" included scurrilous allegations to the effect that a member of Nader's family was anti-Semitic. The document also quoted an informant as saying that Nader's father "had socialistic leanings," and it said that "the family have been repeatedly reported to be very impractical and all are idealists." Of Nader himself, it said he was "not interested in girls" and appeared to be "camera shy by not appearing for group pictures."

At the end of this report a number of handwritten notes contained jottings of instructions, queries, and suggestions concerning the investigation to be undertaken. They included these notes:

"Mention the work with Ribicoff Committee—preparing questions for the hearings July '65 at which FGD appeared with J. Roche" ["FGD" evidently referred to Frederic G. Donner, chairman of the board of General Motors, who, with Roche, had appeared before the hearings on auto safety held by the Ribicoff subcommittee in July, 1965.]

"IRS. Bank checks. Connection w/ATLA" [The American Trial Lawyers Association, of which Nader was a member.]

"Does he drink—?"

"He has nervous habit of sniffing or else he had pneumonia on the day of his press conference Jan. 6, 1965 [*sic*] at the Sheraton Cadillac."

In the deposition that Gillen subsequently made before Nader's lawyer in the Nader libel suit against him, the detective indicated that he and Danner looked over this list of additional notations and instructions and discussed some of them.

"I.R.S." stood for Internal Revenue Service. It is evident from Gillen's deposition that he understood that he was expected to get at Nader's federal tax returns, but he said that he balked at that. "I told him [Danner] that I wasn't making any attempt to get any records out of the Internal Revenue Service, I just wouldn't do it," he said.

The reference to the press conference at the Sheraton Cadillac obviously meant the press conference that Nader had held in that hotel in Detroit on January 6, 1966 (not 1965, as the notation had it) at which Nader had invited officials of G.M. and the other automobile companies to debate the charges he had made in "Unsafe at Any Speed" concerning defectively designed and unsafe automobiles that he said were being produced and sold by the industry. The notation concerning Nader's "nervous habit of sniffing" Gillen took to be a suggestion that he look into the possibility that Nader might be a drug user. At this point, he said in his deposition, "Danner and I engaged in a brief discussion of the various manifestations of dope use." Gillen's excerpts from the transcript of the conversation he had recorded show the detective remarking, evidently concerning the period in which Nader had been attending Harvard Law School, "I know that Dr. Leary was experimenting with students at Harvard about that time . . . was kicked out of Harvard because of it . . ."

The transcript presented by Gillen ended on this note:

[Danner]: Some of those Harvard fellows are very liberal . . . hurt American industry cleverly . . . What they [General Motors] are really after is to get something that will shut him up and get him out of their hair. What gives him [Nader] the expertise to write a book on safety? What is his knowledge of safety? Has he [an] engineering background . . . Where was he during [the] Korean war? . . . girls, who, and if not, boys

. . . What are his motives? What lawyers is he dealing with? They found his name only once a year or so ago . . . Some address in Washington . . . He's not in the phone book here now . . . It's strange . . . There's something somewhere, find it so they can shut him up.

Two days later, according to Gillen, he sent a memorandum of instructions to investigators on his own staff and to the Fidelifacts organization that covered the Washington area. In it, the client was described not as General Motors but as "Vincent Gillen, Esq., co-counsel in this matter with Alvord & Alvord, law firm in 200 World Center Bldg., 16 and K, NW, Washington, DC." Under this heading was this description:

SUBJECT: NADER, RALPH   Born: 2/27/1934
SINGLE—at least not known to marry.
HEIGHT: about 6'2"   Slender

The above apparently is a freelance writer and attorney. Recently he published a book "Unsafe at Any Speed," highly critical of the automotive industry's interest in safety. Since then our client's client apparently made some cursory inquiries into Nader to ascertain his expertise, his interest, his background, his backers, etc. They had found out relatively little about him and that little is detailed below. Our job is to check his life and current activities to determine "what makes him tick," such as his real interest in safety, his supporters, if any, his politics, his marital status, his friends, his women, boys, etc., drinking, dope, jobs—in fact, all facets of his life. This may entail surveillance which will be undertaken only upon the ok of Vince Gillen . . .

14

"Well, Friend, Have Fun"

THE BROADENED INVESTIGATION then got under way, on January 17, and it appears that from time to time someone in Danner's office would get in touch with Gillen to ask for progress reports. It appears that for some time Gillen was not aware of the involvement of Eileen Murphy in passing on the General Motors instructions to Danner, but he said that, through Danner's secretary, a Miss Lonning, he gathered "that it was a woman . . . from Detroit . . . who was pushing her for the information." On January 26, after a conference over the telephone during which it became apparent to Danner that no adverse material on Nader was being uncovered by the investigation, Danner gave Gillen instructions to put Nader under surveillance.

It was this decision that, within two weeks, exposed publicly the existence of the investigation, after Gillen's men followed Nader into the New Senate Office Building. Power, at General Motors, on February 14 ordered the surveillance of Nader to be stopped. But apart from this pullback, the investigation went on. In fact, on February 14, Gillen later swore, he received in New York, over the telephone via Danner's secretary in Washington (Danner himself was out of town that day) a new set of instructions that had come from "a Miss Murphy" in Detroit. They included instructions to him to find out whether

Senator Ribicoff had anything to do with appointing Nader to any government job or to work with his Senate subcommittee and to determine the truth of a statement that Ribicoff had made at the hearing on February 10—that Ribicoff had never seen Nader prior to his appearance there. So now, it seemed— if what Gillen swore to was correct—the investigation by General Motors had widened to the point of investigating the relationship of the chairman of a Senate subcommittee with an adviser to and witness before that subcommittee. The instructions that Gillen said he received on February 14 appear to be consistent with the memorandum prepared by Frederick Condon after he had been interviewed at his office by Gillen on February 21. Condon's notes are perhaps worth repeating:

> He [Gillen] asked also when Ralph had met Senator Ribicoff. He asked if this was right after law school when Ralph returned to Connecticut to practice. I said I didn't know that Ralph even knew Senator Ribicoff, although I had supposed that he probably did now, after having testified before his committee. He seemed quite disappointed that I did not know when Ralph had met Senator Ribicoff, and pursued the question from several different angles before dropping it. I got the idea that the circumstances of Ralph's acquaintance with Senator Ribicoff was quite important to him for some reason. His disappointment that I had no knowledge on the subject was written all over his face.

Condon was not to know the source of Gillen's disappointment, which was, almost certainly, Gillen's feeling of increasing pressure emanating from General Motors, a feeling that he was expected to come up with further adverse information in the Nader investigation—and a realization that no such information seemed to be developing, however hard he and his men might be working. The general counsel and assistant general counsel of General Motors, as well as other lawyers in the general counsel's office, had been examining or had available to them Gillen's reports as they came into Detroit, with some delay, through Danner's office. And complaints were flowing back from General Motors, not that the investigation of Nader had gone too far, but that it hadn't gone far enough.

On February 25, a three-page letter on plain stationery, beginning, "Dear Dick," and signed, "Eileen," expressed to Danner the dissatisfaction of the General Motors legal department with what was being turned up on Nader in the investigation.

"I am still disappointed with the odds and ends we are receiving," the letter started off. The letter went on to complain, "It . . . strikes me that everyone is going overboard to impress us with what a great, charming intellectual this human being is—Eagle-Scout type."

The letter wanted to know more about Nader's Army record. It wanted to know what type of discharge Nader received. Perhaps rather hopefully, it asked, "Is he eligible for recall now?" It wanted to know whether Nader was in a Reserve unit, and if so, where Nader spent his Reserve duty. It wanted to know about Nader's savings account and stock holdings. It wanted to know whether Nader ever had had a motor vehicle registered in Washington, D.C., Massachusetts, Connecticut, Rhode Island, New York, New Jersey, or New Hampshire, and whether he had ever been involved in an automobile accident in those states. The letter instructed:

> On page 877 of the Ribicoff Senate Committee on Traffic Safety transcript for February 10, 1966, he [Nader] mentions an accident which happened a decade ago. *He saw* a child decapitated. This could have happened in Connecticut or in Massachusetts while he was at Harvard. See if this gem can be uncovered as to where, when or how he was involved.

And the letter ended, "Well, friend, have fun. I will be talking to you. Call if anything great appears." The text of the letter contained not a word about the Corvair or Corvair litigation, or about Nader's possible connections with attorneys bringing Corvair product liability suits.

A copy of the G.M. letter containing the instructions—which was written by Eileen Murphy—was sent on to Gillen by Danner on February 28, together with a covering letter from Danner written not on Alvord & Alvord stationery but on the stationery of Danner as an attorney. In it, Danner told Gillen, "As you can gather from the letter and as I certainly note from my telephonic conversations [with Detroit], these people are not too happy with the investigation, nor am I . . . too much time has been spent in detailing long-winded dissertations on the same subject, namely, that Nader is a brilliant fellow who went to Princeton and to Harvard and who wrote a book. . . . You know and I know from what we have learned to date about Nader that this fellow hasn't hit a lick of work in years, apparently lives by his wits and he just couldn't be that perfect."

Danner added, coolly, "Frankly, I think we are going to have trouble justifying your bills unless information is unearthed that hits a little closer to home . . ."

This was a bad sign for Gillen. He responded on March 3 by sending a fairly long letter to Danner explaining, in conciliatory fashion, that because "I do not know your client"—a way of reminding Danner that he, of course, really did know who the client was, and was protecting Danner in this respect—he and his investigators had not been able to judge very well what might be particularly significant to Danner's client. But he said that many of the points raised in the letter from Danner's client had already been dealt with in reports that had been made by his investigators and had been sent off to Danner. He also enclosed a list of what he called "36 new possible additional leads" on Nader.

"This is an interesting and stimulating assignment and I appreciate the opportunity to work with you," he told Danner cordially. "Upon reviewing the entire report to date, I am confident that you and your client will conclude that a satisfactory beginning has been made."

Concerning the incident in which his men had followed Nader into the Senate Office Building, Gillen wrote, "We are dealing with a fellow who will seize upon anything to further his ends. The Washington *Post* item [on February 13 concerning the tailing of Nader into the premises of the Senate] is an example. It so happened that there were few people in the corridor near the TV studio, but there were *two* guards. It is a big building and we wanted to know where Nader went next. Our investigators could not remain in the corridor long and soon went outside . . . The news item itself is largely conjecture . . ."

In the meantime, Gillen's involvement in the investigation had been traced on February 28 by David Sanford of the *New Republic,* who was working with James Ridgeway on the article "The Dick," which appeared in the issue dated March 12. The immediate effect of the article was, of course, the rash of newspaper publicity, initial silence from General Motors, and their eventual statement on March 9 that they had initiated a "routine investigation."

But what had happened to the explanation that, according to Gillen, he and Danner on January 13 had agreed would be offered the public in case the investigation became unmasked? ("Gillen: 'If it blows . . . who will be there to say he is interested in hiring him?'; Danner: 'I'll take care of that.' ") There had been a slipup somewhere. Later on, in a letter to James M. Roche, Gillen expressed regret about that. But he wanted Roche to know that it was no fault of Gillen's. "I was alert to the danger [of discovery of the origins of the investigation] from the beginning," he informed the president of General Motors. "Frankly, I suggested and unfortunately assumed without checking back, that Danner had arranged a cut-out, i.e., a cover organization which would acknowledge requesting the routine background investigation. During the original interview I mentioned that that could readily be arranged through one of the many organizations criticized in the book. Acting on that assumption . . . I immediately characterized the investigation as routine in answering reporters' questions, fully expecting that some Washington agency would acknowledge requesting it. My surprise was about equal to yours when you made the March 9 announcement."

It was really too bad. On March 10, Gillen made a telephone call to Danner to discuss the G.M. statement and other developments. Gillen secretly tape-recorded the conversation. The tape in question was subsequently subpoenaed by Nader's lawyer in the libel suit against Gillen, and this is how the conversation began:

> [Gillen]: Dick?
>
> [Danner]: Vince, how are you?
>
> [Gillen]: As well as can be expected—how's everything with you?
>
> [Danner]: Can you hear me, Vince? [Difficulty with connection.]
>
> [Gillen]: Yes.
>
> [Danner]: G.M. made a statement last night.
>
> [Gillen]:Yes, I saw it in this morning's *Times.*
>
> [Danner]: They called me [from G.M.] and read it off—sounded all right to me. [They] agreed at the time not to mention us—then learned later that they did. And I've been getting innumerable calls . . . and thought I'd better check with you and give you the same information if they come back at you. I've been making some statements down here in the Senate about investigating the alleged harassment . . .

During the course of this conversation, Danner said he was pretty sure that no girls were used to harass Nader during the investigation, and Gillen agreed. The conversation continued:

> [Gillen]: Well, I tell you—are they upset in Detroit?
>
> [Danner]: Well, you can't tell. I have just talked to the legal department—yes, I guess they *are,* but I'm going out there either tonight or the first thing in the morning.
>
> [Gillen]: I thought their statement was very good. Now, did you get a page from me in this morning's mail?
>
> [Danner]: Yeah.
>
> [Gillen]: Is that all right?
>
> [Danner]: Yeah.

[Danner]: Now you see that was the pretext under which
it [the investigation] was conducted.

[Gillen]: Right.

[Danner]: Their statement says this was a routine [investigation] to determine what connections if any he may have
had with attorneys prosecuting these Corvair cases.

Gillen's reference to "a page from me in this morning's
mail" in the context of "the pretext under which it [the investigation] was conducted" is a curious one, and Gillen, in his pretrial deposition in the libel suit against him by Nader, had more
to say about it. In his deposition, he indicated that a day or two
before the March 10 telephone conversation with Danner, but
a day or two after he had forewarned Danner that the *New
Republic* article about the investigation was about to appear on
the newsstands, Danner telephoned him and discussed the cover
sheet of Gillen's investigative report on Nader that was dated
January 31. The cover sheet was supposed to describe the
purpose of the investigation, and as a result of this prior discussion with Danner, Gillen said, "I at his suggestion rewrote
the page . . . and sent him two copies, as was my practice."

"Do you recall now what the original cover page . . . said?"
Nader's lawyer asked Gillen.

"No, we have destroyed all copies of it," Gillen replied. "I
have been unable to find any, but it more exactly spelled out
our purpose, which did not, frankly, tend to confirm the public
image which General Motors apparently wished to project in
acknowledging its participation in the investigation."

Q: You destroyed the copies of the cover page of the January 31, 1966 report at the direction of Mr. Danner, is that
correct?

A: Yes.

Since Gillen did not produce the original cover sheet in his
deposition, and since there is only his memory and sense of
unadorned truth to rely on in this matter, there is no way of
telling just how significant or otherwise the alleged changes in

the cover sheet may have been—except that they were worth two long distance telephone calls made at a time when the General Motors investigation of Nader had been forced into the public view. The cover sheet that Gillen produced as the revised version read:

NADER, RALPH   Born: 2/27/34   STANDARD REPORT ☐   DATE OF REPORT

SPECIAL REPORT ☒   1/31/66

> This investigation was initiated to obtain detailed background information on Ralph Nader, author of the book "Unsafe at Any Speed," and of various articles. The primary objective is to fill in those periods of his life not covered in preliminary information, with emphasis on anything showing prejudice against automobiles or their manufacturers, or any subsidy involved in his writings.

Because March 10, the day of the taped telephone conversation between Danner and Gillen concerning "a page from me," was the very date on which Senator Ribicoff, at 12:30 P.M., sent a telegram formally inviting Roche to testify before his subcommittee on the G.M.-Nader affair; and because Senator Ribicoff, on that same day, made it clear on the Senate floor that he would ask Roche to bring all relevant records of the investigation, the implications of Gillen's story, if it is true, seem serious.

Shortly after the discussion of receipt of "a page from me," the March 10 telephone conversation between Danner and Gillen turned to declarations of innocence by both men of any part in harassing Nader.

> [Danner]: . . . now, I wondered [about] one thing that's not entirely clear—at least I've not been able to dig it out of the report—the two men who were tailing Nader when he was going to that studio over in the Senate, and the guard ran them out. That part is what triggered the whole thing. Now, who were those men? Were those your men?
> [Gillen]: Uh—[pause] You read my report that one man

was on the surveillance and he called his friend and they [pause] decided to go outside. Were our men asked to go outside? [pause] I guess if they were a witness, they would have to testify, they might have to say something. But if I were called I'd testify what they reported to me—

[Danner]: Uh-huh.

[Gillen]: —what the *report* says.

[Danner]: Yeah.

[Gillen]: So—you can figure out the answer yourself.

[Danner]: Uh-huh [chuckling].

[Gillen]: . . . And any harassing—like this four o'clock in the morning deal—we surely didn't do that. Now, the only time that we called him was the day that we couldn't find him . . . About 10:30 in the morning we did get him there. But you see—he has no phone—he has to go to a phone in the hallway or something—so we did call him once. I don't think we called him any other time.

[Danner]: Yes—well, let's just forget that, that he was ever called.

The telephone conversation also dealt with the immediate impact of the General Motors statement of March 9 as it affected the relations of the two men with the news media. Gillen said that an hour or so earlier, he had received a call from a reporter from *Newsweek,* who had asked him if he had been employed by Danner's firm. Gillen said he hadn't denied it— "I just said 'Well . . .' and didn't say anything."

[Danner]: Well, [in the G.M. statement] they say they engaged a reputable law firm in Washington to arrange for the investigation . . .

[Gillen]: . . . This fellow at *Newsweek* said he was trying to locate Nader. They were trying to get ahold of you too. Did they call you in the past hour or so?

[Danner]: Well . . . I have taken some of them and finally told my secretary that I have been receiving so many calls and declining any further comment or any comment, that any further information would have to come from the client, General Motors. Now, as far as you were engaged to conduct this investigation: [a] background investigation to attempt to determine who the fellow was in contact with—had nothing whatsoever to do with the Senate testimony—to try to trace connection between this group that were prosecuting these Corvair suits and Nader, whether he was working with them or for them, and I think they've got some information that a law firm in Detroit had him out, paid his bills, and so on— and they are involved in the suits. There's a little fire there where the smoke is.

[Gillen]: Well, I tell you—I on my own called this re- porter back from *Newsweek,* and I put a little bug in his ear, I said, you guys are missing—you're looking for a story, there is a story here, in Winsted—somebody jumped all over me for asking a question regarding his anti-Semitism, and I said, that's all I'm going to say—and hung up.

[Danner]: Yes.

[Gillen]: Now let him defend his mother and his brother and [chuckling] his father [chuckling].

[Danner]: Yes, that would be good for Ribicoff to know.

[Gillen]: Yes—this may come out, and I want you to know I planted that seed, and that's the only place I found that you may be able to hurt him, if you get those Jewish writers on his neck up there.

[Danner]: Yeah . . .

[Gillen]: . . . I'll say [to inquiries from the media] I did a job for you and I'll refer them to you?—O.K.?

[Danner]: Just say any comments whatsoever will have to come from me and I'm going to pass them on to G.M.

[Gillen]: O.K. . . . [later:] another thing I've been telling these reporters—you know a fellow claims that people are fol- lowing him all over and girls trying to pick him up and people calling in the middle of the night and people are watching him—I said, you know, I said that's very interesting from a medical point of view [both parties laughing].

[Gillen]: I'm trying to get a bill together for you—guess there'll be no trouble getting it paid [laughing].

15

"I Was Not Going to Take the Rap"

RIBICOFF'S ANNOUNCEMENT of his intention to hold a special public hearing and call the president of General Motors was causing some feverish activity out in Detroit. On the evening of March 11, at the request of Danner, who had gone to Detroit earlier that day to confer with the General Motors legal staff, Gillen also flew out to Detroit and met Danner at a motel there. The next day, they went to General Motors headquarters and were intermittently in conference with Power, Bridenstine, and a number of other lawyers on the G.M. staff. Eileen Murphy was also there, according to Gillen, but he said that she did not participate in any discussion in his presence.

"All this time," Gillen said in a subsequent deposition, "I was under the assumption that they [the G.M. legal staff] knew the whole story and that it was up to Danner and me to support their position." However, he said, he found that the G.M. lawyers he was dealing with kept emphasizing, in his presence, that the aim of the investigation was merely the search for information regarding Nader's association with other lawyers bringing lawsuits against General Motors. He said that he remembered, on one occasion when he and Danner were alone in a conference room, Danner saying to him, in effect, "Gee, Vince, I may have goofed here and missed something, but I don't remember any instructions regarding his association with other lawyers."

According to Gillen, he replied in more or less these words: "Well, Dick, that takes a big load off my mind because I have no recollection of it either and I wondered if I had missed something about your instructions."

During the meeting with the General Motors legal people on March 12, according to Gillen's later deposition, he saw "many copies" of the three-page letter of February 25, beginning "Dear Dick," and signed "Eileen," around the conference room at G.M. headquarters, and also on various desks in the legal department. He also saw many copies of the letter he had sent to Danner in reply to this—that is, the letter in which he had suggested thirty-six additional areas that could be explored to help in accomplishing the client's objective in the investigation of Nader.

According to Gillen, during his meeting with the G.M. legal staff "it was decided that it would be rather prudent to eliminate" from material to be given the Senate subcommittee the Gillen letter containing the recommendations for 36 additional areas of investigation "because it tended to contradict the public statement issued by the General Motors officials [on March 9] that the investigation was primarily concerned with his relationship with litigation."

Gillen added, "It was also brought out to me there that I had received Danner's letter after the termination of the investigation, and I, not wishing to antagonize Danner or the client, made no issue of it because it was my definite recollection that I received the letter before any phone call from Danner's office to terminate the investigation . . . Anyhow, I went along with the idea of eliminating this letter of his [Danner's letter of February 28 enclosing Eileen Murphy's "Dear Dick" letter of February 25] and mine." He said he remembered either Bridenstine or Power as being "quite concerned" about the "Dear Dick" letter because, among other things, "it was written on a plain piece of paper, completely contrary to company policy." As for his own answer of March 3 containing the "36 new possible additional leads," Gillen said he "went along with my client. I assisted in rounding up copies that were around on the table, including the ones I had, and handed them to [one of the G.M. lawyers] and I guess they were destroyed." Gillen added, "But I was also conscious of the fact that I had a copy at my office in New York." In the same statement, Gillen swore that all copies at hand of this letter, as well as the "Dear Dick" letter of February 25, signed "Eileen," were rounded up at the G.M. conference for presumed destruction.

Over the next few days, Gillen shuttled back and forth to Detroit for other conferences with members of the G.M. legal staff, who were in a rather frantic process of preparing drafts of statements explaining the company's conduct for Roche and other officers appearing before the Senate subcommittee.

According to Gillen's deposition, at one point Danner told him that Power—in Gillen's words—"had tried to drag up a reference to a case in which General Motors had used Alvord & Alvord some twenty years ago to show that Alvord & Alvord were their regular counsel in Washington."

And Gillen said that in one of his first interviews in Detroit with the G.M. general counsel, Power had shown that he was aware of the fact that Gillen had carried out investigations for General Motors prior to the investigation of Nader. Gillen indicated in his deposition that he found the manner in which Power introduced this matter suggestive. "Mr. Power . . . mentioned that my previous investigations for General Motors had been in personnel work," he said. "I remember very vividly asking him to repeat that. And I said, in effect, 'Well, if you say so, I'll go along with that, that it could be so construed. I'll go along with what your records show.' " Gillen wouldn't go so far as to say to Nader's lawyer that Power wanted him, if he were asked by the Senate subcommittee, to say that he had done previous work for General Motors in the personnel area—only that Power had "asked me the question, and I made it clear to him that I thought he shouldn't push the question too far; put it that way." Gillen, in his deposition, characterized this previous work for General Motors as "not work which I as an investigator would normally consider as personnel work involving employees of the company whom they are hiring or contemplate hiring."

Gillen had his own explanations before the Senate subcommittee to think about. On Friday, March 18, he flew to Washington and met Danner. With him Gillen had his bill for services rendered in the Nader investigation. The bill was on the stationery of Vincent Gillen Associates and was made out to Vincent Gillen, Esq. Gillen presented the bill to Danner. According to Gillen's deposition, "Danner asked me to change the billing so that it would cover my entire expense and to drop the fiction of co-counsel and acting as an attorney . . . I personally erased my name and typed in, in Danner's office, 'Richard G. Danner, Esq.' . . . and changed the supervision expense to cover the amount previously put in for me as a lawyer."

That day, the two men went, as they had been asked to do, to the Senate Office Building to see Jerome Sonosky, the counsel for the Ribicoff subcommittee. According to what Gillen said later, Danner told him that "he was a bit upset" over the fact that during the previous few days Power and Bridenstine had flown into Washington from Detroit without his knowledge and had conferred with Sonosky about the pending hearing. When Gillen and Danner themselves saw Sonosky, Sonosky told Gillen to have a statement concerning his part in the investigation prepared by Sunday, March 20, two days ahead of the scheduled public hearing.

The two men went back to Danner's office. Apparently they weren't in such a bad mood. According to Gillen, Danner told him to "write the most glowing background about yourself that you can, because you're going to wind up as the most famous investigator in the country before we get through with this thing." Gillen began to type out his statement on Danner's typewriter, and in it he did, indeed, give a most glowing account of himself.

In the middle of the typing, according to Gillen, Danner received a telephone call from General Motors in Detroit. When he hung up he had bad news for Gillen. According to Gillen, Danner told him, in effect, that "G.M. had changed their mind about supporting the investigation and that they were going to dump the whole thing on to the investigator."

Gillen was very upset. He was more than upset—he was outraged. "When Danner told me that G.M. was going to apologize and say they were sorry and put the blame on me, I then told Danner for the first time that I had a complete recording of his instructions to me in Washington," Gillen later said in his deposition. He added, "He [Danner] knew what they were. I told him that I was going back to New York to gather some more data and finish preparing my statement and suggested that he take an early plane to Detroit and in no uncertain terms to let the officials there know that I was not going to take the rap for the investigation."

In an amplifying statement in his deposition, Gillen said, "I told him in no uncertain terms that I wouldn't permit that [the scheme "to dump the whole thing on to the investigator"] . . . and I urged him to go to Detroit early the next morning to inform Mr. Bridenstine and Mr. Power and Mr. Roche of this, and that I would arrive in Detroit later in the day, perhaps about two o'clock, and I wanted the matter straightened out, that I was not going to take the rap for doing what I had clear instructions to do and which I had done and which Danner knew I had done and which Danner knew as an investigator had been done in a competent manner with all the risks involved in any investigation."

Gillen flew back to New York that afternoon and on March 19 he flew out to Detroit, in the company of his wife, Irene. He arrived at G.M. headquarters at about three o'clock, together with his wife, whom he insisted on having with him in the meetings that weekend. ("There was a reason for this . . . I didn't have a recorder on me," Gillen later stated.) Danner was already there in the G.M. legal department. So were Bridenstine and a number of other members of the G.M. staff. The people in the assistant general counsel's office had now drafted the statement that, it was proposed, Roche would give the Senate subcommittee at the open hearing on March 22. As he later stated, Gillen asked Danner in an aside if he had not told the G.M. lawyers that he, Gillen, had made a recording of the original instructions Danner had given him. According to Gillen, Danner told him that they knew about it. In a further statement, Gillen said that later on that day, "I recall having a sandwich or a cup of coffee with Danner and my wife, at which time Danner repeated that he had told them [the G.M. lawyers] about our discussion in Washington on January 13 and his instructions to me. He said that their [the G.M. lawyers'] reaction was, 'Well, it's only [Gillen's] word against yours.' Then Danner said, 'I told [them] you had a recording of it.' "

At the Saturday meeting with Bridenstine and other members of the G.M. legal staff, Gillen later said, "their [the G.M. people's] attitude was to disassociate themselves completely from the [Gillen] investigation." During the early part of the meeting, Gillen said, Bridenstine read out Roche's proposed statement, which contained a declaration "to the effect that the investigative information was of no value and worthless." Gillen said that when he read that he interrupted Bridenstine. "I stopped him [Bridenstine] there and told him that we had obtained some evidence of association of Nader with Corvair attorneys, the very thing which their press release of March 9th . . . had indicated," Gillen said. He told Bridenstine that the proposed statement by Roche was thus inconsistent with the G.M. statement of March 9. Gillen declared, furthermore, that "I would not permit Mr. Roche to say such a thing"—to say, that is, that Gillen's investigative information was of no value and worthless.

From Gillen's deposition, it appears that the point that Gillen made to Bridenstine to the effect that the investigation had revealed a connection between Nader and attorneys in Corvair suits—the supposed evidence of this actually consisted of one mention in the scores of pages of the Gillen report, to the effect that Nader *knew* lawyers engaged in Corvair litigation—had been spotted only rather late in the proceedings.

At any rate, Gillen said that after he made these representations to the assistant general counsel of G.M. at the Saturday meeting, "in half an hour or so, Bridenstine came back into the room with a different version of the role of the investigators and submitted it for our consideration. Nothing they had at that time was satisfactory."

That day, when Gillen was having a snack with his wife and with Danner, he said that he and Danner "discussed the fact that we couldn't understand the persistence of Mr. Bridenstine reading a draft which threw the blame on me and Danner because he, Danner, several times felt that he had been used only as a messenger boy, and he was very unhappy about it." And, according to Gillen, Danner repeated that he did not recall any instructions from Eileen Murphy at General Motors to show any connection between Nader and lawyers engaged in Corvair litigation and mentioned how "damn lucky" they were that "something like that" had been found.

It appears that besides Roche's proposed statement, Gillen's statement for the Senate subcommittee, which Gillen had drafted and had brought along with him to Detroit, also was a subject of discussion at this and probably other sessions at G.M. headquarters. According to a later deposition by Gillen, he was asked by the General Motors people about the content of this statement. According to Gillen, "I read it to them and after outlining what activities I had conducted in the investigation, I had written in something to the effect [that] 'what I have done I would do again under the same circumstances.' " He said that "both Danner and one of the G.M. lawyers present asked that that be deleted because it would only anger the senators."

Gillen said he also recalled having been asked by this same G.M. lawyer at one of the sessions at G.M. what he would say to the Senate subcommittee if he were asked "what I planned to do about the statement Ribicoff had made on Feb. 10 [at the Senate subcommittee hearing] that he had not met or known

Nader before." Gillen said he told the G.M. lawyer, "I would endeavor to establish whether or not that was true." This, he said in his deposition, was in accordance with his understanding of the instructions that he had received from Danner's office on February 14.

At that, according to Gillen, "The G.M. lawyer and everyone else in the room said in effect that I should not say that. I did not." (This particular matter was not raised at the subcommittee hearing, for some reason.)

Gillen said that, in the original draft of his statement to be made before the Ribicoff subcommittee, "I had some remark about the fact that a young man in Washington should feel insulted if he was not approached by a girl in the supermarket, because that is the way girls meet men in Washington." However, he said, "everyone thought it would be inappropriate to make such a statement and I omitted it."

Also, he said, he told the General Motors people that it was ridiculous that he should be charged with hiring women to entrap Nader, and told them that he "felt like saying, 'Do you think that if I wanted to entrap Nader that I would use women?'" He said that this statement caused "a horrified reaction" among the General Motors representatives present, because "it tended to imply that I thought that he could be tempted by boys." Gillen said he denied to those present that this was what was on his mind. He said all he was saying was that in the entire investigation of Nader there was no indication that he was interested in women. "I pointed out that it was not my fault that people might interpret it in the manner in which they did, but G.M. counseled me against saying that [before the Senate subcommittee] and I did not say it," Gillen said.

He added, "Along the same lines, the General Motors lawyers pointed out that John F. Kennedy had not been married until he was about thirty-four and it would not be a good idea to play up the fact that Nader was single and he was not yet thirty-two. I agreed with them on this and therefore played down this angle as much as possible in my statement and testimony. All the time I kept informing them that we had obtained no definite information about Nader's sexual proclivities one way or the other, although it was clear to them as it was to me that that was one of the most important aspects of the entire investigation."

Apparently Gillen's adamant attitude toward accepting the drafts of Roche's statement that he said Bridenstine had read aloud on Saturday afternoon had some further effect on the G.M. legal staff's literary efforts, but these did not sway Gillen. According to Gillen, Bridenstine "read other drafts until about six o'clock, when I told him that I was not satisfied and I was going to the hotel and that if it [the Roche statement] was not written to my satisfaction when I returned about two o'clock Sunday, or the next day, that I was going to go to the Senate subcommittee and tell them the whole story."

Besides the draft changes that Gillen alluded to, he indicated in his deposition that certain other changes were afoot too, at General Motors headquarters. At some point—Gillen couldn't remember whether on that weekend or during one of the conferences at G.M. that preceded it—Gillen said that the question was raised, he thought by Danner, about unfortunate interpretations that someone not an investigator might make concerning the written instructions that Gillen had given his investigators in the Nader case. In his deposition, Gillen declared that, in connection with these instructions, "Bridenstine somewhere along there suggested changing it, rewording it."

This is the way Gillen elaborated on this matter:

> You see, these instructions were originally written in conformance with our subterfuge that I was co-counsel, and I, as an attorney, was retaining Vincent Gillen Associates to make a report to me.
> So the suggestion came from Bridenstine that maybe something could be done about it. He said it in a very nice way. I got the meaning. I asked him for an appropriate typewriter. Incidentally, my wife was there at the time and can confirm this. Some hours were spent intermittently on Saturday or

Sunday trying to find a typewriter which approximated the type of my original memorandum . . . When he located an appropriate typewriter, I retyped the first page and had it come out so that it looked substantially like the original first page. I pointed out to him that I had to have it Xeroxed if I was going to submit it to the Senate because it would be difficult for a typewriter expert to compare copies but not difficult to compare originals. He [Bridenstine] arranged to have me go to another floor with [another lawyer on the G.M. legal staff] and [he] operated the Xerox machine and made copies on that machine of all the pages of the report . . . He helped me to collate them . . . but we didn't discuss what I was doing. It was obvious to me that he knew what I was doing, but we didn't—frankly, we didn't discuss it. We just said nothing.

It seems only fair to observe, concerning these particular allegations in Gillen's deposition, that Gillen produced no copy of the alleged altered instructions; that he gave no concrete details as to the nature of the alleged alterations, and that his word is all that exists to bolster these assertions. Further, he did not say that Bridenstine actually saw the instructions before or after the alleged alterations—"I told him I thought it would be better if he didn't see it, and I don't know specifically that I ever gave him a copy of the instructions . . ." That is pretty vague. The only things that evoke one's curiosity about these particular allegations are the description of the search for a typewriter and the detail about the double-Xeroxing of what he said were the altered instructions. What does seem important about this part of Gillen's deposition is the question of whether *any* changes—major, minor, or inconsequential—were made in documents that everyone involved surely knew had been requested to be produced before a public hearing by the chairman of a Senate subcommittee. As far as Gillen's own eventual handling of this material is concerned, he has said that the copy of his instructions to his investigators that he eventually delivered to the subcommittee counsel was the original, and not an altered version of it.

Gillen said that he returned to General Motors headquarters on Sunday afternoon at about two o'clock, and that about fifteen minutes later Bridenstine read to Danner, himself, and Irene Gillen another version of the statement Roche was to make before the Ribicoff subcommittee. (It is reasonable to assume that, at this stage of the proceedings, with the public hearings less than forty-eight hours off, the drafting had been taken over by Sorensen somewhere behind the scenes, presumably in collaboration with Bridenstine, Power, and Roche himself.) "I knew it [this latest version] was not acceptable," Gillen later said, "and told Danner privately that if the wording was not changed to my satisfaction I was going to go to Washington and play the record of instructions which I received from Danner and [that] Danner's voice came through 'loud and clear.' " He added, in his deposition, "Danner has a well-modulated, strong voice."

About 4 P.M., Gillen said, Bridenstine eventually came down to see him in the public relations department of the G.M. building and read to him the final version of the Roche statement. Gillen said he took exception to the sentence, which Roche was to utter before the subcommittee: "I deplore the kind of harassment to which Mr. Nader has apparently been subjected."

> I told him that it would be seized upon by the press, ignoring completely the word "apparently." I urged that it be rewritten to contain in the earlier part of the sentence something such as "I deplore the alleged harassment to which Nader claims he has been subjected." Bridenstine pleaded with me to accept it, saying that they had considerable difficulty in drafting it and that the entire staff of the organization was busy trying to get sufficient copies run off. I was extremely tired, of course, at that time and was working with the girls in the public relations section who were typing up my [own revised] statement on stencils to be run off. There were about eight girls there . . . and they had to type Roche's statement, Mr. Power's statement, Danner's and mine.

Gillen said that he finally agreed to go along with Bridenstine in the latest version of the Roche statement, and that Bridenstine then left the room. That night, Gillen returned to New York.

16

"They've Dumped the Whole Thing on You, Vince"

THE FOLLOWING DAY—the eve of the Senate subcommittee hearing—Gillen flew to Washington with his wife and took a room at the Mayflower Hotel. As it happened, several of the General Motors executives who were to testify at the hearings the next day—including Power and Bridenstine—were also staying at the hotel. According to Gillen, about five o'clock in the afternoon he received word from Sonosky, in Senator Ribicoff's office, that he had not yet received copies of Gillen's prepared statement. Gillen had assumed that his statement would have been handed over to Sonosky by the G.M. people, at whose headquarters the statement had been amended, typed and mimeographed along with the statements of the G.M. executives who were to testify. It appeared that Sonosky possessed the G.M. statements, but that nobody had given him Gillen's. However, Gillen had several other copies with him, and he took a cab to the Senate Office Building and delivered a copy to Sonosky. During the meeting, Sonosky glanced through Gillen's statement, and, according to Gillen, "told me that he had Mr. Roche's copy, [about which] he said several times, 'It is a very, very clever statement. They've dumped the whole thing on you, Vince.'"

Gillen was upset. He returned to the Mayflower, called Aloysius F. Power, and told him that he wanted to see him. According to Gillen, Power asked him to come to his suite and

Gillen and his wife went there. Gillen said that Power and Bridenstine were in the room together, near a TV set, which was on. Gillen said he told Power, concerning Roche's statement, that he still strongly objected to the wording of Roche's apology, which, Gillen insisted, implied that his detectives had caused Nader harassment. According to Gillen, Power "urged me to accept it and forget it and added that the [Roche statement] had already been filed with the Senate and that nothing could be done with it. He said, 'Look, Vince, what they had done to me. I threatened to resign, but they're afraid to let me resign. If I can take this, you can take it too.' "

Gillen, in his deposition, declared that he then said to Power, in Bridenstine's presence, "Didn't Dick Danner tell you what my instructions were? That I was told to get this guy out of your hair and to get anything I could on him—boys and girls, narcotics or anything else, as long as you can get something to shut him up?"

According to Gillen's deposition, Power, when he heard this, "pretended to be very indignant, and said that he was going to go 'right down there tomorrow and take the entire responsibility.' " In a subsequent telephone conversation with Danner, two days after the subcommittee hearing, on March 24 (which Gillen, as usual, recorded), Gillen further described Power's reaction this way: ". . . he jumped up and said, 'By God, if Dick says that I'll go in there and take the rap for everything —admit everything.' " At that, according to the detective's deposition, "I told him that he would ruin the company and indicated to Bridenstine that he should use his influence with Power to have him reconsider."

Perhaps Gillen's later allegation, during the Nader libel suit, that Power had "pretended" to be very indignant at the Monday night confrontation at the Mayflower when Gillen questioned him about his knowledge of the instructions to "get anything I could on [Nader] . . . to shut him up" was influenced by what Gillen learned from his March 24 telephone conversation with Danner in which this incident was discussed. Gillen wanted to know from Danner just who it was on the G.M. legal staff Danner had informed that Gillen had a recording of his instructions from Danner:

> [Gillen]: Who was there, who did you tell it to?
> [Danner]: Bridenstine, and Power—no one else.
> [Gillen]: Aha!—because the night before the testimony, you know, Power indicated he didn't know anything about it.
> [Danner]: [Laughing in the manner of a man shaking his head in disbelief] He was damn sure sitting there.
> [Gillen]: I said you—I quoted you as saying you wanted to get something on him and get him out of your hair, did you use those expressions to talk to him?
> [Danner]: No—no, I told him Vincent had substantially repeated the conversation that I'd had with Eileen, wherein she had used the expression repeatedly, whom does he [Nader] sleep with, and if not, what does he do for sex?
> [Gillen]: Uh-huh—meaning boys.
> [Danner]: Yeah.

When Gillen, in this same conversation with Danner, persisted in asking for details of what Danner had told Power and Bridenstine concerning the instructions Danner had given Gillen, Danner became wary. "Well—now are you recording *this* conversation?" he asked. "No, not necessarily," Gillen replied quickly. But Danner backed away. He said that he had only repeated to Power the conversation in which Gillen had informed Danner that he had recorded the instructions concerning the investigation. Danner now told Gillen over the telephone that he had told Power he couldn't recall the details of the instructions he had given Gillen, but that he and Power had "just discussed it [the investigation] professionally." However, this backtracking came perhaps a little late; since Danner had already conceded, in this discussion, that Gillen's version of the instructions Danner had given him was substantially a repetition of the instructions Danner had received from General Motors through Eileen Murphy.

If the revelations in these and other conversations as sworn to by Gillen can be considered as reflecting the true state of affairs in the General Motors investigation of Nader and the preparation of the official explanations thereof, they certainly place the sworn testimony of the General Motors executives— not to mention the testimony of Gillen and Danner—before the Ribicoff subcommittee on March 22, 1966, in a most interesting light.

One has to say for Gillen himself that he possessed a certain irrepressible quality, an almost fathomless, ever-flowing well of sheer gall, and his conduct before the hearings, during the hearings, and after the hearings ended are all of a piece. As soon as the hearings were over on the afternoon of March 22, Gillen pushed his way forward and attempted to socialize with two of his principal adversaries. He subsequently described these encounters in a letter to Roche at General Motors:

"I was walking toward the exit [of the hearing room]," he wrote Roche, "when I noticed Senator Kennedy near the door, apparently waiting for me. I went up to him and shook hands and said, 'Bobby—pardon me, Senator, you gave me a rough time up there and I think I gave you a few rough minutes, too.' He smilingly said, 'Well, maybe it will help your business,' and went out the door. I turned back into the room and walked out with Mr. Power."

And then, in the hallway outside the hearing room, Gillen approached yet another familiar figure. "I walked up to Nader in the hall," Gillen wrote Roche, "and shook his hand, saying, 'I'm sorry that the investigation created any embarrassment. We did not intend to cause you any trouble.' Nader looked at me in a manner which indicated that he did not know me. I said, 'I'm Gillen.' He did a typical movie-style double-take. This was strange, because I had been testifying for over an hour. Apparently, he paid little attention to me.

"Nader said, 'Oh, let me show you my driver's license,' and pulled it out."

(This was clearly a gesture of irony on Nader's part, as he remarked to an acquaintance not long after the hearing, "They interviewed scores of people and spent $6,700 and didn't find out if I had a driver's license." But it seems that the irony was wasted on Gillen.)

"He held up the card," Gillen continued in his letter to Roche, "and I examined it to see that it had been renewed on or about Feb. 28, 1966.

"I asked Nader if he had an unlisted phone. He did not respond the first time so I asked him again. He said, 'It is listed under someone else's name.' This is the landlady's phone in the hall."

The day after the hearing, most of the principal witnesses received typewritten transcripts of their testimony—a courtesy normally given to witnesses before congressional committees, who may then correct minor errors in spelling, syntax, and so on. On March 24, when Gillen and Danner were on the telephone, Gillen as usual recorded the conversation:

> [Gillen]: How you feeling today?
> [Danner]: I've been reading the testimony.
> [Gillen]: Yeah, I read it. I read mine and yours. I didn't read the others yet. Any feedbacks from any people round town?
> [Danner]: No, I haven't heard anything other than the— of course you read the press reports. They make a hero out of Nader and I guess the whole drift of the thing is that we came off a bad second.
> [Gillen]: (laughs heartily)
> [Danner]: It's amazing that these things can go on, but they do.
> [Gillen]: Well, it's a great life. I think we got bad timing . . . we testified beyond the time the papers were closing, apparently. I imagine that some of these magazines will handle it a little differently.

At another point in the conversation, Gillen let Danner know how poorly the press had treated him and how this attitude was in marked contrast to that of Gillen's professional peers:

[Gillen]: I wanted to get to that [congressional committee] hearing on wiretapping which was going on on electronic devices [on March 23] but I got there too late. Three different people in the hall recognized me. Apparently people hang around at those hearings, and they said, 'Gee, you were the star of the show yesterday,' and they said that was great; 'haven't seen anything like that in ten years,' one guy said. And yet the press did not give us any coverage at all—any favorable coverage, anyhow.

[Danner]: [A sigh] Well, of course, if . . . they'd taken our advice [at General Motors] we would have had a sharp, tough interview there, but we would have come off on top, we'd have made that committee look like a bunch of jerks. We'd have made them have to *defend* Nader—instead of making a hero out of him, we'd [have] made *them* put him *up*— and I'm convinced now that his late showing was deliberate, they didn't want him to go on first. Everybody would have *seen* that he was a kook, this would have made the early press . . .

At one point in the conversation the two men discussed Gillen's bill, and how Gillen was to be paid—whether directly by General Motors or through Danner. Danner said that whichever way it was to be, the G.M. people wanted the matter settled immediately.

[Gillen]: Oh. Well, something has come up very greatly disturbing to me. I got a little inkling of—some of the boys from the B will be around shortly.

(The "B" is F.B.I. men's talk for the Bureau; the F.B.I., at the request of Senator Ribicoff, was presumably looking into possible violations of law in the G.M. investigation of Nader.)

[Danner]: Uh-huh.
[Gillen]: And it suddenly occurred to me that it could be on this civil rights kick. If they [General Motors] admit that it was harassment [in the Nader investigation] it may be some of these new laws cover that. [Quickly] Did you ever think of that?

[Danner]: No, I hadn't.

[Gillen]: You know, some of these concerning voting in the South, and so forth. I'll bet it could be so construed. May be that we're all right. I feel [here Gillen gave a sort of sigh] I'll have a lot of good company if I'm indicted.

[Danner]: Well, of course, this is . . . where they ought to get Mr. Sorensen off his big, flat, cold ass doing some work. Everything that was done, it must be imputed to General Motors, I mean they can't *divorce* themselves—

[Gillen]: Yeah . . .

[Danner]: Well, I keep hearing the same thing . . . that the F.B.I. is going to take a look at this thing . . .

Gillen then went on to discuss an encounter that he had had the day before with yet another of the principals in the Nader affair and about whom, as it has been shown, Gillen himself had been making certain investigative inquiries:

[Gillen]: You know what I think—this case is full of the damnedest series of coincidences. I was sitting with the wife on the bench there, sitting at Capitol Hill . . . yesterday afternoon in the sun reading this transcript [of Gillen's testimony] and someone went by, and he said, 'Are you enjoying your visit to Washington?' and I looked up and who the hell was it but Abe Ribicoff.

So I said, 'Oh, yeah, I'm enjoying it.'

[Danner]: Huh!

[Gillen]: [continuing] —'Did *you* enjoy yesterday?' or something like that. And he [Senator Ribicoff] continued [on his way], then I called after him and I said, 'Say, Senator, did you know we got a lot of publicity on this statement [in which, at the hearing, Senator Ribicoff had held up in his hand a copy of the Gillen investigative report on Nader as he addressed Nader] holding up that report and saying, 'They didn't prove a damn thing against you'.

I said, 'you know'—I wish I had thought to say [here Gillen attempted a sort of Seventh Avenue accent in uttering the name]—'*Mister Abrahams-Ribicoff*, do I understand you to mean that it's all right to be . . . anti-Semitic in Connecticut?' [Brief chuckle on the line] . . . Now, do you think I should have said that to him?

[Danner]: . . . I think they just went overboard to protect Nader.

[Gillen]: Yeah, I'm glad—you know, I read your testimony and mine and they were quite in harmony.

[Brief laugh from the other end of the line.]

[Gillen]: We laid it in, uh—right in Eileen's lap. Wonder why they didn't call her. I guess they were afraid.

17

"Miss Murphy—Whoever She Is"

"WONDER WHY THEY DIDN'T CALL HER"—that was an intriguing question. Why Eileen Murphy was never questioned by the senators at the public hearing on March 22 has remained something of a mystery ever since, at least to those not a party to the decision not to call her. The testimony that Eileen Murphy could have given before the Senate subcommittee concerning the actual instructions that she gave Danner from General Motors for the investigation of Nader was obviously crucial to a proper understanding of the whole subject of the March 22 Ribicoff subcommittee hearing. Considering the relentless way in which Senator Robert Kennedy questioned Gillen during the detective's appearance, it seems rather remarkable that the Senator should have shown such a lack of curiosity concerning Eileen Murphy. In fact, he seems almost to have been turning the subcommittee's attention away from Miss Murphy. At one point, when Senator Harris began to question Roche about Miss Murphy's role in conveying instructions concerning the Nader investigation and the extent of Roche's knowledge of the investigation at the time of the March 9 G.M. public statement, Senator Kennedy had interjected, "Let's not focus on Miss Murphy, whoever she is." And even in discussing with Roche the content of Danner's formal statement to the subcommittee, Senator Kennedy had touched on Eileen Murphy's role in such a glancing fashion as this:

Senator Kennedy: Let me just give you what, according to Mr. Danner's testimony, he said, talking again of poor old Miss Murphy . . .

Senator Kennedy then went on to quote from Danner's version of Miss Murphy's instructions to him on behalf of General Motors. It would have been a simple matter for Senator Kennedy to have Miss Murphy testify concerning these instructions, but one has a sense that the Senator had no great desire to hear this testimony. Why should a figure who obviously knew all about the inner workings of the Nader investigation in the General Motors camp not have been called upon by the Senate subcommittee to give her version of what really happened? Things might have been different if the members of the subcommittee had had access to the seven-page dossier on Nader, with its imputation of anti-Semitism and the handwritten notations at the end, that Eileen Murphy conveyed to Danner along with the oral instructions from General Motors concerning the investigation of Nader. But the senators appear to have been unaware of the existence of this rather telling document when the hearings were conducted. It is possible that Senator Kennedy's apparent lack of interest about the precise instructions Miss Murphy gave Danner was attributable to the fact that, having the president, the general counsel, and the assistant general counsel of General Motors—not to mention Gillen—sitting in the room and testifying as to their roles in the Nader investigation, he didn't want to divert attention to what the law librarian of General Motors did or did not do at various times.

General Motors did not submit the Eileen Murphy annotated background summary on Nader to the subcommittee before the March 22 hearings. The corporation probably did not do so because its legal officers placed a strict interpretation on what the subcommittee chief counsel told them to submit. What Jerome Sonosky had asked them to submit was less than what Senator Ribicoff, in his speech on the floor of the Senate on March 10, had said would be called for—which was all of

G.M.'s records including the detective reports concerning the Nader investigation. Sonosky merely asked the G.M. executives to bring with them the prepared statements of the G.M. people who were to testify at the hearing, and the detective reports on Nader.

However, on February 13, 1967, an article by Morton Mintz in the Washington *Post* revealed that Sonosky actually had come into possession of the Eileen Murphy annotated memorandum on Nader four days before the March 22, 1966, hearings. According to the Mintz article, Sonosky acknowledged that he had not shown the seven-page memorandum to the subcommittee members. He was reported as telling Mintz that he was under great pressure at the time and that the document was in the nature of a "synopsis" of what General Motors knew about Nader and that it had not struck him as being as significant as it later might have appeared to be. Sonosky has refused to say publicly just how the document came to him. But he has conceded that the document "surfaced" after a meeting between himself, Danner and Gillen on March 18. As to whether Gillen gave it to him, Sonosky refused, even when questioned about it recently, to answer this question directly. When pressed, he said that he was "shown" the document. He then conceded that he had the document copied, but as to how this was done, he refused again to go further ("I'm always hesitant about talking about my own investigative techniques"), leaving the impression that he had had the document copied surreptitiously. This seems rather remarkable, considering that Sonosky was the chief counsel for a Senate subcommittee and had every right— and indeed duty—to require the production of such a serious piece of evidence. It seems remarkable, also, that Sonosky, having made a copy of the Eileen Murphy memorandum in a manner he declined to talk about even six years after the event, should have treated as "routine" a G.M. investigative document replete with annotations that included mention of Sonosky's own name, Nader's advisory connections with the Ribicoff subcommittee, and Nader's drinking habits, not to mention his sniffing habits. Sonosky's disregard of the Eileen Murphy memorandum may have been just as inadvertent as he says it was. Nader and his former aide Gary Sellers, who handled much of Nader's liaison work with people in Congress, have plainly been suspicious that political pressure was brought to bear or extraordinary guile used on people associated with setting up the March 22 hearings, with the effect that, in consideration of a public apology by Roche, the subcommittee members would not humiliate the corporation and its president unduly at the hearings. Whatever the facts may be, there is little doubt that making the Eileen Murphy memorandum public at the hearing on March 22 could have had a shaking effect on the credibility of the prepared testimony of the G.M. people, from Roche on down.

During that hearing, Roche specifically denied being aware of the subject matter of Eileen Murphy's meeting on January 13 with Danner, even as this was described in the rather sanitized version that Danner offered the subcommittee: "Miss Murphy went into details as to the type of information needed, including the date and type of government employment, sources of income, type and locale of law practice, if any, business associates, movement, and, in short, a complete background investigation of Mr. Nader's activities." In reply to a question by Senator Harris, Roche said that he knew nothing of all this; "I was given to understand it was a routine investigation into the areas that I have mentioned"—that is, Nader's possible association with Corvair litigation and his potential appearance as an expert witness in such cases. What Roche seemed to be saying, in essence, was that his general counsel and assistant general counsel had let him down and kept the facts about the investigation from him. The only difficulty one has in accepting Roche's claim that he approved G.M.'s March 9 Detroit statement under the impression that the Nader investigation was merely a routine legal inquiry lies in what were, by most accounts, Roche's working habits. A former G.M. employee who has had considerable contact with the G.M. legal staff has said,

"It was well known at G.M. that the moment a problem hit Roche's desk, the first thing he did was to call for *everything*— *all* the facts—on the problem. And when the president of General Motors called for the facts, you can be sure that everybody scrambled to supply them." Something like these doubts may have entered Senator Kennedy's mind when, during the hearing, he remarked of the G.M. statement of March 9, "I can't believe that with the record that General Motors has made in the United States . . . they would be so inefficient that that kind of a statement went out carelessly."

"No, the statement did not go out carelessly, Senator Kennedy," Roche replied. "I assure you it is one of the most difficult statements that I ever had anything to do with."

"So, therefore, you must have talked to the people who knew about it, and the people who knew about it, knew it was inaccurate," Senator Kennedy pressed.

". . . They can answer that only for themselves, Senator Kennedy," Roche replied.

Yet even after the publication of the obviously inaccurate statement of March 9 concerning the nature of the Nader investigation caused Senator Ribicoff to announce the public hearing on the facts of the G.M.-Nader affair, when Roche had ten days in which to exercise anew, and with the utmost rigor and vigilance, his well-known insistence on having every available fact concerning the problem at hand presented to him, the simple truth about the instructions given Danner, and through Danner, Gillen, somehow eluded the president of General Motors, if one is to have faith in his testimony before the Ribicoff subcommittee. Throughout all those conferences in the ten days before the public hearing, had his general counsel, assistant general counsel, and assembled lawyers— a force augmented toward the end by the shrewd reasoning powers of Sorensen—*still* kept the basic facts from Roche? "They can answer that only for themselves, Senator Kennedy" was surely a curious way for the president of the biggest corporation in the world to accept responsibility for his company's having ordered up a most intensive investigation into the background and personal life of a citizen who had gained attention as a critic of the safety of the corporation's products. Could it conceivably have been something like this puzzling thought that might have impelled Aloysius F. Power allegedly to have exclaimed to Gillen (when Gillen confronted him on the evening of March 21 with the G.M. instructions he swore he had received through Danner to "get anything . . . boys and girls, narcotics or anything else" to silence Nader), "Look, Vince, what they had done to me. I threatened to resign, but they're afraid to let me resign. If I can take this, you can take it too"?

Before the denouement in the investigation of Nader, Eileen Murphy was considered, within the legal department of General Motors, to be in the good graces of the general counsel, and it appears that afterward the professional relationship between them continued to be good. At least, Miss Murphy was reported to have retained a sense of loyalty to Power throughout all the corporate uproar caused within G.M. by the Nader affair. But if Eileen Murphy was so miraculously or skillfully spared an appearance as a crucial witness before the Ribicoff subcommittee, she did not appear especially thankful for the mercy that had fallen on her. The day after the hearing, according to a man who says he was present, Miss Murphy is reported to have gone to lunch with several other members of the G.M. legal staff at a steak house near G.M. headquarters in Detroit. "This is what horrified me at that lunch," this man says. "Eileen lifted her glass and offered a toast to 'the end of James Roche, that son of a bitch.' " Such a toast certainly seemed like a poor expression of support for the man who, twenty-four hours earlier, had sorrowfully informed the Senate subcommittee that "I hold myself fully responsible"—or fully responsible with various reservations— for the investigation of Nader.

18

"The Boys from the B"

IT WAS A DAY after the utterance of this reported malediction that Vincent Gillen, who also in his own way had a feeling of having been let down, was expressing his anxiety to Danner over the telephone about the "greatly disturbing" development that had reached his ears—namely, the little inkling, as he put it, that "some of the boys from the B will be around shortly."

As it turned out, there was no great need for Gillen to have been so worried about visits from the F.B.I. As early as March 11, the Department of Justice had announced that as a result of the request by Senator Ribicoff for an investigation by the Department of Justice of possible violations of federal law concerning the harassment of a congressional witness, the F.B.I. was entering the G.M.-Nader case. On June 17, Fred M. Vinson, Jr., head of the criminal division of the Department of Justice, wrote Senator Ribicoff that the F.B.I. had pursued "every logical and relevant lead" in the case, but that the Department of Justice had concluded on the basis of the investigation that "criminal prosecution is not warranted" in the affair. If the wide-ranging investigation by the resourceful F.B.I. followed every relevant lead in the case, it seems that it did not, however, point "the boys from the B" in the direction of some of the principals. Thus, as far as can be ascertained by the author, Vincent Gillen was never interviewed by the

F.B.I.; nor was Richard Danner; nor was Jerome Sonosky; nor was Senator Ribicoff; nor was Frederick Hughes Condon, who had written such a detailed report on the investigative interest Gillen had shown in the history of Senator Ribicoff's acquaintance with Nader; nor was former Attorney General of Iowa Lawrence F. Scalise, who in January, 1966, had himself ordered an investigation of Nader's complaints that he believed himself to be under surveillance in Des Moines. Under these circumstances, one is forced to ask oneself how zealously the Department of Justice really pursued this investigation into the activities of General Motors and its agents.

On February 6, 1967, as a result of information uncovered by the depositions made in the Nader libel suit against Gillen, Senator Ribicoff asked the Department of Justice to investigate whether any witnesses at the March 22 subcommittee hearing had perjured themselves. Once again, the F.B.I. went to work, this time more intensively and seriously than before, but the result was the same; and after eighteen months Nathaniel E. Kossack, first assistant of the criminal division in the Department of Justice, wrote Senator Ribicoff that the department's investigation and review of the information obtained (including all documents that had been filed in the meantime in State Supreme Court in New York in the civil suit by Nader against General Motors) obliged the department to conclude that there was insufficient evidence to justify any prosecution under federal law relating either to perjury or obstruction of justice. However strongly the case may have seemed to a layman to have reeked of misrepresentations, then, the U.S. Department of Justice couldn't see that the department could make even a *prima facie* criminal case that would get so far as a grand jury room. And one could see that the Department of Justice really was in a difficult position in considering criminal action over the Nader investigation, at least if one considered the doors such action might have opened into the ways of investigators. After all, this was an affair in which F.B.I. men were looking into the activities of (among others) former F.B.I. men who were using investigative techniques not too dissimilar from those the F.B.I. itself was customarily using. At one point during the March 22 hearing, when Senator Kennedy tried to get Gillen to admit that Gillen's use of what the detective called a "preemployment pretext" in investigating Nader consisted quite simply of telling lies to the people he was interviewing, Gillen became quite indignant. "Oh, Senator, come on, come on," Gillen exclaimed. "For goodness sake, where did I learn to do this? In the F.B.I.!" Gillen may have had a certain point there. Two days later, in a telephone conversation with Danner (which, of course, Gillen taped), Gillen put the matter more succinctly when he remarked to his former F.B.I. colleague that "It takes a good liar to be an investigator." Gillen was saying this to a man who had been an agent in charge of F.B.I. offices, and he spoke as though he knew Danner would understand what he was talking about.

The point involved is hardly an academic one, because a protective attitude toward investigative techniques employed against private citizens reaches up into the highest levels of government. To cite an example other than the Nader affair, one may refer to the news that broke in November, 1971, that F.B.I. agents had been investigating the background and personal life of the experienced Columbia Broadcasting System correspondent in Washington, Daniel Schorr, who was known to have been incurring the resentment of members of the White House staff by his reporting on Administration policy matters. On orders that came down from the White House, F.B.I. agents visited the president of C.B.S. News and a number of present and former C.B.S. officers, Schorr's neighbors in Washington, and even those of his brother in New York, and sought all manner of information on Schorr with the explanation that Schorr was being considered for what was variously described as "a very important job" and a "position of trust and confidence" in the government. The only flaw in this story was that Schorr had not applied for any such job and had no intention of doing so. The day after the news of this investigation became public, Ronald L. Ziegler, the Presidential press secretary, when questioned about the affair, declared that Schorr was being considered for a position in the Administration that Ziegler described rather vaguely as being in the "environmental area." An unnamed White House official said that the F.B.I. investigation had been initiated "routinely" by the office of Frederic V. Malek, the chief recruiter for the White House. But when Schorr happened to meet Malek at a dinner after the investigation was under way and asked him if he really was being considered for a job with the government, Malek's re-action was one of complete surprise. He assured Schorr he would check into the matter and let Schorr know the answer to his question. He didn't call Schorr, who then rather logically came to the conclusion that the "very important" government job for which he was being investigated probably never existed.

The Schorr investigation and the Nader investigation thus seem cut from the same bolt of cloth, and in each case the course of the investigation, the pretext used, and the subse-quent attempt at covering up involve the imposition of layer upon layer of deception and misrepresentation. The question thus arises: if in 1971 the imposition of such layers of deception and misrepresentation about the investigation of a citizen-critic should originate with and be deliberately compounded by the White House itself, can it really be all that surprising that the investigation of Ralph Nader in 1966 by former F.B.I. men, on the orders of General Motors, and the subsequent attempts at cover-up by the officers and agents of the corporation before and during the March 22 hearing did not arouse the Depart-ment of Justice in a case that would certainly involve detailed public discussion of the kind of practices the F.B.I.'s own agents were routinely carrying out against citizens?

Clearly, people who have been trained in surreptitious tech-niques and activities in the service of the federal government are of value to industry, and the services of former F.B.I. men, who form a considerable private investigative fraternity through-out the country, are always in demand by big corporations because of the former connections of these agents with national and local law enforcement officers and their insights into the whole nether world of shadowing, pretext-manufacturing, and dossier-compiling. Often, too, they are in demand because of their savvy in delicate political matters. Thus two or three years after the General Motors people picked him to be the legal go-between in the investigation of Nader, Danner went on to become an aide to Robert Maheu (also a former F.B.I. man), who for a time was the proconsul for the Howard R. Hughes empire in Las Vegas. Maheu was eventually fired by Hughes, but Danner survived as a Hughes management man; he is at present said to be in charge of a company controlling Hughes's hotel interests in Las Vegas. Danner surfaced in the national news in mid-1971, when the columnist Jack Anderson asserted that Danner was the emissary used by Maheu during the 1968 presidential campaign to transfer $100,000 that Anderson alleged had been siphoned off from the Silver Slipper, a Hughes gambling house in Las Vegas, to C. G. ("Bebe") Rebozo, an intimate of Richard M. Nixon, as a contribution to the 1968 Nixon presidential campaign. (After the appearance of the Anderson column, Danner refused to comment on this matter to the press.) Whatever the facts may be, it appears that Danner enjoys good relations with the President himself. President Nixon is reported to have spoken warmly of Danner in private conversation and to have referred to him as "a dear friend."

Nader was not overly surprised at the failure of the Department of Justice to act concerning the charges of illegal behavior that were raised as a result of the original G.M. investigation of him and the Senate subcommittee inquiry into that investigation. However, Nader is a most tenacious man. In August, 1970, his suit against General Motors for invasion of privacy was settled out of court, with G.M., while admitting no wrongdoing, agreeing to pay Nader $425,000 "to avoid the very substantial additional expense and demands upon the time of corporation personnel" if the case were to drag on. This money Nader, after deducting his lawyers' fees and other expenses, has used to finance a number of projects to monitor the activities of General Motors "in the safety, pollution and consumer-relations area." Thus, as Nader has observed dryly, the General Motors people, in settling his suit for invasion of privacy, are "financing their own ombudsman."

19

"Not Like His Brother and His Father"

DESPITE THE SETTLEMENT of his suit against General Motors, Nader's interest as a student of corporate life in the facts surrounding the original General Motors investigation of him has not waned, even though the subject is one that he seems personally reluctant to hark back to, and one that he talks about only when pressed. (Nader's suit against Gillen as a co-defendant in this case, as well as his libel suit against him, had been withdrawn earlier.) Nader seems to be interested in the facts around the G.M. investigation of him primarily because the affair represents what he calls "a matured situation"—that is, it is not one of those situations in which a critical and detailed examination of a particular form of corporate wayward behavior has to start from scratch. He feels that the already extensive record of that investigation deserves to be filled in so that the history of the case may be reasonably complete.

In April, 1971, Nader's staff aide on legal and congressional liaison matters, Gary Sellers, who had been assigned to keep track of any developments concerning the original G.M. investigation, came across, more or less by accident, certain discrepancies between recordings of the statements and examination of G.M. witnesses at the March 22, 1966, Ribicoff subcommittee hearing and the actual official printed record of the hearing. This led Nader to ask Sellers to make a close comparison of what the G.M. witnesses actually did say in the hearing and what they said according to the official printed record. As a result, on May 20, 1971, Nader sent a letter to Senator Ribicoff listing these discrepancies and asking for an investigation of what Nader's letter said appeared to be "significant alteration" in the printed record of testimony actually given to the subcommittee in the March 22 hearing.

The most startling of these discrepancies had to do with James Roche's declaration to the subcommittee that "the investigation initiated by General Motors, contrary to some speculation, did *not* employ girls as sex lures, did *not* employ detectives giving false names . . . did *not* follow Mr. Nader in Iowa and Pennsylvania, did *not* have him under surveillance during the day he testified before this subcommittee . . ." Nader's letter pointed out that in the official printed record Roche's words "did *not* employ girls as sex lures" had been omitted. Nader's point was that the elimination of this and other phrases was a particularly serious matter because, he said, the Department of Justice investigation of possible perjury before the subcommittee had been based on the department's perusal of the printed record of the March 22 hearing, and also because the just discovered discrepancies raised the suspicion that the hearing record had been deliberately tampered with.

Unfortunately, there was no quick way for Ribicoff's staff lawyers to determine what changes had or had not been made, or by whom, in the original transcripts, which, according to custom, had been shown witnesses shortly after the hearing for the purpose of allowing them to correct obvious minor errors. By the time Nader made these latest representations to Ribicoff, all the corrected typescripts and galley proofs of the March 22 hearings had been thrown out of the Senate subcommittee files as no longer useful. And even the original stenotypist's tapes had gone astray. However, it is quite probable that most of the deleted words or phrases in question had been left out either by errors committed by the stenotypist or in the typesetting process in the Government Printing Office, where the final record was set, proofread, and run off on the press. A Xerox copy of the typescript of the G.M. witnesses' testimony as corrected at the G.M. end in Detroit has been produced by G.M. and it shows that the corrected copy of Roche's testimony contains no deletion of the "sex lure" phrase from the typescript.

However, a look at a copy of the changes in the transcript as corrected by G.M. does show one interesting alteration of the original transcript. When, during the subcommittee hearing, Senator Ribicoff pressed Aloysius F. Power about the employment of "the most intimate questions" that had been made about Nader's personal life in the course of the G.M. investigation, Power replied:

> Now, on that I want to first point out that from the reports that we got and the understanding of the man who was engaged by Royal [Royal-Globe Insurance] up in Connecticut, he did not present any questions, as I understood, along those lines. The point was made by different people that were talked to—"Now, remember this fellow is not like his brother and his father," and then they commented that they were anti-Semitic. That is what started some of this.

In the typewritten transcript of Power's testimony this reply was altered at the G.M. end to read as follows (the inserted words are italicized here):

> Now, on that I want to first point out that from the reports that we got and the understanding of the man who was engaged by Royal up in Connecticut, he did not present any questions, as I *understand,* along those lines. *Subsequently, when Vincent Gillen Associates took over the investigation,* the point was made by different people that were talked to— "Now, remember this fellow is not like his brother and his father," and then they commented that they were anti-Semitic. That is what started some of this.

Aside from the gratuitous intrusion by the general counsel of General Motors into the public record of the repetition of scurrilous allegations put together by investigators concerning members of Nader's family—which Power left unchanged in the record—what seems to be involved in these changes is an attempt to lay responsibility for "the most intimate questions" about Nader's personal life and that of his family at the door of Gillen's later expanded investigation of Nader, rather than on the early and more perfunctory investigation conducted by O'Neill. But the change also gives the effect of having the record indicate that the question of anti-Semitism never arose in the G.M. investigation prior to the hiring of Gillen. However, this implication as it is conveyed by Power's altered testimony is simply at variance with the facts on record, and it has the further effect of steering the content of Power's testimony before the subcommittee away from an interesting discrepancy in the G.M. account of events.

The O'Neill report was only *one* of two documents, copies of which Eileen Murphy gave to Danner along with verbal instructions from G.M. for the Nader investigation—the other document being the seven-page report bearing the handwritten annotations by Eileen Murphy concerning Nader's drinking habits, his income tax reports filed with the I.R.S., and so forth. This report on Nader is in dossier form and is the one that Power described as "biographical data concerning Mr. Nader" and that Danner described as "some background data that [Eileen Murphy] had apparently compiled from press, magazines, and other publications." This second report may well have included some biographical details on Nader gleaned from press clippings, but it became apparent to me, when I examined a copy of the report toward the end of 1971, that the report was much more than that. I saw that it incorporated and repeated many of the principal details of the O'Neill report, but it went considerably beyond the O'Neill report both in tone and content and (unlike the O'Neill report) levelled allegations of anti-Semitism against members of Nader's family, and it contained details that could only have been gathered by investigators or informants on the lookout for derogatory material on Nader's personal and family life.

20

"You Were the Ones That Were Caught"

THE SERIOUS QUESTION THEREFORE arose in my mind as to whether, between the original O'Neill investigation and the far more intensive Gillen investigation—and before Danner ever gave Gillen the original G.M. instructions—some other sort of investigation of Nader was carried out, on behalf of General Motors or on behalf of someone else. In this connection, certain observations by one of the detectives employed by Gillen to shadow Nader in Washington seemed to me most interesting. The name of this detective is J. Donald Remmert. He is a former F.B.I. agent. Normally working for Gillen in the New York area at the time the G.M. investigation into Nader got under way, Remmert was assigned by Gillen on Sunday, February 6, 1966, to begin shadowing Nader in Washington that very day.

Remmert flew to Washington that day and went to a point near Nader's rooming house where, together with another Gillen detective, named Morley, he took over surveillance of Nader's residence from a couple of private detectives from the Arundel agency, which had been hired by Gillen to investigate and tail Nader. Remmert and Morley maintained their surveillance of Nader's movements and contacts for the next several days. Remmert and Morley were the two Gillen men who followed Nader's trail into the New Senate Office Building on February 11. In 1967, Stuart M. Speiser, Nader's lawyer in the suits against

General Motors and Gillen, had a talk with Remmert about his [Remmert's] activities during this period, and he found Remmert, who was by then no longer with the Gillen agency, reasonably cooperative. Speiser has preserved an account he later dictated on this meeting with Remmert.

According to Speiser's account, Remmert said that while he had Nader's rooming house under surveillance, he saw, at various times on two different days, a car that he remembered as being probably a 1964 Plymouth or Dodge driving slowly around in the area in which Nader lived. Remmert told Speiser that the car, after cruising around, would park near Nader's residence, and the detective said that, relying on his "general instinct about such matters," he developed as he noticed this car "the definite feeling that somebody else had Nader under surveillance."

In the meantime, Remmert and Morley were doing their own best to keep up with the details of Nader's daily life—following him, for example, to restaurants, banks, office buildings, and noting whom he met where and when—in short, keeping track of his movements. ("Movement" is a term used by F.B.I. agents to connote not only the general habits of a subject in going from place to place but the actual physical surveillance of these motions; thus, when Danner testified that Eileen Murphy had requested, on behalf of General Motors, information on Nader's "movement," a reasonable assumption is that Danner considered the prospect of at least some physical daily surveillance of Nader to be inherent in the instructions he had received from G.M. In fact, if one thinks about it, how could Nader's "movement" be catalogued *without* his being put under physical surveillance?)

Remmert said that, during his period of surveillance of Nader, he and Morley read in the Washington press (on February 9) that Nader was going to testify before the Ribicoff subcommittee the following day. According to Speiser's account, Remmert said that he and Morley telephoned this information in to Gillen's New York office on February 9, only to discover that the New York office already was aware of Nader's impending appearance as a witness. According to Remmert, the two detectives were definitely instructed to continue to keep Nader under surveillance despite this foreknowledge at Gillen headquarters. As to the trailing of Nader in the New Senate Office Building on February 11, this is how Speiser's memorandum summarizes Remmert's recollections of this event:

> Remmert states that Morley was following Nader at the time, and followed him into the Senate Office Building, but lost him in there. Morley then asked a guard where Nader had gone, and the guard told a reporter about it, thinking that the reporter was Nader. About that time, Morley called the hotel [where the two detectives were staying] and had Remmert join him. They stood around for forty-five minutes to an hour, whereupon an entirely different guard, a sergeant or lieutenant, came up to them and asked them if they were following someone. They stated that they were "working" or were there "on business," whereupon the officer told them that they could not conduct a surveillance on Senate property. Nader's name was not mentioned at that time, since this guard was a different one from the one of whom Morley had asked Nader's whereabouts. They were asked to leave by the guard. When they left, they did not want the guard to see them get into their car and take the number of the car, so they walked around awhile, and then Remmert came back with his hat and coat off and was observed by the guard but not recognized as he got into the car and drove away . . .

On February 16, still on the Nader case, Remmert went to the Ribicoff subcommittee office in the New Senate Office Building to examine the transcript of Nader's testimony before the subcommittee on February 10. Remmert later told Speiser that when he identified himself to the receptionist in the subcommittee office and explained what he wanted to see, he was told he would have to wait and that "four other investigators had reviewed the transcripts the same day."

Remmert said that in fact, when he did get an opportunity to examine a copy of the February 10 transcript, a man he took to be yet another private investigator arrived to ask to look at the transcript also. Speiser, in his talk with Remmert, asked if he knew just who the other man was. According to Speiser's memorandum, Remmert replied that "he did not find out, but he was positive that the man was a private investigator for two reasons. First of all, he said that the man was wearing 'delicatessen shoes,' which I [Speiser] took to mean that he was dressed and had the look of a private eye. More important, Remmert had noticed, when this other investigator came into the room, that he had been asked to show identification to the receptionist, and that he had shown an identification card similar to the one which he [Remmert] carried and was required to carry as a private investigator licensed in New York . . ."

If what Remmert had said about the presence of other investigators on the Nader trail was true—and his detail about the man with the "delicatessen shoes" to me had a certain persuasive quality that precise descriptions of height, weight, and color of eyes perhaps could hardly match—I reasoned that the other private investigator or investigators who were seemingly concerned with Nader's doings must have been representing a client or clients paying well for their services. Who could such a client be, and could the alleged or real presence of one or more investigators on the scene somehow have a connection with the surveillance which Nader had complained he had been subjected to on the plane journey between Philadelphia and Washington; with the incidents in which he had been approached by girls in stores; and with the harassing night telephone calls preceding his testimony before the Ribicoff subcommittee on February 10—all of which incidents had occurred within one week preceding Remmert's inspection of the Nader transcript on February 16?

In his March 22 testimony before the subcommittee, president Roche of General Motors had denied, of course, that G.M. had anything to do with telephone harassment or out-of-town surveillance of Nader, but so far as Nader has been concerned, that hardly has put the matter conclusively to rest. In his testimony, Roche also asserted that the G.M. investigation of Nader was an unusual, indeed unique, case and that he had ascertained from a search he had ordered of the records for several years back that the company had undertaken investigations of people only on "minor matters" concerning genuine preemployment checks or job applicants and internal security matters within the company. But it seemed to me that this hardly conforms to strict truth if material uncovered in the Gillen deposition in the Nader libel suit was a fair sample. Gillen admitted that prior to the Nader investigation he had carried out a number of other investigations for G.M. These included an investigation "under a suitable pretext" of the Reverend O. D. Dempsey, a well-known figure in antipoverty work in Harlem, after Dempsey had written a letter to the General Motors Acceptance Corporation complaining that the New York branches of the corporation discriminated against Negroes in its employment practices. And another assignment that Gillen had carried out on behalf of General Motors was an investigation into the life history and political beliefs, with particular emphasis on possible "subversive or communist activities," of a man who had left regular employment at General Motors to become a member of the international board of the United Auto Workers. Considering that Vincent Gillen Associates was but one of a number of private investigative agencies whose services General Motors could call upon, it seemed reasonable to me to suspect that the investigative activities initiated by G.M. in the past against critics or potential critics of the policies of the corporation were considerably greater than the president of General Motors indicated to the Senate subcommittee.

Whether or not G.M. might have been connected with some investigation other than that admitted to by the company, my own feeling has been after reading Gillen's deposition and after considering the circumstances surrounding Nader's story of being put under surveillance in various states, systematically harassed by telephone, and being made the object of apparent attempts to compromise him sexually, that the chances of Gillen's men having been responsible for such acts are pretty slight. This feeling has been founded less in any great faith I might have in Gillen's avowals of innocence than my notion of Gillen's sense of practicalities. Gillen was not a man with a disdain for the financial rewards of his labors. If, on behalf of General Motors, he had had Nader trailed in various states and had indeed used girls to try to entrap him, he certainly would have put in a handsome bill to G.M. for his services. But his itemized bills in the Nader investigation appear to have been scrutinized pretty carefully by Nader's lawyers, and there seems to be no known record of his having demanded or received payment for any such services. Thus, perhaps one should seek another explanation for the additional acts about which Nader has complained. Toward the end of 1971, while working on this book, I received from a person formerly with General Motors information that, shortly after the revelations in March, 1966, of the G.M. investigation of Nader, an employee of the G.M. legal staff had been told in confidence by a man from another auto company, "You at G.M. weren't the only ones. You were the ones that were caught. But you weren't the only ones."

Thus, even after six years, after a special public hearing of a Senate subcommittee, after two investigations by the Federal Bureau of Investigation, and after the facts brought to light by the two lawsuits brought by Nader against G.M. and Gillen, respectively, the full ramifications of the famous investigation of Nader are still not known. Perhaps some of them never will be known. But it seems certain that, if one draws back and, for the sake of fairness, gives General Motors the benefit of almost every doubt on unresolved issues and certainly where allegations of corporate misconduct have been made but have not been substantiated by concrete evidence—for example, the allegations concerning the alteration of documents, or the question of whether some further intensive investigation and/or harassment of Nader was involved in addition to the O'Neill and Gillen investigations ordered by G.M.—what remains beyond the realm of reasonable doubt or speculation is an almost classic case history in the misuse of corporate power. It was a sub-rosa operation carried out with trappings of conspiracy, with the employment of former F.B.I. agents, with a hardly unconscious abuse of the privileges and immunities of the lawyer-client relationship to conceal the corporate origins of the operation—for the purpose not only of investigating but of possibly discrediting and, if Gillen's taped instructions are a guide, of silencing a critic of the corporation at a time when the automobile industry was facing, for the first time in its history, the spectre of strict federal regulation. Under such an intimidating barrage, who but a Nader could have emerged without having had his personal integrity and critical reputation destroyed?

PART THREE

21

"It Could Have Been Toothbrushes"

HAVING READ OVER the testimony offered by the G.M. witnesses, and that of Danner and Gillen, I gave considerable thought to the question of pursuing various leads suggested by the internal evidence of the testimony and sworn statements offered. Should I try to visit the principals who had testified—Roche, Power, Bridenstine, Danner, Gillen—to seek their version of how the whole investigation had really come about and had been conducted? Aloysius Power had retired in 1967. Roche had retired at the end of 1971, to be succeeded as chairman of the board of G.M. by Richard C. Gerstenberg. (Until the preparation and issuance of the statement of March 9, 1966, on the investigation, Roche and Power, I had been led to believe, had been intimate friends, but by the time the March 22 hearing was over, I have been told, that friendship was virtually at an end. Precisely what brought about such a breach I would naturally have been interested in hearing about, especially as it might illuminate some of the circumstances leading up to the March 22 hearing.) As this is written, Louis Bridenstine is still in the G.M. legal department as associate general counsel. Of the other witness on the G.M. side during the March 22 hearing, Danner, as I have said, is an important figure in the Howard Hughes empire in Las Vegas, although he apparently retains an association with Alvord & Alvord in Washington. As for Gillen, Senator Robert Kennedy's smilingly ironic remark when Gillen accosted him after the March 22 hearing, "Well, maybe it will help your business," seems to have been a prophetic one. Gillen's private-eye business appears to be flourishing. At the end of 1966 he cooperated as a principal subject of a fairly long article in the New York *Times* Magazine on the private investigative business and was photographed posing, unabashed as ever, amid all sorts of elaborate wiretap-detection equipment presumably used by his operatives. I certainly felt that I might succeed in interviewing Gillen, as long as I didn't mind the thought of that pocket recorder reeling away as the interview progressed.

All these people, I decided, had had ample opportunity clearly and deliberately to state their cases on the record before the Ribicoff subcommittee on March 22. I came to the conclusion that I should let the record speak for itself. But having come to that conclusion, I reflected that there was one area that really might be worth exploring and that was the testimony that could have been, and indeed surely ought to have been, offered at the March 22 hearing—that is, the account of the mysteriously non-testifying witness, Miss Eileen Murphy, concerning the investigation of Nader. Eileen Murphy, I had heard reliably, was a very ill woman. After the March 22 hearing she had continued in her job as law librarian in the General Motors legal department until August, 1970. The previous year, she had developed a serious heart condition, and in August, 1970, she suffered a severe heart attack and was retired from the company. I had heard that in retirement, she had, while continuing on the job, consistently and firmly refused to discuss the Nader investigation with the press. And I heard that after her retirement, when, in response to Nader's various allegations of perjury, tampering with documents, and deliberate withholding of relevant information, the Ribicoff subcommittee counsel had wished to interview her formally, they had been told by the G.M. people that Miss Murphy's state of health was indeed precarious and might be rendered even more so by the strain of such an interview. Further, I had heard that Miss Murphy herself had resisted such an interview and the making of a sworn affidavit that would almost certainly be requested as a result.

In spite of all this, early in February, 1972, I made an approach to Miss Murphy through a person I had heard had some contact with her. My intermediary visited Miss Murphy and let her know that I was aware of her frail state of health, did not intend to subject her to a distressing interview, but did want her to know that I was ready to listen attentively to any observations she might care to make concerning her part in the Nader affair. To my surprise, I was told that Miss Murphy was willing to see me, on the understanding that while she didn't intend to volunteer information about the Nader investigation, she would try to answer questions about it that she thought appropriate. I went out to Detroit early in March to see Eileen Murphy at her home—a comfortable light-filled apartment in a modern building complex. I found Miss Murphy to be a dark-haired woman in her late forties—a woman that one would not call beautiful, perhaps, but there was no doubt that she was a person of considerable presence. She seemed less physically frail than I had expected, although her movements had an economy and deliberateness that I assumed were connected with her state of health. Miss Murphy's living room was filled with books and paintings, and it appeared that most of the paintings were by Eileen Murphy herself—Miss Murphy told me that in her retirement she'd taken up art and was working hard at it.

We sat down. I asked Miss Murphy how the investigation of Nader had got under way. She said that it began in July, 1965, in the legal department of General Motors, when "one of the attorneys walked in and said, 'Who the hell is this guy?'" —meaning Nader. At that point, Miss Murphy said, the interest in Nader was "strictly a library problem"—she, as the law librarian of G.M., was there to dig out whatever references to his name were occurring in legal literature. She said that she had recourse to the usual sources, such as Martindale-Hubbell, the standard directory of the legal profession, and that she'd found out very little about him that way. But, she said, "his name kept popping up" as a critic of the automobile business in general and G.M. in particular, and in October, 1965, she saw an item in the San Francisco *Chronicle* about Nader's writings on auto safety and "how we [General Motors] were going to be blown out of the world," presumably by these writings. By October, Miss Murphy said, she had obtained a set of pre-publication galleys of "Unsafe at Any Speed," and she made it clear to me that the company's ability to get its hands on that sort of thing long before publication was considered routine—"They'll see the early galleys of the book *you're* writing, too, you can be sure of that," she said to me.

As for the investigation of Nader by outsiders hired by the corporation, she said that "it was Aloysius [Power] who started that." But she said that she herself had been unaware of the existence of the O'Neill investigation out of Hartford until after the O'Neill report had been completed. I talked for some time with Miss Murphy about the atmosphere that was prevailing in the G.M. legal department at the time. There was, I gathered, a growing uneasiness in the department about Nader's widespread activities, at a time when product liability litigation was looming as an increasingly serious problem for the corporation. "Here this guy was, and we didn't know from *nothing* about him. A *shadow!*" Miss Murphy said. G.M. attorneys would come in, she went on, and ask her what she knew about this young man. She had continued compiling whatever information came to hand about Nader. As Eileen Murphy talked on, I found myself confounded by her strange mixture of attitudes concerning Nader and by her often remarkable candor. My astonishment grew as she touched on the expanded investigation of Nader that had been ordered by Power late in December, 1965, and her mission to Washington on behalf of the legal department to hire Danner and, eventually, through Danner, to contract for the services of Gillen.

"I really, in a way, enjoyed what he [Nader] was doing," she said. "I'd say, 'Keep it up, baby!' or 'Keep it up, Ralphie baby!'—I would often just speak of him as 'Ralphie baby.' I have nothing against Ralph Nader. I think he's quite a guy. Even when the hearing was going on I felt that. I liked the fact he even did the book—although not in the sense that he was exposing the corporation. That was something else. But he had no money. He had the stamina, the self-discipline, to see something. I liked that. It could have been toothbrushes. He just happened to pick the biggest one of them all."

Again: "I thought they [at G.M.] should give him a lab, and all the facilities he needed, let him design a car in every way he wanted it to be. And then turn him into the division that would be marketing it. And see how successful he'd be."

Then again, quite breezily: "I used to go around [at the time, presumably, when Nader was under intensive investigation] saying, 'I wish that bastard's father had never met his mother!' "

And again: "It was a professional challenge. And I *like* hard work."

And again: "There was no malicious intent. I never had it. I never had it in my mind to do harm to the boy. What the hell, without Murphy he might never have made it!"

Some time later, and in a perfectly matter-of-fact way: "He was an unknown quantity. I can remember when I first saw him on TV. It was on CKLW, which is a Canadian TV station in Windsor, Ontario, right across the river from Detroit, on [speaking precisely] December 10, 1965. And this guy appeared on a talk show, between two people; a silicone-treated girl dancer, and Wayne Lonergan—you know, the guy who went to jail for killing his wife back in the forties? And this boy appeared on the screen. That's when I got the idea, that I thought that he was queer. I thought there had to be something about him—the way his socks fell down. The way he held his head. The way his hands hung limp."

Again: "Around Christmas, Aloysius decided we should do something [about Nader]. He's spouting off at press conferences, TV question-and-answer shows. [In the G.M. legal department] they laughed at me when I said, 'Maybe he's queer —did you ever think of that?' "

And yet again: "As true as God is my judge, I never had any animosity toward him . . . that homo jazz—that was in the sense that he was an unusual person."

These observations on Nader himself were scattered through our talk. I don't wish to convey the impression that the subject of the inquiry into Nader's sex habits was prominent in our interview. In speaking of the investigation of Nader, Miss Murphy kept stressing the theme that, at least in the early stages, the legal department of General Motors knew virtually nothing of Nader and that its lawyers who were engaged in Corvair litigation had become increasingly curious during the latter part of 1965 as to Nader's technical qualifications on automotive safety matters, and that the expanded investigation of Nader undertaken by Gillen as a result of the instructions conveyed by Miss Murphy to Danner was fundamentally a proper one for which, she felt, General Motors needed to make no apology. In fact, she told me, she herself felt so strongly on this matter that she had been opposed to the company's eventual settlement of the lawsuit brought against G.M. by Nader.

I touched on various aspects of the events leading up to the full-scale investigation of Nader. I took it from what Miss Murphy said that she had been given, from the beginning, ample encouragement and authority to compile whatever information she could from open sources on Nader, and that in doing so, certain resources of the corporation were helpfully made available to her. "That's one thing in General Motors," Miss Murphy told me. "You just press a button, and you get what you want." By December, Miss Murphy had, in addition to whatever other information she had been compiling, been given access to the O'Neill report. I was interested in this. I told Miss Murphy of the strong feeling I had arrived at from examining both documents that the second report, on plain paper, that she had given Danner, along with the O'Neill report, was something of a continuing dossier that had been compiled within General Motors after the receipt of the O'Neill report; that it incorporated the principal facts of the O'Neill report and some material from the public domain; but that it showed, also, evidence that some other inquiries had been made into Nader's personal and family life in addition to whatever had been unearthed in the O'Neill report. Miss Murphy said that this, in fact, was true. She indicated that these additional inquiries about Nader weren't too extensive, but she made it clear to me that she wasn't going to say who made them or how they found their way into the report that contained, on the last page, all those handwritten notations about the I.R.S., Nader's drinking habits, and his "nervous habit of sniffing."

I asked whether Miss Murphy felt General Motors had been responsible for other acts of harassment of Nader, outside of the activities admitted to by the G.M. executives at the March 22 hearing—the annoying and ominous telephone calls at night, the alleged attempts at entrapment by girls, and the alleged tailing of Nader in various states. Miss Murphy said that to the best of her knowledge the corporation had nothing to do with those acts. I remarked that from what I myself had seen of Nader, I'd noticed that he was usually very much aware of what was going on around him, and that I doubted if all of these alleged incidents were merely the product of an overheated imagination. "Oh, I believe him on that," Miss Murphy said. "He's a very sensitive man. Those incidents [concerning the girls] were just blatant. I don't think he was making all that up."

I asked Miss Murphy who, apart from agents employed by G.M., she thought could have been responsible for such acts of surveillance, for the apparent attempts at entrapment, and for the harassing night telephone calls to Nader. She said she really didn't know, and wouldn't even care to guess. "That phone call about, 'Why don't you go back to Connecticut, buddy boy?'— they came right after *me* about that at G.M. [after the Nader affair had hit the news]—they thought that I might have been responsible for having that call put in," Miss Murphy said.

"Because of the 'buddy boy' phrase that was used. That's the way I talk. But I had nothing to do with it, I assure you."

I wanted to know how Miss Murphy had hit upon Danner as a go-between, and finding her reluctant to discuss this matter, I let it drop. During the ensuing conversation, the subject of the instructions she had given Danner on behalf of General Motors came up. She recalled specifically having asked Danner to determine whether Nader was an engineer, and she said that she did tell Danner that G.M. was interested in Nader's connections, if any, with the American Trial Lawyers Association, which, she said, in her mind was almost synonymous with Corvair litigation, since much of this was being undertaken at the time by members of ATLA.

Speaking of her handwritten annotations at the end of the dossier that she had given Danner, along with the O'Neill report, Miss Murphy denied unequivocally that in making the notation, "He has nervous habit of sniffing or else he had pneumonia on the day of his press conference . . . ," she had meant to imply that Nader might be a drug user. "It never crossed my mind!" she exclaimed. " 'Sniffing'!—here I was using that word. I'm a native-born New *Yorker,* and it never even crossed my *mind* that it might mean drugs! My God, how could you be on dope and do all that work that Nader was doing? His sniffing was a nervous habit to me, and that's what I noted down. And it got turned into sniffing dope."

I found myself impressed enough with this explanation to make a point, when I got back to New York, to look up the transcript or partial transcript of the conversation that Gillen swore he had had with Danner while receiving his instructions on the investigation of Nader. And I read over this passage apparently bearing on some of Eileen Murphy's handwritten notations:

[Danner]: Well, you know a lot of people like to play investigator . . . There is a lot of stuff listed there and I don't know just what it all means . . . Sniffing gave someone the idea that maybe he's on . . . [sentence unfinished in Gillen's transcript].

[Gillen]: I know that Dr. Leary was experimenting with students at Harvard about that time . . . was kicked out of Harvard because of it.

[Danner]: Some of those Harvard fellows are very liberal . . . hurt American industry cleverly . . . What they are really after is to get something that will shut him up and get him out of their hair.

From this, Miss Murphy's explanation of the "sniffing" reference could very well make sense. Yet if it did, why, I wondered, had Miss Murphy raised no objection when she had read in Detroit the reports resulting from Gillen's instructions to his investigators in various states to "determine 'what makes him tick,' such as his real interest in safety . . . his women, boys, etc., drinking, dope, jobs"? For the same reason that, in the legal department of General Motors, "they laughed" at her suggestion that Nader might be a homosexual, and yet "they" took no steps whatever to put an immediate stop to persistent inquiries by Gillen's agents concerning anti-Semitism and Nader's sex habits?

In discussing Gillen's reports in general, Miss Murphy seemed rather offhand. She said that as these came in she would take them in to the general counsel, leave them on his desk, and tell him what had been found thus far on Nader. She was emphatic on one matter. She denied that she had given instructions to Gillen to investigate the truthfulness of Senator Ribicoff's assertion at the February 10, 1966, subcommittee hearing that the senator had never met Nader prior to that hearing. "What I had asked was whether Nader was ever in the employ of the subcommittee," Miss Murphy said.

Miss Murphy went on to observe that part of the trouble that G.M. got into on the Nader investigation had to do with a time lag between instructions that came from General Motors and the forwarding of Gillen's reports through Danner's office. "Gillen was crazy, taking as much time as he did in the investigation," she said. "He was leaving tracks all over." She added, "If you want to make an investigation like this, you make it *fast*." (I found this remark interesting. It reminded me that I had read concerning the F.B.I. investigation of Daniel Schorr, the C.B.S. correspondent who had aroused people in the White House by his critical reporting, that the investigation had begun at 8:30 on the morning of August 20, 1971, and by 3:30 in the afternoon twenty-five people had been interviewed by F.B.I. agents on the job. Fast work, but even then not quite fast enough?)

Miss Murphy reflected a little further on Gillen's work and her feelings at the time about his progress. "What made me so damned mad about Gillen," she told me, "was that we already *had* nearly all of that background stuff on Nader, in the way of documentation, at General Motors. We had every tape, every piece of film, everything he'd written, from the time he'd been in Harvard. Gillen didn't have to get all that. We *had* that. I can remember three tape-recording machines going at the same time, just transcribing tapes of interviews or talks that Nader had given. We had volumes of Nader transcripts that would be, altogether, about sixteen inches thick, and then we had a four-inch-thick binder on him. We had a *lot*."

I asked Miss Murphy about the events that had occurred in the G.M. camp when the investigation of Nader had become public knowledge, and when the Ridgeway article concerning the investigation and Gillen appeared in the *New Republic*. Miss Murphy indicated that "the fat was really in the fire" at G.M. headquarters when all the publicity started pouring in. "I used to cringe when I read that *New Republic* piece and another one that followed it," Miss Murphy said. She added, "And I still buy the *New Republic*."

I expressed interest at this.

"Yeah, I like the *New Republic*," Miss Murphy said. "I'm a *reader*."

As for just what happened, in what order, at G.M. headquarters when the Nader affair broke, Miss Murphy seemed disinclined to volunteer much information, and I didn't push her on the subject. But she did say that "when the whole thing hit the *Congressional Record* [on the day following the G.M. statement of March 9] I offered to resign. I said, 'Why not put the blame on me?' "

I didn't pursue this any further with Miss Murphy. In any event, it was clear that her offer to resign hadn't been taken up by the G.M. general counsel, who, according to Gillen's account, himself had offered to resign sometime before March 21, "but they wouldn't let me." I moved on to the subject of Miss Murphy's presence at the March 22 Senate hearings and told her that I'd be interested in her impressions of the event.

She talked quickly, and unhesitatingly, about the experience. "We [the people from G.M.] arrived in Washington the day before the hearing. We were flown in G.M. planes into Baltimore instead of Washington, so that there wouldn't be all the reporters there at the airport. Then we were driven to Washington in G.M. cars. I had, like, a Panzer division around me, so no reporters could get at me. They put me in a room at the Mayflower, with the TV blaring all the time in case the room was wired."

Here, I remembered with interest Gillen's observation that when he confronted Power on the evening of March 21 at the Mayflower concerning Gillen's deepening conviction that Roche's prepared statement had the effect of making Gillen the scapegoat in the G.M. investigation of Nader, the TV set in Power's room was turned on. I asked Miss Murphy if, that evening, she had any inkling of the confrontation with Power that Gillen described in his deposition in the Nader libel suit.

"Well, I knew, the night before the hearing, that something blew," Miss Murphy said. She went on to indicate that she had been invited to go to Power's suite that evening to sit around and talk with him, but that this invitation had been hurriedly withdrawn before the time that she was to go to see Power, and withdrawn in a manner that made her feel that something had gone seriously amiss.

The next morning, she said, the G.M. people, under instructions, went to the Senate subcommittee hearing in pairs, so as not to attract too much attention from the press and not to create opportunities for photographs of the G.M. party *en masse*.

"God, I remember it so well," Miss Murphy told me. "The nervousness. The klieg lights. The TV camera crews. The electric cables all over. The men in the black leather jackets rushing out with reels of film that had been shot. The reporters, the still photographers. The big crowd. And everybody [from General Motors] separated from one another. And in the middle of all this those visiting children, who were brought in to the committee room for a while during the hearing as part of some tour of Capitol Hill. I remember that my hands and feet were freezing, and yet at the same time it was so hot with all the lights that my body was perspiring. I was scared to death. But I wouldn't have missed it for the world."

I asked Miss Murphy if she'd had a good view of Nader, and had been able to hear his testimony fairly clearly in the hearing room. She said she had, and then she made the comment about Nader's appearance before the subcommittee, "There's something that's wrong." Before I could ask what that was, Miss Murphy went on to make a remark about Nader that perhaps could only have come from her: "He should hold his head up more when he's speaking. He's so tall, I suppose he's used to hitting his head on door jambs." She continued, "After the hearing was over I went up to him as near as this [indicating the short distance between Miss Murphy and myself as we were sitting]. He didn't look at me. A G.M. attorney grabbed me at that point. If Ralph had looked at me I'd have put my hand out and said, 'No hard feelings, doll.' "

I asked Miss Murphy if she could explain why she hadn't been called upon to testify at the hearing.

"That's an interesting question," Miss Murphy said, without expression. She volunteered no answer.

"Were you told that you wouldn't be called upon to testify?" I asked.

"I was never told I wouldn't testify. But I was never prepared," Miss Murphy said, presumably referring to the rather
elaborate legal preparation that counsel for a corporation customarily gives witnesses due to appear before congressional
committees or the courts.

I had one further matter to take up with Miss Murphy in
connection with the March 22 hearings. It had to do with the
response of James Roche to this question put to him by Senator
Harris:

> *Senator Harris:* Were you aware of these facts of Miss
> Murphy's instructions about how the investigation was to be
> conducted, and into what areas? Were you aware of that at
> the time you issued the March 9 press release?
> *Mr. Roche:* No, sir, I was not. I was given to understand
> it was a routine investigation into the areas that I have men-
> tioned.

I asked Miss Murphy whether the substance of this answer
agreed with what she herself understood the situation to be at
the time of the March 9 press release. But I received no answer.
Whatever the state of Miss Murphy's knowledge might or might
not be in this area, it was clear to me that she had no intention
of volunteering any information on the subject, and so I let
things go at that.

Next we talked about the general atmosphere in the G.M.
legal department during what could be called the pre-Nader
period. She said that the size of the G.M. legal staff actually was
very small in relation to the amount of legal work that had to be
handled directly, or, when parcelled out to outside attorneys,
supervised in one way or another. Thus, she said, at the time
when Nader became active, the legal staff in G.M. headquarters
in Detroit consisted only of between fifty and sixty lawyers. I
had already formed the impression, from information that had
been given me previously by a couple of people who had some
familiarity with the workings of the G.M. legal department, that
the rising number of product liability suits against General
Motors arising out of Corvair accidents for some considerable

time had been causing the G.M. legal people anxiety about their ability to cope with the successful defense of so much complex litigation. And I had the impression that this anxiety had helped bring about an air of acute apprehension, in which, eventually, the idea of the investigation of Nader originated. Nothing that Miss Murphy told me contradicted this impression. As far back as 1964, she said, people on the legal staff had seen, "like a cloud on the horizon," a potential crisis threatened by the gathering number of Corvair design suits. By mid-1964, some thirty such suits were pending, and it looked as though many more might be brought.

I made it clear to Miss Murphy that I was no lawyer or engineer, but that I wondered why the impending Corvair crisis feared by the legal department couldn't have been averted by the relatively simple process of recalling those models of the Corvair over which so much litigation had been arising. "Was there anybody at G.M. who considered that recalling the product might turn out to be the most desirable answer to the problem?" I asked.

Miss Murphy lit a cigarette, smoked it for a while, and told me that she knew of such a person. She said that his name was Daniel Boone. She said that Daniel Boone had been a close friend of hers, and that he had been the attorney in charge of general litigation for General Motors. Miss Murphy said that in 1964 Boone told her several times that he thought that the Corvair (I assumed that Miss Murphy was referring to the 1960-63 model Corvairs, over which nearly all of the Corvair design litigation was then arising) should be recalled by the corporation. " 'Call them all in'—that's what he said," Miss Murphy told me. And again, later: " 'Recall them.' He told me that."

I asked Miss Murphy what had come of Mr. Boone's expressed views on the Corvair. Miss Murphy then told me the following story:

"Dan and I were very close friends, as I've said. In December of 1964, a week or so before Christmas, we had a

Christmas party for the legal staff one evening at the Detroit Athletic Club. Daniel was supposed to be my escort. But he was late, and I remember that we had to delay dinner because of that. The reason he was late was that on the same day he and a group of other attorneys had been out at the proving grounds. One of the attorneys with the group told me what had happened. He said that Daniel had been driving a Corvair around the proving grounds and that he'd flipped [over] the Corvair he was in. When Daniel turned up at the party he didn't mention what had happened. I brought the subject up with Daniel a few days later, when he was driving me somewhere. He confirmed that he had been driving the Corvair and that it had turned over. He didn't go into details—he wasn't the kind of guy you'd try to push if he didn't want to give details."

Approximately three weeks after the accident, Miss Murphy said—specifically, on the morning of Monday, January 11, 1965—Daniel Boone was found dead in bed by his wife. Miss Murphy told me that his death was attributed to cerebral thrombosis. According to Miss Murphy, Boone, rather characteristically, had not told his wife about his Corvair rollover. Miss Murphy told me that she is a close friend of Boone's widow, and that a few weeks after Boone's death she had told Mrs. Boone of the incident at the proving grounds—and then regretted having done so because of the extreme distress this story gave Mrs. Boone. Miss Murphy made it clear to me that she did not intend to imply a direct cause-and-effect relationship between Daniel Boone's Corvair rollover and his death; she simply was telling me what the sequence of events was.

"That's Danny Boone," Miss Murphy told me, pointing to one of two framed photographic portraits on a bookshelf behind her. The portrait was of a round-faced, smiling man in glasses. The other portrait was of Aloysius Power. Miss Murphy said that Daniel Boone had been fifty-four when he died, and that after his death the sense of his loss was such that "it was just as though a bulldozer had been driven through the G.M. legal staff."

22

"Corporate Manslaughter"

I TOOK MY LEAVE of Miss Murphy, who was beginning to show signs of fatigue and strain, and walked out into the forlorn streets of downtown Detroit, quite shaken by what I had just heard. As I walked, I reflected on the tragic irony of the circumstances involved. If what I had heard was true, here was the very attorney in charge of general litigation for General Motors at once supervising before the courts the vigorous defense of the safe design of the Corvair, bringing out and preparing, from inside and outside General Motors, expert engineering witnesses to testify as to the car's safe design, and yet privately expressing such serious doubts about the Corvair that he considered the best solution to be the recall of the car. And then he had himself driven a Corvair—what model year it was Miss Murphy never did learn—and himself had had the car roll over. Of course, it is possible that this happened through some gross error of judgment on his part. However, from all that Miss Murphy told me, Boone was a prudent man, and I could not easily believe that he would have driven recklessly and certainly could not believe that he would have rolled the car over deliberately. He was a skilled lawyer, not a skilled test driver, and the safety rules at the G.M. proving grounds would not have permitted him to drive in a deliberately dangerous manner. Nor did he seem remotely like the sort of man who would violate such rules. However, roll over he did, according to what I had just heard, and this could scarcely have altered his views on recalling the Corvair.

But the sudden death of Daniel Boone three weeks later seems not to have spurred the G.M. legal department to make prompt recommendations for the recall of Corvairs. On the contrary, it seems to have marked an effective end to any movement within the legal department toward recommending such a solution to top G.M. management. The energies of the department were now concentrated instead on masterminding the defense of the ever-growing number of Corvair suits. And as the suits piled up, the people in the legal department became increasingly nervous. By the end of October, 1965, the number of Corvair lawsuits against G.M. had climbed to more than a hundred; they involved potentially about $40 million in damages against the company. If the suits had been settled—probably for considerably less than this—the cost to G.M. in terms of its annual profit, which was $1.7 billion in 1964, would not have been even a trifling one; it would have been zero, because G.M. was insured against such losses. However, such seems to have been the weight of corporate prestige tied up in the Corvair program and the overriding organizational push of the people responsible for producing the car within the Chevrolet Division that those in the legal department saw no practical alternative but to struggle on with litigation—settling the most gruesome of the Corvair cases out of court here, winning one or two there, and fighting out the rest tooth and nail. But by the time "Unsafe at Any Speed" was published, the atmosphere of nervousness in the legal department seems to have deepened until the responsible people there seem to have been seized by a kind of panicky feeling that they might soon be overwhelmed by a tidal wave of Corvair litigation that they simply would not have anything like the proper staff to supervise. It was in such an atmosphere, it seemed to me, that the dream must have arisen within the legal department of an almost magical solution to the problem: rather than seek out and fix whatever design defects might exist in the Corvair, why not seek out whatever defects might exist in the professional and personal life of the chief critic of the Corvair—in effect, to fix Ralph Nader himself? And it seemed now to me the bitterest, the saddest irony that the chosen instrument of this' undercover corporate exercise should have been Eileen Murphy, the close friend of perhaps the one man in the G.M. legal department with both the strong authority and strong feelings on the subject to have made a serious attempt to bring about the recall of the Corvair—the strangely fated Mr. Boone.

"It was a professional challenge, and I *like* hard work," Miss Murphy had told me. A professional challenge! What can the loyalty a corporation demands of people bring them to! Here Miss Murphy was, a year after Daniel Boone's death, busily ordering inquiries into what girls Nader might possibly be sleeping with, "and if not girls, boys," and sending off letters asking for an investigation of the circumstances in which Nader, years before, had witnessed an automobile accident in which a child had been decapitated: "See if this gem can be uncovered . . ." And this was the same woman I had just been interviewing—bright, interesting, very human: I really had found it hard not to like her. But the aberrations of civilized behavior brought about in Miss Murphy's display of loyalty to G.M. in the Nader affair seemed to me only indicative of the amazing degree to which people can become separated, in large corporations, from their normal personal standards and can surrender their will to a kind of collective corporate consciousness. I remembered having talked, some time before I had met Miss Murphy, with one man familiar with the operations of the G.M. legal staff, who had told me he had become most disturbed by the apparent detachment into which members of the legal staff seemed to drift from their sense of responsibility as citizens as well as their professional oaths as attorneys. "It's amazing to see how corporate manslaughter becomes an impersonal thing," he said. "The people in the corporate hierarchy don't see the paraplegics. I understand that at one time in the G.M. legal department there was some casual discussion of whether it might not be advisable for the company quietly to buy up Corvairs in used car lots so as to keep them out of the hands of potential litigants. But that came to nothing. I can remember talking some time back to one attorney on the G.M. legal staff who mentioned, in connection with the current state of Corvair litigation, that the people who by then were driving Corvairs—driving them in the Detroit area, anyway—were, increasingly, the poor and the black. The only thing that seemed to be on this man's mind in making this observation was that accidents involving these people's cars would cost General Motors less from product liability suits because of the economic status of those driving the Corvairs."

23

"Loyal Soldiers in the Ranks"

IT ALSO HAD COME to me from someone who was working within the corporate structure in the mid-sixties that several of the younger people in the G.M. legal department had become distressed at the prevailing attitude in the company toward the Corvair safety problem. In 1967, according to this man, a "dedicated, knowledgeable man in New Mexico" wrote a letter to G.M. saying that the heater used in the 1961-and-on models of the Corvair [a type called a direct-air heater, in which the air that cooled the motor was heated by contact with the hot engine manifold and taken into the vehicle] was hazardous to the occupants because it was prone to leak carbon monoxide and other products of combustion into the interior of the car. This same source who had been in G.M. had told me, "The thing that shocked me was that they [at G.M.] knew that the Corvair carbon monoxide problem was ongoing and incurable, and that the people in the legal department concerned with the letter of complaint seemed to feel that the only choice open to them in a practical way was to . . . divert the attention of the man who had raised the problem . . . to send someone out to wine and dine this man and hope that he would drop the matter. I remember being so upset about this whole situation at the time that I stayed up all night, pouring out to two very close personal friends of mine my doubts and anxieties about what was going on."

But 1967 was by no means the first year in which the problem of the carbon monoxide leakage connected with the Corvair direct-air heater had been raised with General Motors. As far back as 1962, Edward L. Wolf, a lawyer in Philadelphia representing a man called John P. Petry, of Chester Springs, Pennsylvania, had contended in a suit against General Motors that carbon monoxide leaking from the heater in the 1961 Corvair Greenbriar van that Mr. Petry had been driving regularly had caused Mr. Petry permanent and irreversible brain damage. The suit was settled by General Motors out of court in 1966 for $125,000, but not under conditions that an attorney possessing the information that Mr. Wolf did concerning the carbon monoxide problem in the Corvair heater could rest easily with. As part of the settlement, Mr. Wolf was obliged to turn over to the G.M. side all the very considerable and detailed evidence he had assembled in the case, and to agree not to discuss the specifics of the case with anyone. The lack of willing promptitude attributed to G.M. by the ex-G.M. man to whom I had talked concerning the production of evidence called for in Corvair cases somehow seems to have been interestingly exemplified in the Petry case. According to Mr. Wolf's later testimony before a Senate subcommittee hearing presided over by Senator Vance Hartke of Indiana, a formal demand by Mr. Wolf during pretrial proceedings in the Petry case for information possessed by G.M. concerning complaints or customer notification of dangers or problems having to do with engine fumes in 1961 Corvairs had brought forth a sworn statement from G.M. that the company had knowledge of one complaint, on a 1961 Greenbriar.

However, in April, 1971, a couple of junk dealers in the Detroit area who had come into possession of cartons of microfilmed records that had been somehow discarded by General Motors took a look at some of these records. After this, they had quickly got in touch with Ralph Nader's people, and apparently also had the nimbleness to let the General Motors people know they had done so. In no time at all a G.M. representative turned up at the premises of the junk dealers with a cashier's check for $20,000 and a truck, which promptly whisked the microfilmed records away. According to press reports at the time, the records were of G.M. customer complaints covering the years from 1962 to 1965. And, according to the same press reports, these microfilmed records had been disposed of by General Motors on August 18, 1966—rather an interesting date, it would seem, because that happened to be the very date on which the House of Representatives had passed the Motor Vehicle Safety Act of 1966—and the Act contained certain provisions that would have made it possible for such customer-complaint records to have been called for by the Department of Transportation and be subject to examination by the department. Due to publicity surrounding the discovery of these junked microfilmed records, the Department of Transportation did in fact eventually examine the records. They contained seventeen thousand letters of complaint having to do with the Corvair, and Mr. Wolf, who in 1966 had been given to understand by G.M. that the company had knowledge of only one customer complaint relating to fumes and similar problems connected with heaters in 1961 Corvairs, must have been interested to learn, as he subsequently did, that in the junked and recovered G.M. microfilm records 545 complaints referred in general terms to fumes or odors in the Corvair, and an additional 143 complaints referred specifically to exhaust fumes noticeable in the vehicle. (As for 1961 Corvairs in particular, a G.M. statement in June, 1971, admitted to the company's having received 215 customer complaints concerning fumes or odors, 67 of these complaints being, by G.M.'s own estimates, related to engine and exhaust fumes.) In September, 1971, *Consumer Reports* printed a detailed article on the problem of carbon monoxide in the Corvair. The magazine said it had invited Corvair owners to bring the cars in to its parent organization, Consumers Union, for testing, and 221 owners had done so. The article reported that 25 of the 221 Corvairs tested produced carbon monoxide concentrations in the passenger compartment in excess of street level concentrations when driven with the windows closed and the heater on full. Six of those 25 produced carbon monoxide concentrations of between 100 and 200 parts per million, and seven others produced in excess of 220 parts per million—ten times more the concentration of carbon monoxide prevailing at street level. In October, spurred on by this information, the Department of Transportation notified G.M. that the heater systems in 1965 Corvairs (on which the department had concentrated its research) could, by delivering carbon monoxide into the passenger compartments, create "an unreasonable risk of accidents and injury," upon which G.M. did agree to issue a safety defect notification letter to some 750,000 current owners of 1961-69 Corvairs concerning possible carbon monoxide leakage, but the company declined to remedy the defect at its expense. (Production of the car was discontinued in 1969.) Since the average expense of correcting the defect is $170, or about $20 more than the average trade-in value of a Corvair nowadays, it is unlikely that many of these defects are going to be corrected, especially as the current owners of Corvairs are in many cases people of low income.

Such a solution to the carbon monoxide problem in the Corvair seemed, if nothing else, consistent enough with what one former G.M. employee to whom I had talked had told me about the attitudes prevailing within the G.M. legal staff. "The problem I found with the G.M. legal department was really that these people didn't think of themselves so much as lawyers as of loyal soldiers in the ranks of General Motors," he had said. When I heard these words, I was already aware that Ralph Nader had been making, in letters to Senator Ribicoff during 1971, a series of charges detailing alleged failures by G.M. to produce, as Nader claimed the corporation should have produced in certain Corvair cases, particular proving ground tests and other engineering data that Nader claimed to be relevant and important to the proper trial of these cases. (Since I wasn't a lawyer, and since I knew that these and other charges made by Nader, involving very complex legal matters, were being investigated by counsel for Senator Ribicoff—they still are, as this is written—I felt that I could afford to wait and see how Senator Ribicoff's people viewed the substance of these charges.) I knew, also, that within the previous twelve months, one by one, certain engineers and other people who had been concerned with the production and testing of early models of the Corvair had been coming forward with information that did not exactly accord with the position consistently taken by General Motors that the Corvair was not a defectively designed car. For example, there was George Caramanna, who had been a design and development technician in the Chevrolet Division of G.M. from 1957 to 1970, who was interviewed by Alexander Auerbach, a writer for the Los Angeles *Times,* in May, 1971, concerning his connection with the development of the Corvair. Caramanna was quoted in Auerbach's report on the interview as saying that executives at General Motors, including Edward Cole, now president of G.M., knew, before the car was put on sale late in 1959, that it had handling problems affecting its safety. According to Caramanna, the first prototype Corvair built rolled over the first time it was driven; he also said that a front roll stabilizer bar, which was intended to make the car less likely to roll, had been designed for the car and was installed on the prototype, but that the bar was removed, for what Caramanna understood to be reasons of cost, before the Corvair went into production. The Auerbach article said that the reporter had contacted representatives of General Motors for comment on Caramanna's statements. The article quoted a G.M. spokesman as having given out a statement saying that "allegations of improper design of the 1960-1963 Corvair . . . have been refuted on a number of occasions in the courtroom following the examination and cross-examination of qualified expert witnesses." The G.M. statement concluded, "General Motors has never denied that the 1960-1963 model Corvair may be rolled over after it substantially exceeds its limits of control, which is equal to or better than the limit of control of competitive cars of the same era."

24

"A Most Unusual Occurrence"

WHEN THIS G.M. STATEMENT about the relative controllability
of the Corvair and "competitive cars of the same era" appeared
in a version of the Auerbach article printed in the Detroit *News,*
there were repercussions displeasing to G.M., for this statement
was read by Harley F. Copp, the engineer at the Ford Motor
Company who had had the responsibility for the engineering
of the 1960 Falcon, the car that Ford had put out in competi-
tion with the Corvair. Copp, who now was director of engineering technical services for Ford, was upset at the comparison
that G.M. had made. He felt that it reflected unfairly and inaccurately on the controllability of the Falcon, and on June 3,
1971, without consulting his superiors at Ford, he wrote a personal letter to Senator Warren G. Magnuson, chairman of the
Senate Commerce Committee, refuting the implications of the
G.M. statement. He told Senator Magnuson that, as a routine
matter, Ford evaluated and tested competitive cars along with
its own, and he said that prior to the introduction of the Falcon
in 1959 Ford, to make such comparative tests, had exchanged
five production Falcons for five production Corvairs with the
Chevrolet management. Then he told the Senator: "Of these
five and some additional Corvairs bought through dealerships,
three Corvairs rolled over during our early customer type
evaluations. None were rolled due to abusive driving, none were
considered driver error, and all came as surprises to the drivers

and passengers. These rollovers were a most unusual occurrence because of their frequency." Some time later, at Senator Magnuson's request, Copp provided more specific information on the Ford comparative evaluation of the Corvair and Falcon. This included a description of a presentation that had been made to the executive committee of the Ford Motor Company in October, 1959, on the comparative handling characteristics of the Falcon and the Corvair, which, Copp said, had been illustrated by films made at the Ford proving ground at Dearborn, Michigan, of several vehicles of competing models. Copp gave excerpts from the commentary that had been provided the executive committee of Ford at this session:

> These pictures have shown only that the Corvair exhibited instability under extreme cornering conditions, under which the Falcon remained stable . . . While the [average driver of the Corvair] will not encounter difficulty under most normal driving conditions, there are frequently encountered emergency conditions such as slippery pavement or emergency maneuvering in which the driver cannot maintain control of the vehicle. The Corvair falls considerably short of our handling standards.

Copp also enclosed an internal Ford Motor Company memorandum dated June 17, 1960, addressed to the principal executives of Ford, from Fred J. Hooven, who had the reputation of being one of the most competent engineers in the automobile manufacturing business. Hooven had formerly worked at G.M. and in 1960 was executive engineer of advanced engineering at the Ford Division. Hooven's memorandum was entitled "Handling of Chevrolet Corvair." It said, in part:

> A question arose in the Advanced Product Planning meeting of May 31, 1960, as to whether the poor handling and stability characteristics of the Chevrolet Corvair had adversely affected its sales. It was agreed by all present that there had been little or no adverse effect on sales and that the unfavorable characteristic of the Corvair did not emerge in normal customer-type driving.

The time was not appropriate for a more thorough discussion of the implications of poor vehicle stability but I believe there should be some mention of the relationship of this characteristic and safety. One of the outstanding characteristics to emerge from our comparative tests of the Corvair and Falcon was the fact that not only did the Corvair have a low limit of maximum permissible speed in a turn but once this limit had been exceeded, the vehicle became totally uncontrollable. The penalty for a misjudgement of speed in a turn, or of insufficient attention on the part of the driver, is therefore not only more often encountered in a Corvair but is much more severe . . .

Other reports, which I am in a less fortunate position to verify, also support the conclusion that such vehicle instability is in truth a serious accident risk and safety factor. While such factors have less direct effect on vehicle sales than more easily discernible product characteristics they certainly constitute a highly undesirable condition which we at Ford should make every effort to avoid.

After Copp's initial letter to Senator Magnuson concerning what he said was foreknowledge at Ford concerning the relative instability of the 1960 Corvair in the hands of the average driver under certain unusual driving conditions, General Motors issued a statement saying that "Mr. Copp's statements . . . are essentially a repetition of the statements made by witnesses who have testified in behalf of plaintiffs in Corvair litigation over the years. Some of the testing done at the Ford proving ground in 1959, including the matter of a Corvair rolling over, was part of the testimony of plaintiffs' witnesses in Corvair lawsuits which were decided in favor of General Motors over five years ago."

The G.M. statement then quoted from the judgment in one key Corvair case—the case of Mary Jane Drummond vs. General Motors, which was tried in Superior Court in California —the opinion of Judge Bernard S. Jefferson:

It is the Court's conclusion that the Corvair automobile of the 1960 through 1963 variety is not defectively designed nor a defective product; that no negligence was involved in the manufacturer's adoption of the Corvair design; that the Corvair matches a standard of safety which does not create any unreasonable risk of harm to an average driver . . .

The Drummond case concerned an accident occurring in 1960. The suit had been filed in 1962 and had been tried over a period of months in 1966—as a matter of fact, some 3,000 out of an eventual 8,000 pages of testimony in the case had been taken in court by the date of the March 22 Ribicoff subcommittee hearings on the G.M. investigation of Nader. This case was clearly an important one for both sides, and it evidently involved long and meticulous legal preparation for the defense by the General Motors camp. The Drummond case had been one of the Corvair cases pending when Daniel Boone died.

Had Daniel Boone lived, would the Drummond case have gone to trial as it did in 1966, and if so, would the evidence and the defense be such that Judge Jefferson would still have found, as he did, "that the Corvair matches a standard of safety which does not create any unreasonable risk of harm to an average driver . . ."?

As a layman who had never read the thousands of pages of such sworn testimony as was given and arguments offered in the case—which was, I am sure, most carefully, skillfully, and fairly considered by Judge Jefferson—I could hardly even venture to guess the answer to such a question. I could only wonder about the late chief of general litigation for General Motors, upside down in a Corvair on the G.M. proving grounds.

In any event, the verdict for General Motors in the Drummond case had been a landmark in Corvair litigation. A few months after the verdict, when another verdict in a Corvair case, this time for the plaintiff, was set aside by a court in California, an attorney in California handling many such cases pretty much threw in the towel and was obliged to settle with the defendant corporation forty-seven Corvair cases that his firm then had pending against General Motors.

To revert to the allegations made by Harley Copp to Senator Magnuson concerning the relative handling characteristics of the Corvair and the Falcon, one would find it reasonable to assume that the chief executives of the Ford Motor Company would be gratified by the spirited manner in which such a senior engineer of the company had defended the good name of a Ford product that he so strongly felt had been unfairly clouded by the G.M. statement following the publication of the Auerbach interview with Caramanna. But this turned out not to be the case at all. Shortly after Copp sent his initial letter to Senator Magnuson, I had heard from a reliable source that when Henry Ford II himself had heard of Copp's letter, instead of congratulating Copp on his frankness, Ford had become annoyed at the initiative taken by this senior company engineer. And, I had heard, the chairman and chief executive officer of the Ford Motor Company had telephoned James Roche, and had told the chairman of the board of General Motors that Copp's action in writing Senator Magnuson about the findings of the Ford 1959 handling tests of the Corvair had been taken without his, Ford's, knowledge and did not have his approval.

25

"You're Rocking the Boat!"

SOME TIME LATER, I myself had gone out to Dearborn and had talked to Copp, whom I found to be an interesting, intelligent man who appeared to have, in the automobile manufacturing business, a reputation as a maverick. Copp talked to me about such automotive engineering matters as G forces, polar moment of inertia, displacement in the horizontal plane, spin tendencies, roll couple distribution, and differential tire pressures, and he explained in great detail why he was convinced and, he said, had been convinced all along that the Corvair was an unduly hazardous car for the average driver to handle under certain unusual or difficult conditions. (I will not go into this detail here, nor will I myself make any attempt at assessing the comparative handling characteristics of the Corvair as against the Falcon or any other car.) I had been interested in finding out from Copp what life had been like for him after he had written Senator Magnuson about the 1959 Corvair handling tests at Ford. Copp told me that the first reaction of some executives had been that he and Henry Ford must have had some arrangement under which he had revealed the alleged comparative deficiencies of the Corvair, but that when they discovered he hadn't made such an arrangement, "the general reaction was that 'Harley's gone off his rocker.'" Other Ford executives who had previously been cordial to him began to give him a wide berth. " 'Don't get too near that man, he might have poison ivy'—that was the air," he had told me. A neighbor on the very pleasant, tree-lined street where Copp lives—there are a lot of Ford executives living on the street, in $60,000 to $100,000 homes—had advised Copp's wife that he thought it the best course "to let sleeping dogs lie." One high executive at Ford had said to him, "What have you done, Harley? You're rocking the boat!" Another high executive at Ford had explained to him, after Copp had gone into a lengthy explanation of his engineer's reasoning concerning the Corvair, "Right now, it looks as though G.M. is wearing the black hat and Ford is wearing the white hat. But, Harley, you do the sort of thing you've done, and before you know it *both* companies could be wearing black hats." After the implications of Copp's letter sank in, Copp's position at Ford had become so delicate that Senator Warren Magnuson thought it advisable to indicate in a letter to Henry Ford that Copp was a potential witness before the Senate Commerce Committee. Until that happened, some people at Ford had been speculating that Copp's days as a responsible executive there might be numbered. In the meantime, at home, Copp and his wife had been subjected—and as this was written still were being subjected, according to both people—to harassing telephone calls (for the most part, calls in which the caller would hang up when the telephone was answered) at all hours of the night. And their home intermittently had been put under surveillance from cars, each occupied by two men, that would park for hours outside the Copp residence, but which, when Mrs. Copp would approach them to try to get a license number, would take off suddenly with a screech of tires, and even cut across the grass divider that runs along the center of the street on which the Copp residence lies.

It appears that George Caramanna, the former G.M. technician whose press interview on the Corvair had triggered Copp's letter to Senator Magnuson, had a not too dissimilar experience. In a pre-trial deposition in August, 1971, in a Corvair case, Caramanna had this to say about events occurring around his home prior to his having been subpoenaed by lawyers for G.M. in the pre-trial proceedings: "Well, a week or two ago . . . I observed a Mustang automobile sort of on one part of the street, and I would notice it at another part and then I would observe other automobiles. And the people that work for me observed automobiles; people coming in, asking where I was, and then taking off. And then they would drive down the street where I live and turn around—come down to the dead-end street, and come around, and they would go away . . . I don't like people watching my house, and my business and my family. I don't know what they are up to."

Between the cars and the telephone calls, the atmosphere surrounding the Copps was a little reminiscent of the air in or about Ralph Nader's rooming house in Washington in February, 1966. All in all, it was as though somebody was trying to tell Copp something, and perhaps the message was that it wasn't a good idea at all to rock boats. That was just about what Copp had done. He had been heedless of the fact that while the giant corporations in the automotive industry might compete vigorously on one plane, on another they maintained tight solidarity. He had been heedless, even, of the grave reminder delivered by James M. Roche, chairman of the board of General Motors, in a speech before the Executive Club in Chicago on March 25, 1961. In that speech, Roche had warned that certain critics of business "are now busy eroding another support of free enterprise—the loyalty of a management team, with its unifying values of cooperative work"; that these same critics were "inflaming any issue that promises attention"; that, indeed,

> Some of the enemies of business now encourage an employee to be disloyal to the enterprise. They want to create suspicion and disharmony and pry into the proprietary interests of the business. However this is labeled—industrial espionage, whistle blowing, or professional responsibility—it is another tactic for spreading disunity and creating conflict.

And here was Harley Copp, writing Senator Magnuson all about those Corvair and Falcon handling and proving ground tests and about questions of safety—apparently oblivious of the thought that instead of engaging in an act of professional responsibility, he might actually be a means of spreading disunity and creating suspicion and disharmony in the automobile manufacturing business!

Some time after hearing Copp's story, I had checked in with Fred J. Hooven, the Ford engineering executive whose 1960 memorandum Copp had sent to Senator Magnuson. Hooven was now retired from Ford and living in Norwich, Vermont, where he was enjoying the countryside, playing Bach on his piano, and working part time as an adjunct professor of engineering at Dartmouth. I had been hopeful that Hooven, having worked at General Motors as well as at Ford, might speak from a certain perspective, especially since he was retired from the automobile manufacturing business. I had found him as outspoken in his way as Copp had been in his. He told me that at Ford in the late fifties the engineering staff had been under considerable pressure from top management to design and build a rear-engined compact car of the general type G.M. came up with in the Corvair, but that the Ford engineers had resisted this pressure. "*Everybody* knew this design was susceptible to roll-over," he said. "We were shocked when we got the Corvair [for testing purposes at Ford]. I must say that I didn't know they [the G.M. people] had done such a bad job as they did."

Hooven had gone on to talk about what he considered to be the inherent risk of rollover, loss of control, and failure to reestablish control once control was lost—a factor he considered far more important than rollover—in a car of the Corvair type, and of his conviction that the G.M. people could not be unaware of such risks.

"Do you mean that a company producing such a car was rolling dice with the safety of the customers who bought it?" I asked.

"They weren't rolling dice. It was an absolute certainty," Hooven said. He added, "Let me say what I have in mind when I'm talking about certainty. If I say that we're putting out a car that nine hundred and ninety-nine times out of a thousand is safe, that sounds pretty good. But if I say that we're putting out a million cars and that there'll be a thousand fatalities, that sounds pretty horrible. But it's the same sort of statistic that you're talking about in each case." He added, about the engineers at General Motors, "Let me tell you, we weren't any more shocked by their cars than they were by ours. They were incredulous at G.M., I've heard, about the Falcon. We thought the Falcon was an engineering tour de force—the lightest and cheapest car of its size around. At G.M., they thought this thing [the Falcon] would break up when it rode down the road. Part of the trouble [at both companies] was that you had no really technologically competent people at the top level of management. That was a very important factor. They didn't know whether to believe the engineers or not. In the case of the testing of the Corvair that was done at Ford, management didn't know whether to believe the [Ford] engineers or not. They thought that perhaps we engineers weren't telling the truth [about the Corvair]—that perhaps we were just trying to make ourselves look good."

And Hooven had told me, "I know why the decision was made [at Ford] to keep quiet about the Corvair. Everybody knew the truth would get lost. And Ford's credibility would be challenged, and that would institute an era of dirty advertising and dirty P.R., and Ford said, in effect, 'We're in no shape to tell the truth about this.' "

Hooven had added, "Keeping secrets—this is an endemic disease. It's positively pathological."

Surely, this was a most perceptive, most wise observation, and I have thought of it again and again while going over in my mind the story of the investigation of Ralph Nader by General Motors, and of what I had been hearing and reading about the Corvair, and the corporate lawyers, and the back room deliberations, and hired detectives piled on hired detectives— thinking, too, of Eileen Murphy and her G.M. instructions, and Richard G. Danner and his instructions, and Gillen and *his* instructions; thinking of the surreptitiously taped telephone conversations; of Daniel Boone flipping over in a Corvair; of documents that might have been produced before the courts and before Senate subcommittees but that somehow weren't; of strangely evanescent microfilm records of customer complaints; of the "proprietary interests of the business" that James Roche had spoken about so gravely and protectively; and of cars that are shown to be safe in the courts but not so safe, perhaps, in comparative handling tests on the proving grounds. And I have thought that what we are dealing with is, indeed, a disease, a serious industrial disease, and one that is surely in need of a broad program of treatment.

APPENDIX

---

*Statements Before the Special Hearing,
Subcommittee on Executive Reorganization,
U.S. Senate, March 22, 1966**

STATEMENT OF GENERAL MOTORS CORPORATION, MARCH 9, 1966

General Motors said today that following the publication of Mr. Ralph Nader's criticisms of the Corvair in writings and public appearances in support of his book "Unsafe at Any Speed," the office of its general counsel initiated a routine investigation through a reputable law firm to determine whether Ralph Nader was acting on behalf of litigants or their attorneys in Corvair design cases pending against General Motors. The investigation was prompted by Mr. Nader's extreme criticism of the Corvair in his writings, press conferences, TV and other public appearances. Mr. Nader's statements coincided with similar publicity by some attorneys handling such litigation.

It is a well-known and accepted practice in the legal profession to investigate claims and persons making claims in the product liability field, such as in the pending Corvair design cases.

The investigation was limited only to Mr. Nader's qualifications, background, expertise and association with such attorneys. It did not include any of the alleged harassment or intimidation recently reported in the press. If Mr. Nader has been subjected to any of the incidents and harassment mentioned by him in newspaper stories, such incidents were in no way associated with General Motors' legitimate investigation of his interest in pending litigation.

At General Motors' invitation, Mr. Nader spent a day at the GM Technical Center, Warren, Michigan, early in January visiting with General Motors executives and engineers. He was shown a number of engineering and research testing and development programs in the field of automotive safety. A number of the accusations in his book were discussed at length, and a presentation was made of the evidence used in the successful defense of the only two Corvair lawsuits tried.

Mr. Nader expressed appreciation for the courtesy in providing him with detailed information, but he nevertheless continued the same line of attack on the design of the Corvair in a number of subsequent press conferences, TV and other appearances. This behavior lends support to General Motors' belief that there is a connection between Mr. Nader and plaintiffs' counsel in pending Corvair design litigation.

Testimony of James M. Roche, President,
General Motors Corp.:
Accompanied by Theodore C. Sorensen, Counsel

. . . I am here today at the chairman's invitation issued in conjunction with his March 10 statement to the Senate. That statement ordered hearings concerning this corporation's responsibility for a private investigation of Mr. Ralph Nader, a witness before this subcommittee who has been critical of the automobile industry's efforts on traffic safety and particularly the GM Corvair. I immediately stated our intention to cooperate with this subcommittee in every possible way.

Let me make clear at the outset that I deplore the kind of harassment to which Mr. Nader has apparently been subjected. I am just as shocked and outraged by some of the incidents which Mr. Nader has reported as the members of this subcommittee.

As president of General Motors, I hold myself fully responsible for any action authorized or initiated by any officer of the corporation which may have had any bearing on the incidents related to our investigation of Mr. Nader. I did not know of the investigation when it was initiated and I did not approve it.

APOLOGY TO SUBCOMMITTEE AND NADER

While there can be no disagreement over General Motors' legal right to ascertain necessary facts preparatory to litigation, as I shall discuss in a moment, I am not here to excuse, condone, or justify in any way our investigating Mr. Nader. To the extent that General Motors bears responsibility, I want to apologize here and now to the members of this subcommittee and Mr. Nader. I sincerely hope that these apologies will be accepted. Certainly I bear Mr. Nader no ill will.

To the best of my knowledge—and I have made every effort to obtain all the facts since learning about this some 2 weeks ago—the investigation initiated by General Motors, contrary to some speculation, did *not* employ detectives giving false names, did *not* employ Allied Investigation, Inc., did *not* use recording devices during interviews, did *not* follow Mr. Nader in Iowa and Pennsylvania, did *not* have him under surveillance during the day he testified before this subcommittee, did *not* follow him in any private place, and did *not* constantly ring his private telephone number late at night with false statements or anonymous warnings.

At the time the investigation was initiated last November, Mr. Nader's book had not yet been published, he had *not* appeared nor was he scheduled to appear as a witness before this subcommittee and he was *not* regarded to anyone's knowledge as a consultant to this subcommittee. In short, this investigation was wholly unrelated to the proceedings of this subcommittee and Mr. Nader's connections with them.

There has been no attempt by, and it has at no time been the intention of, General Motors Corp, or any of its officers or employees to annoy, harass, embarrass, threaten, injure or intimidate Mr. Nader, to invade his privacy, to defame his character, or to hinder, impugn, coerce, or prevent his testimony before this or any other legislative body. Nor was any attempt made along those lines with respect to any other critic of General Motors.

I personally have no interest whatsoever in knowing Mr. Nader's political beliefs, his religious beliefs and attitudes, his credit rating or his personal habits regarding sex, alcohol, or any other subject. Nor for the record was any derogatory information of any kind along any of these lines turned up in this investigation.

While I do not personally know Mr. Nader, I am informed that he is an articulate attorney and citizen who is deeply interested in traffic safety and has written and spoken extensively on the subject.

We in General Motors certainly would not want any private citizen to think for one moment that he was not free to criticize our corporation or products, before this subcommittee or anyone else, without fear of retaliation or harassment of any kind. While we do not agree with many of the opinions and allegations Mr. Nader has put forward, General Motors has responded to his public criticisms not by responding in kind or ignoring the problems but by inviting him to meet with us to discuss those questions of safety which concern us all. Mr. Nader spent a day at the GM Technical Center, Warren, Mich., early in January visiting with GM executives and engineers. We hope we will have the opportunity to meet with him again in the future.

CORVAIR CASES PROMPTED INVESTIGATION

Under the circumstances, I believe we owe this subcommittee an explanation of exactly what happened and why it happened, as best as I have been able to ascertain. As of November 1 of last year, General Motors Corp. was a defendant in over 100 lawsuits involving potentially about $40 million in damage claims relating to the design of Corvair cars of the 1960 through 1963 models. Although the only two cases actually tried and decided on the basis of the Corvair's design resulted in verdicts in our favor, both State and National legislative bodies have respected our wish not to discuss in public any issues involved in pending litigation. While I am not a lawyer, I am certain that the learned lawyers on this subcommittee understand that practice in keeping with the canons of ethics. As the U.S. Supreme Court has aptly put it, "it is impermissible to litigate by day and castigate by night." (In Re Sawyer, 360 U.S. 622, 635.)

Suffice it to say that the general counsel of our corporation has a responsibility to the stockholders to defend all such suits with all his strength and ability and with every proper method and measure. I understand that both State and Federal courts have consistently held that most lawsuits, and particularly product liability cases of this kind, necessarily and customarily require considerable investigation—investigation of the accident, the damages, the parties, the witnesses, the qualifications of experts and related facts.[1]

Troubled by what appeared possibly to be a concerted effort on the part of a few trial attorneys handling most of the Corvair cases to

---

[1] *Miller* v. *United States* (192 F. Supp. 218, 222): "The weight and value of the testimony of the expert witness depends largely upon the qualifications (of) such expert, and these qualifications may be the subject of intensive investigation by the opposing counsel."

Hare v. *McGue* (174 Pac. 663, 664); in upholding propriety of man threatened with lawsuit employing a detective to shadow, investigate, and otherwise check on the other party and potential witnesses: "Anyone has a right, when threatened with litigation, or desiring himself to sue, to employ assistance with a view of ascertaining facts as they exist. * * *"

stimulate both additional cases and the kind of sensationally adverse publicity that might influence juries against the Corvair—and troubled further by requests from shareholders as well as from both satisfied and worried Corvair buyers that the corporation counteract the harsh attacks on this product which had been continuously made outside the courtroom—our general counsel felt called upon, *first,* to ascertain whether any actions for libel of the corporation or its products or bar association grievance procedures, based on violations of the canons of ethics, should be instituted against members of the bar (including Mr. Nader) who publicly discussed pending or anticipated litigation; *second,* to ascertain whether any witness, or author of any book or article which might be offered as evidence in any court (including Mr. Nader) was entitled to the legal definition of "expert"; and *third,* to ascertain whether any of the individuals (including Mr. Nader) who were most often said to be cited or consulted by these attorneys, or to be publicizing their allegations, could properly be cross-examined in any trial in which they might appear as expert witnesses to show bias, lack of reliability or credibility, if it were a fact that they had a self-interest in the litigation or had been attempting deliberately to influence public opinion.[2]

In Mr. Nader's case, and only in Mr. Nader's case, the general counsel felt that he could not ascertain the answers to these questions— and they were only questions, not charges—without using a private investigating agency to check on Mr. Nader's credibility, reliability, and qualifications as an expert witness and his ties, if any, with these attorneys. A brief inquiry in Mr. Nader's hometown in Connecticut revealed nothing. Inasmuch as he gave a Washington address on a brief filed against General Motors in a product liability case, but could not be found in any Washington telephone or legal directory, the general counsel requested a Washington attorney, Mr. Richard Danner, to secure an investigation of the facts needed. At that time Mr. Nader had not yet been announced as a witness before this subcommittee; and the general counsel, treating this like all other investigations of fact related solely to pending and anticipated litigation, did not consider it necessary to inform the other officers of the corporation.

ROCHE DID NOT KNOW OF INVESTIGATION

This investigation was initiated, conducted, and completed without my knowledge or consent, and without the knowledge or consent of any member of our governing committees. To say that I wish I had known about it earlier is an understatement—and I intend to make certain that we are informed of similar problems of this magnitude in the future.

Mr. Danner secured the services of Vincent Gillen Associates, an investigation agency in New York City, a decision which was not ratified by or made known to me. Nor was I informed of the preem-

---

[2] In *Hatch* v. *Ooms* (69 F. Supp. 788, aff'd. 338 U.S. 318), for example, investigation revealed that an article by a supposedly disinterested person had actually been arranged by the attorneys for one side.

ployment investigative methods which would be employed by Mr. Gillen and his associates. Most of the information gathered in this effort, which was terminated last month, was, not surprisingly, irrelevant for the very narrow purposes which our general counsel had originally intended.

When I first read in the press on March 6 that Mr. Nader was apparently being shadowed and investigated, and his friends questioned about his beliefs, I was just as surprised and disturbed as all of you must have been. Two days later, in the process of ordering a formal statement denying our involvement, I discovered to my dismay that we were indeed involved. I immediately ordered an investigation and release of the facts as we then knew them.

We earnestly hope, Mr. Chairman, that you will not interpret this episode as reflecting GM's response to the issues raised by your subcommittee and by others concerned with traffic safety. We deeply share that concern. We want to consider all complaints and suggestions on their merits, not on the basis of personalities. We know that any automobile is subject to accident and that we must be constantly devising and improving ways to protect the occupants and others. If our concern for safety has not always come through with sufficient clarity and vigor in previous statements, including our statement before this subcommittee last summer, then I can assure you that we regret that failure.

Without straying too far from the purposes of today's hearing, I do want to stress that General Motors is expanding its research engineering and testing in all areas of safety, including that of the second collision and the causes of both accidents and injuries. We are stressing safety in our advertisements and consumer contacts, and adding new safety features to our cars as fast as they can be effectively developed, carefully tested, and thoroughly proven to be practical. We are in every other way devoting more time, imagination, attention, manpower, and statistical studies than ever before to this all important safety factor. We are, in short, in all our plans and calculations, giving safety a priority second to none. And we consider this to be our duty.

In every endeavor at General Motors, we are always striving to do better, and this includes safety. But we take great pride, Mr. Chairman, in your recent comments on GM's leadership in introducing the collapsible (energy absorbing) steering column and in providing for dual braking systems on all cars. Other safety features which need not be detailed now are also being provided as standard, as well as optional, equipment for 1966 and 1967 cars.

The traffic toll, of course, is still tragically high. As the President has pointed out, the car, the driver, and the highway environment all have a role in accidents, and all must be improved. Automotive design is our responsibility. I am urging our engineers and experts on to greater heights, to be pioneers in automotive safety. But in this broad effort the entire automobile and insurance industries, the universities and research centers, the various voluntary organizations, and the State and Federal Governments all have important roles to play. General Motors will cooperate fully in all these endeavors, including the support of constructive State and Federal legislation. It is in that spirit of cooperation that I have come before you today not only to report on this unhappy episode, but also to pledge our continuing effort to work with all those concerned with improving traffic safety.

TESTIMONY OF RALPH NADER

Mr. Chairman, members of the subcommittee, I owe you a deep apology for being late this morning. I ought to explain it briefly to you and to anyone else in this room. I usually take no more than 12 minutes to come down from my residence to the Capitol by cab. In this instance I gave myself 20 minutes. And I waited and waited and waited and waited to get a cab, and as my frustration mounted, I almost felt like going out and buying a Chevrolet. But that is the simple reason I am late.

I am grateful for this opportunity to comment briefly on the issues before you and the allegations of General Motors with respect to my declarations concerning the hazards of their automobiles.

I do not intend to present the details pursuant to General Motors' probings, on false pretexts given by their agents, into wholly irrelevant aspects of my personal life. I think that has been elaborated already. It is not easy for me to convey in words what I had to endure and what my family has had to endure, as anyone subjected to such an exposure can appreciate. However I certainly stand ready to reply to questions which the subcommittee may wish to ask.

This is not the first, nor the last, time when issues transcending in importance the particular individual find a focus for serious treatment and resolution through an individual case. This happens frequently in the courts, of course, and it is a refreshing reminder of the unique organization of our Federal Government that it can happen also judiciously, though less formally, before legislative committees.

In the few minutes available, I want to make several observations about the importance of dealing with or limiting the kinds of penetrations into individual lives as engaged in by General Motors in this case. I also wish to reply to General Motors' statement of March 9, 1966—a peculiarly convulsive premidnight announcement purporting to explain their investigation.

OTHERS RELUCTANT TO SPEAK OUT ON SAFETY

During the course of gathering materials and information for my book, "Unsafe at Any Speed," I was encountering continually a profound reluctance, in not a few cases it could be called fear, to speak out publicly by those who knew the details of neglect, indifference unjustified secrecy and suppression of engineering innovation concerning the design of safer automobiles by the manufacturers. Such severe inhibitions operated in varying but usually decisive degrees to those within the industry, to those working for other companies close to the industry, to many in universities and Government service.

Although this was not the phenomenon about which I originally intended to write, I soon realized that the stifling of candid expression embracing dissent from the suffocating orthodoxy of the times was the key reason why auto design safety took until 1965–66 to receive public attention and the serious concern of Government, instead of 1936 or 1946 or 1956. The price paid for an environment that requires an act of courage for a statement of truth has been needless death, needless injury and inestimable sorrow.

INDUSTRY ENFORCES SILENCE

What seriously contributed to such an environment is the absence of adequate insulation or protection for individuals against corporate transgressions into their privacy and personal status. It is unfortunate that I cannot reproduce the responses of those with whom I spoke or the elaborate arrangements which often had to be made in order to make contact with them. But I can convey my astonishment at hearing such comments as "They can get me, like they've gotten others," or "It pays to keep one's mouth shut in this business." I can convey my initial incredulity at the descriptions of the farflung apparatus of private detectives and security agents deployed by the auto companies, especially General Motors, in areas far removed from the protection of design and trade secrets. For many outside the industry, there was the contact of superiors by auto industry officials heaping abuse or tendering warning about those few who dared speak out.

At first, I was prone to be skeptical of such excuses. In particular, within the industry, meek surrender to the system is facilitated by the ample salaries that render the conformity of withdrawal and resignation to the status quo quite irresistible. But before long, it became apparent to me how privacies of a past error, misfortune or human frailty that attach to, indeed, almost inhere in the human condition, can be exploited to silence criticism and dissent. It is often too little recognized that as the complexity of our lives and interrelationships increase, the exposure to unfair and malicious manipulation of personal information wholly unrelated to the subject matter under contention grows commensurately. Those who perpetuate such a reign of restraints can succeed in establishing authoritarian pockets within our overall democratic framework from which no assistance to the afflicted proceeds. In the days of the cavedweller, restraint came in the form of the motivated club or the directed rock. With the development of modern society, the restraints can be less visible, less tangible, less preventable by an undeveloped legal order and an untutored people, especially as the technical instruments of investigation and surveillance become more ingenious.

How much has this Nation lost because there are men walking around today with invisible chains?

The trademark of modern society may be the organization but its inspiring and elevating contributions still flow from individual initiatives. Unless multiple sources of initiative and expression are kept open and asserted, the creative and humanizing infusions of a peoples' energies will atrophy.

CONFRONTATION BETWEEN INDIVIDUAL AND CORPORATION

Yet in a confrontation between an individual and a corporate organization, between myself and General Motors if you will, the systematic immunities accrue to the corporation which has outstripped the law that created it. This problem of legal control over corporate action is one of increasing interest to a number of legal and economic scholars. I am responsible for my actions, but who is responsible for those of General Motors? An individual's capital is basically his integrity. He can lose only once. A corporation can lose many times, and not be affected. This unequal contest between the individual and any complex organization, whether it is a corporation, a union, government, or other group, is something which bears the closest scrutiny in order to try to protect the individual from such invasions.

CORPORATE SHIELD

The requirement of a just social order is that responsibility shall lie where the power of decision rests. But the law has never caught up with the development of the large corporate unit. Deliberate acts emanate from the sprawling and indeterminable shelter of the corporate organization. Too often the responsibility for an act is not imputable to those whose decision enable it to be set in motion. The president of General Motors can say he did not know of the specific decision to launch such an investigation. But is he not responsible in some way for the general corporate policy which permits such investigations to be launched by lower-level management without proper guidelines? The office of the general counsel can put forth a document outlining the limits of a "routine" investigation merely to protect the interest of the company's shareholders. A second shield in front of the corporate shield comes in the form of a law firm commissioned in the nonlegal task of hiring a private detective agency. In this case, apparently, GM did not wish to hire agents directly. The enthusiasms of their detectives, the law firm would have us believe, were unauthorized frolics and detours. Besides, the law firm could assume responsibility in the last analysis since there was little burden to such an assumption. Aside from the Federal statute under which this subcommittee is proceeding in this matter, there are few sanctions to protect the principle of privacy in American society against such new challenges largely unforeseen by the Founding Fathers.

INVASION OF THE SELF

I do not particularly care for this word "privacy" because it indicates something superfluous. I would rather call it invasion of the self rather than invasion of privacy.

I should be the last to expect that after General Motors tripped over my book, it would respond as one chastened. Any critic must expect a focused interest in his doings, as they pertain to the subject, by the object of his criticism. But certainly there should be, in all decency, an economy to be observed in the exercise of such corporate curiosity. Surely the questioning by private detectives of people who know and have worked with me (including the crippled and pained person to whom my book is dedicated) as to my personal life in an attempt to obtain lurid details and grist for the individious use and metastasis of slurs and slanders goes well beyond affront and becomes generalizable as an encroachment upon a more public interest. One wonders what some shareholders would think on learning that their management spends money for such purposes. One wonders as well how far this "routine" General Motors investigation would have gone had it not been abruptly curtailed.

It is beneficial to explore the working of such a routine investigation and its framework of operation. People all over should know that things like this go on so that they can, quite apart from laws, apply the customary social sanctions in a community which can operate to discourage or stifle such probings. But unless some definitions and sharpened values appear soon in our Nation to limit such inquisitorial excesses, the employment of this essentially arbitrary power will continue its undermining of individual expression.

MARCH 9 STATEMENT DISCUSSED

Turning briefly to the allegations contained in General Motors' statement of March 9 1966, the company declares that because of my "extreme criticism of the Corvair," it initiated a routine investigation to determine whether I was acting on behalf of litigants or their attorneys in Corvair design cases pending against General Motors.

This seems to be the crux of their case, and their attempt to try to provide a particular motive for my statements and articulations, so I would like to reply.

First, I should like to declare that there is nothing more legitimate and honorable in the practice of law than the representation of clients in products liability cases. Not only does a proper and successful representation secure the rights of injured parties against the manufacturer of defectively designed or constructed products, such as automobiles in whole or part, but such cases have a significant disciplinary effect on the manufacturer which leads to greater consumer protection.

Moreover in many cases, and this is easily documentable, many hazards which flow throughout the community attached to a particular product in our mass production marketing economy have been uncovered only through court procedure. This in a sense is an indication of really how primitive in some respect our organized protection of the consumer is that design defects hazardous to health have to wait for a particular law case to come up in order to be disclosed.

DENIES REPRESENTING CORVAIR LITIGANTS

Second, I want to say that I do not represent any clients nor act on behalf of any of their attorneys in the Corvair litigation. I informed General Motors executives as much during my meeting with them on

January 14, 1966, at the General Motors Technical Center right after—
a moment after the assistant general counsel led me to believe that he
was satisfied that I was not engaged in this litigation, and therefore,
apparently, could enter the room, the precincts of a room where some
displays about the Corvair were to be shown. I also explained to General Motors executives, which included four vice presidents, when and
why I became interested in the subject of auto design safety and the
flagrant lack thereof. But General Motors executives continue to be
blinded by their own corporate mirror-image that it's "the buck" that
moves the man. They simply cannot understand that the prevention
of cruelty to humans can be a sufficient motivation for one endeavor-
ing to obtain the manufacture of safer cars.

Third, I want to correct a misleading impression given in the GM
statement about my reaction to their Corvair presentation. I was
singularly unimpressed by this presentation and by the evasive responses, and on one occasion dealing with tire pressures, an out-
rageously erroneous assertion by the lecturer. A similar presentation,
replete with statements which can be described either as true but
meaningless or full but false, was given last month before a committee of the Michigan Senate in Lansing. I might add about that meeting at the General Motors Technical Center, when I was first introduced to the General Motors vice president he indicated his wish that
everything that went on that day would be off the record. I told him
that since I was here at his invitation, and on the premises of General
Motors, I would certainly respect that. You can imagine my reaction
when I began hearing the comments and responses which I was alleged to have made to their presentations iterated by GM in public
forums only to advance the particular cause of the General Motors
people there.

If General Motors wishes to know why I spent an inordinate
amount of time on the Corvair, it is because the Corvair is an
inordinately dangerous vehicle. The making of the Corvair provides a
spacious and instructive case study of the subordination of safety considerations to the tyranny of the cost accountants and the creative
lethality of the stylists. As such, the Corvair was an insult to the
suppressed engineering talent within the Chevrolet division.

It also illustrated how diffused responsibility for design decisions
are, and where the responsibility is not focused, care tends to be over-
collectivized, and therefore diluted.

I shall not try to catalog all the defects of the Corvair design. Such
an endeavor could approach a trespass on eternity. But since they
make it the basis from which they are calling into question my motives,
I will provide the following information. I want to rebut the implication by General Motors that the Corvair is a sound, safe car that is
being harassed, intimidated, and otherwise persecuted by a lawyer.
The fact that Corvair sales in the current model year are nearly 40
percent under Corvair sales of a year ago is not insignificant. After
having sent so many victims to the cemetery and hospital, the Corvair
may be nearing its death dive by an aroused and informed consuming
public acting through the marketplace. But the marketplace is a
slow and inefficient taskmaster in this area. It should have been a
governmental function to forbid the placement and design of the fuel

tank in the Corvair without a show of safe performance. Corvair fuel tanks have ruptured in otherwise survivable accidents and incinerated occupants struggling to get out of the car. This hazard was recognized in the technical literature by GM engineers, H. M. Crane in 1939 and Maurice Olley in 1953, the hazard of the forward position of the fuel tank. Mr. Olley said that the forward fuel tank is "a collision risk, as is the mass of the engine in the rear." Even with a forward placement, a stronger and rupture-resistant fuel tank would have been a substantial safety advance. GM neglected even using what was available in the engineering art.

It should have been a governmental function to rule out the positioning of the Corvair steering column from a point about 2 inches in front of the leading surface of the front tire and so constructed that it can be routinely driven backward in a left front collision to impale the driver. Seat belts offer no aid here.

It should have been a governmental function to rule out the deadly design of the Corvair dash panel.

CORVAIR SWING-AXLE REAR SUSPENSION

Best known of the Corvair's hazards is the simple swing-axle rear suspension of the 1,124,076 Corvairs produced between 1960–63. This type of suspension leads, under certain expected evasive or cornering maneuvers, to dangerous vehicle instability characterized by tuck under of the rear wheels and rear end breakaway that frequently leads to rollover. For 1962 model Corvairs, GM offered a little-publicized regular production option 696 comprising a heavy-duty suspension kit to improve handling characteristics and cornering stability. RPO 696 is now claimed by GM to have been for the auto enthusiast who takes his handling seriously as in racing. Safety accessories for the wary, no warning for the unwary is the moral of RPO 696. GM improved the suspension of its 1964 and 1965 cars— the latter model and the 1966 model embodying a dual-link suspension system which substantially improved handling and which could have been placed on the first Corvairs which came out in 1959. It might have cost a bit more, however. The know-how and techniques were available years before 1959.

Likewise, more responsive steering could have reduced the poor recovery potential of the Corvair when it exceeds its limits of controllability. At this point, and in the interests of time, I want to submit three important exhibits for inclusion in the record which reveal some important points of relevance to safer auto design through a comprehensive rule of law. . . .

Testimony of Vincent Gillen, President, Vincent Gillen Associates, Inc.

Mr. Chairman and Honorable Senators, my name is Vincent Gillen. I am president of Vincent Gillen Associates, Inc., with offices in

New York City, Paramus, N.J., and Garden City, N.Y. I appreciate this opportunity to inform you frankly and fully about the investigation of Ralph Nader. It involved no harassment; no intimidation; no attempt to defame; no following him around the country; no telephone harassment, no recordings, and no women.

Many statements have been attributed to Mr. Nader in the press and on the floor of Congress. Some have appeared so often that what Mr. Nader originally mentioned as "suspicious" or "strange coincidence" have been repeated so often that they are now quoted as facts—an excellent example of the big lie. I even have been accused of being engaged in a "seamy trade."

GILLEN QUALIFICATIONS

In view of that, I believe it appropriate to inform this committee of my qualifications to undertake investigations. I am completing 40 years of work experience, almost half of it as an investigator. I attended Fordham University and Brooklyn Law School. After receiving a master's degree in law I was admitted to the New York Bar. I have also been admitted to practice before the U.S. Supreme Court. Incidentally, all of my schooling beyond high school was at night. I was elected president of my class at college and at law school.

After receiving my bachelor of law degree, I spent almost 3 years as a special agent of the Federal Bureau of Investigation. Thereafter followed about 7 years of investigative work for the legal department of the Metropolitan Life Insurance Co., and during World War II, as Assistant Chief of the Special Services Section of the Office of Alien Property Custodian, and as an inspector in the Air Force Intelligence. The following 9 years I was a personnel executive with Otis Elevator Co., the Rexall Drug Co., and the final 4 years personnel director of Reeves Instrument Corp., the 2,800 employees division of the Cynamics Corp. of America. During this period, I was elected by about 80 of my peers as president of the Long Island Personnel Association.

I resigned that job in September 1954 to become professor of management and industrial relations at Hofstra University, Hempstead, N.Y. (then about 7,000 students, and now has over 10,000), and to act as a labor and personnel consultant to industry. In June 1958, I resigned the professorship to establish a corporation licensed to conduct a private investigative business. A thorough character investigation of applicants for a license is conducted in New York to make sure a license is not issued to anyone not meeting the high standards set by the State.

All members of our board of directors have at least two college degrees. Almost half our investigative staff have college degrees. Almost 60 percent of our work is conducting preemployment and background investigations for employers in all facets of our great economy.

The rest of our work covers myriad management problems and a few personal, such as investigating prospective sons-in-law. The management problems range from counterespionage, including debugging of electronic devices, to proxy or stockholder matters, preparation for lawsuits, and criminal defense investigations. We do not handle divorce cases.

I am a member of the board of directors of the Long Island Association of Commerce & Industry; only 2 weeks ago, March 9, I was elected president of the Long Island Industrial Job Development Corp., organized by leading citizens under a law sponsored by Governor Rockefeller to make low-cost mortgage money available to industry expanding and creating jobs on Long Island. I am also a member of the American Management Association; the Society of Professional Investigators; past vice president of the 5,000-member American Society for Personnel Administration; former chairman of the Long Island Chapter of the Society of Former Special Agents of the FBI; a member of the Rotary International, and of the American Society for Industrial Security.

In 1942, I was foreman of a Kings County (Brooklyn) grand jury.

In 1952 I was elected president of the Parent-Teachers Association of my daughter's high school in Brooklyn. That year the New York City teachers refused to perform extracurricular activities without compensation. Representatives of some 80 New York City high school PTA's met to determine what they could do to resolve the teachers' dispute with the board of education. I was selected spokesman of a committee of that citywide group to mediate between the striking teachers and the board of education.

We lived a few years in Glen Cove, N.Y., and the mayor appointed me a member of the five-man board of zoning appeals.

I am listed in Who's Who in Commerce & Industry, the only private investigator listed, I believe.

NO "SEAMY TRADE"

I have made this lengthy statement of my background, because I deeply resent the statement on the floor of the Senate that I am engaged in a "seamy trade." I resent it for myself and every other licensed private investigator in the country and for every State which licenses private investigators. Senator Nelson's statement is an insult not only to me but to the citizens of every State which licenses private investigators.

I did not trail Ralph Nader, nor any of my employees in Des Moines, Iowa, on January 10. I never heard of Ralph Nader until January 13, 1966. On or about December 22, 1965, Richard G. Danner, of Alvord & Alvord, phoned and asked if I was in a position to conduct an investigation in several Eastern States. I told him that we have a full-time staff of 25 and could handle almost any type of investigation, anywhere. On January 12, he telephoned and asked me to meet him in Washington.

On January 13, we conferred in his Washington office. He said that he was representing General Motors Corp. and wished to find out something about the background of Ralph Nader, who held himself out as an expert in the safety field. Nader claims not to represent claimants in lawsuits, but the language of Nader's writing and speeches seemed identical with those appearing in papers filed in suits against General Motors. General Motors had made some investigation of Nader but had not found out much. He is not listed in any phone directory in or about Winsted, Conn., his hometown, nor in Washington, D.C. Danner wanted to learn all he could about Nader's background, his expertise in safety, his source of income, and his associates especially in the legal profession.

PREEMPLOYMENT PRETEXT

Mr. Danner and I discussed the fact that people are reluctant to give information about a person who may be engaged in a lawsuit or an argument with an insurance company, or when the client is a large corporation. Therefore, we decided to tell no one the name of the client, a standard investigative practice. We knew that the information we wanted could be uncovered in a normal, routine preemployment-type investigation. We decided to use that pretext. Every bit of investigation was conducted with that understanding, because no one else knew the name of the client.

As you gentlemen are aware, whenever any investigation is made, people interviewed invariably jump to the conclusion that something is wrong with the person being investigated, especially if no reason for the inquiry is given. On the other hand, if people are told the person is being investigated for a position, no stigma is attached to the inquiry. We do it every day. The principal reason for using the pre-employment pretext was to prevent any inference of wrongdoing on the part of Mr. Nader and to prevent any "character assassination."

We began the field investigation in the Winsted-Hartford, Conn., area on January 25, and continued there until January 27. This was by one of our own agents who used his name and the name of our company, Vincent Gillen Associates, Inc. All of our men used their names and the company name. No one, not a single person we interviewed in Connecticut, knew where Nader could be found, except possibly in Washington.

I had sent, on January 20, a request for investigation in the Washington area to my associate, Mr. D. David Shatraw, former FBI agent, president of the Arundel Investigative Agency, Severna Park, Md.

This request for investigation in Washington contained the following rather prophetic words:

> We must be careful not to arouse the ire of Nader. Keep in mind that he is a brilliant fellow and a good writer and he could, no matter how unjustly, write something about us which would be rather damaging.

I repeat, "no matter how unjustly."

> Hence it is important that interviews be handled with great discretion and under a suitable pretext.

On January 28, I phoned Mr. Shatraw to inform him that our investigation in Connecticut indicated Nader was in Washington and inquired about the progress of the investigation there. Mr. Shatraw explained that through some delay in the mail, he had not received my request until January 26 and had nothing to report. He promised action the next week.

There was a severe snowstorm here that next weekend, and Mr. Shatraw's office was closed Monday and Tuesday.

As I recall, on Thursday, February 3, I read in a New York paper an item, or saw a TV program, which lead me to believe that Nader had testified before this committee the day before. I phoned Mr. Shatraw and expressed myself rather strongly about his men not finding Nader when he was testifying in public. This, gentlemen, and to every fairminded person in the world completely refutes any implication that there was any connection between our investigation and Nader's testimony. I owe an apology to Mr. Shatraw because it was not until this past week when all the publicity arose about this matter, and I learned Nader did not testify here on February 2.

Senator RIBICOFF. That should give a testimonial to the competence of detective agencies.

Mr. GILLEN. Senator, I hope you are listening and reading carefully.

Senator RIBICOFF. I sure am.

Mr. GILLEN. They couldn't find him if he wasn't testifying. He wasn't testifying. I think you missed that point.

Senator KENNEDY. You thought he was testifying?

Mr. GILLEN. No, sir.

Senator KENNEDY. Who thought he was?

Mr. GILLEN. I said I read on February 3, or I saw a TV program which led me to believe he had been here the day before.

I did not know that Nader might testify before this committee when I began this investigation. Our report of January 31, you have it right there, look at page 21, mentions that we hoped to find Nader before his scheduled appearance in Albany, N.Y., "in midmonth," midmonth meaning the succeeding month of February, midmonth I assume meaning the 14th or 15th.

That would be a strange report to make to a client who allegedly knew he could be found here on February 2, 2 days later. In fact, I did not learn of his appearance on February 10 until late in the afternoon of February 10.

Meanwhile, inquiries were being made in the Boston area through my associate, Mr. Charles B. Allen, a certified public accountant and former FBI agent, of Management Consultants, Inc. These inquiries, like all others, were made openly and not secretly and with no attempt to hide who the investigators were. These inquiries continued, intermittently, as their workload permitted, until February 18, when their report was mailed to me. About half of this work was performed before Mr. Nader testified here on February 10.

SURVEILLANCE BEGAN FEBRUARY 4

We found little about Nader's source of income or his activities. Hence we decided, on January 26, to institute a surveillance when we located him to find out what he was doing. We had an address in Washington for Nader which appeared on some legal papers filed many months before. On Thursday, February 3, Mr. Shatraw or one of his agents, made a routine telephone call to the landlady of the roominghouse at that address to ascertain if anything was known of Mr. Nader. To his surprise, the landlady said he was rooming there but was not in.

Keep in mind, gentlemen, Mr. Nader has been quoted in the press quoting him as saying he was harassed in January. I did not know where he was in January, or his unlisted phone. We began the surveillance the next day, Friday, February 4. Two Arundel Investigative Agency men handled this surveillance.

An Arundel agent on the surveillance telephoned me—I live in Garden City—about 11 p.m. Saturday, February 5, to advise that due to manpower shortage and the heavy workload in Mr. Shatraw's office, that they could not continue the surveillance. Hence, I dispatched two of our men from New York to take over, which they did about 4 p.m. Sunday, February 6. All other surveillance and investigation in Washington thereafter was conducted by our own employees. We conducted no surveillance outside Washington.

This surveillance was continued until 4:30 p.m. Wednesday, February 9. It was discontinued then because Nader had not appeared since 3:30, when he entered the office of the *New Republic*. Upon phone instructions from Mr. Danner, we discontinued the full surveillance because it was not being very productive. Mr. Danner suggested a "spot surveillance," and that we might pick Nader up after he had testified sometime in the future before this committee. Mr. Danner did not know the date. Remember, gentlemen, that was the day before. About 4:55 p.m. February 9, I instructed one of our agents in Washington to call the committee office to ascertain when the hearings would be held and whether or not Nader was scheduled to appear.

Late February 10, I learned that our agent had called this committee about 11:55 that morning and was informed that Nader was then testifying and was almost finished. [Laughter.] I am sure the audience is getting the wrong impression. Our men made no attempt to find Nader that day but conducted interviews here in Washington and followed leads developed through the surveillance. They weren't sitting around watching.

NADER FOLLOWED INTO SENATE OFFICE BUILDING

Late February 10, I instructed our men to start the spot surveillance about 11 a.m. February 11, because Nader usually did not go out until noon. About 1:30 p.m., one, I repeat, one of our men saw Nader enter the New Senate Office Building. He followed. The man on the scene makes a quick decision and you have to live with it.

That sort of thing can happen in any investigative organization. I am sure Senator Kennedy knows this from his experience as Attorney General when he was responsible for all Government investigative agencies.

Senator KENNEDY. I am glad that you brought me into this.

Mr. GILLEN. I did, Senator, because I think you know more about investigations than the rest of us.

It is always easy to second-guess others, particularly regarding a surveillance, one of the most difficult assignments in the investigative business.

I assure you that I did not know of this episode until sometime later. I was in New York and they were in Washington. We were in frequent contact, for guidance and instructions, but it was not feasible for them to phone while on an active surveillance. I am sorry and apologize to this committee and to the entire Senate that we entered the Senate Office Building to keep track of Mr. Nader but I wish to assure you that the published version of what happened did not occur.

They are accused of clumsily following a newspaper reporter by mistake.

Gentlemen, I remind you that our investigators are investigators.

That is fantastic. These men had followed Nader several days and knew him well. They did not tell a guard that they were looking for Nader. They did not tell a guard that they had been following him all over the country, because they had not. One agent did describe Nader to a guard and the guard said a man fitting that description had entered the TV studio. Our agent then phoned his associate to join him. They were both in the corridor, some distance apart, when they were, independently, asked to leave. They left. I sincerely regret this incident and again apologize to the Senate for it.

We conducted no surveillance on Mr. Nader after Friday, February 11, 1966. One agent, you can guess which, returned to New York that night. The other agent remained in Washington and continued to openly interview people about Nader in Washington. That agent finished his work about 4:30 p.m., Friday, February 18, and returned to New York on February 18.

DENIES USE OF WOMEN

I have read of the incidents reported by Mr. Nader concerning two women who allegedly approached him one Sunday, February 20, and the other Wednesday, February 23, while he was buying cookies. Neither I, nor any of my former FBI colleagues, used any women during this investigation. I had no one, male or female, working on this case those days in Washington. I am sure the Senate and all fair minded people in the world will appreciate that it is as impossible for Mr. Nader to prove the alleged incidents occurred, as it is for me to disprove involvement if they did—the ladies are unknown. I invite complete examination by anyone you wish to send, of all my business and personal disbursements, and those of my employees, and all pertinent company records, to refute this dastardly implication.

INTERVIEW WITH FREDERICK CONDON

On Friday, February 18, I drove to Cambridge, Mass., with my wife, to visit our son, William, an architect. We were on a brief holiday in connection with Washington's Birthday. Monday, February 21, I visited the office of my Boston colleague, Mr. Allen. He said they had not talked with Mr. Frederick Hughes Condon, Concord, N.H. I told Mr. Allen that we had found no one who ever saw Mr. Nader drive a car, or any proof that he had a driver's license. Keep in mind, we were investigating a safety expert. It was a nice day. We had never been to Concord. I decided to phone Mr. Condon to ascertain if he was in Concord and could be seen that day.

Let's put the Condon interview in proper focus. One does not dedicate a book to a stranger. Condon should know if Nader had ever owned or driven a car. That's all I want to find out. For almost a month, investigators from my office, using my name, showing credentials with my name, and handing out cards with my name, had interviewed numerous friends and acquaintances of Nader. I assumed he had long since learned of this investigation and knew my name. We made no attempt to hide it.

I referred earlier to the reaction of people to investigative interviews. Imagine the reaction of Nader, if he believed that I, personally, made a round trip of over 500 miles from New York to Concord to interview his best friend, or one of his friends. There was no point in mentioning my name unless Mr. Condon could be seen that day. I was returning to New York the next day. Mr. Condon, when I called him, insisted upon knowing who was calling and why before he granted an interview. Therefore, I had to use a fictitious name. He then said he would be available at 3:30 that afternoon. Immediately upon meeting Mr. Condon, I told him my name and explained how it happened that I was there, and assured him that I had not driven from New York to Concord in the middle of winter to conduct one interview. We had a pleasant chat for about 25 minutes.

ATTACHÉ CASE

Now, about that attaché case. After waiting in the lobby for a half hour to see Mr. Condon, I went to my car, got my attaché case (the same one I have here today), and did some paperwork. I took the case with me to his office at 4:35. Mr. Condon has an adequate, but small, office and if I had put the case down, it would have been in his way. I did not "insist on holding" it on my lap. I would have been glad to put it down. I wasn't invited to. It did not contain a recorder although I now wish it did; because some of my questions have been characterized as "lurid."

NADER'S DRIVER'S LICENSE

I asked once, not four times, about Nader's driving and his driver's license. It would be insulting to ask an attorney the same question four times. Incidentally, this question is still open in our report. We have received conflicting information. My Connecticut colleague, Mr. Thomas F. Skinner, a former FBI agent, of Confidential Research

Associates, Stamford, received an official letter from the licensing office in Connecticut stating that Ralph Nader of Winsted, Conn., driver's license expired in February 1964. We have received other information from Connecticut that his license was renewed in February 1964 and was due for renewal in February 1966.

Let me recall, as best I can, the questions to Mr. Condon regarding Mr. Nader's marital status. I asked if, at Harvard where they had been law school classmates, they had "double dated." Condon said "no" and explained that he, Condon, was married then and living with his wife off campus. He believed that Mr. Nader lived in a roominghouse. I asked if he had ever met any of Nader's girlfriends or has seen him with a girl. Condon said, "Oh, if you are concerned about that, don't worry about Ralph. He's all right," or words to that effect. I asked no other questions along that line.

We then had a casual discussion regarding the difficulty such an intelligent fellow, with a wide range of interests, has to find a suitable girl to marry. It certainly was not my intent in that casual talk to pry any further into that aspect.

Many published stories indicate a complete lack of how an investigator conducts an interview. You don't walk into a man's office and ask: "Does Nader drive or own a car?", get his answer and walk out. You endeavor to establish rapport with him. You discuss anything to do so. I did not know Condon uses a wheelchair. While waiting to see him, the company receptionist volunteered that information. She said he had an auto accident 3 or 4 years ago.

We all know it does not require much persuasion to have someone tell you about their operation, or their accident. Any questions I injected into his story were only those of a polite listener.

Please keep in mind the pretext, and I urge you so strongly to keep in mind the pretext. Any investigator conducting a preemployment background investigation of a mature, healthy, intelligent unmarried man who apparently has sufficient income to support a wife, must ask questions of this nature. They are essential questions in every Government background investigation.

Let me put this ridiculous subject to rest by categorically stating that no investigator asked any embarrassing questions or intimated anything lurid.

Senator KENNEDY. Mr. Chairman, could I interrupt there because I think that we are proceeding here in a way that really disturbs me. You are just going on. Your testimony, Mr. Gillen, is proceeding on the supposition that this is a preemployment background investigation, isn't it? Were you trying to hire Mr. Nader for something?

Mr. GILLEN. Well, the earlier part of my statement, Senator Kennedy, clearly states why I used it, and I knew what we were doing it for.

Senator KENNEDY. But then you go ahead and excuse all of the steps that you take thereafter on the basis that this was a regular preemployment investigation or a regular Government background investigation.

Mr. GILLEN. That is covered, if you will let me proceed, sir.

Senator KENNEDY. But here you deal with the subject:

Any investigator conducting a preeemployment background investigation of a mature, healthy, intelligent unmarried man who apparently has sufficient income to support a wife must ask questions of this nature.

You weren't in fact conducting a preemployment investigation, were you?

Mr. GILLEN. I repeat, sir, that I have it covered in the next paragraph or so, and unfortunately in typing up it got out of context.

Senator KENNEDY. I would like to have an answer to the question. You were not in fact conducting a preemployment investigation?

Mr. GILLEN. I have testified that I knew that, sir. I was not.

Senator KENNEDY. Why do you excuse all of these steps that you take?

Mr. GILLEN. I will read it now, sir.

Senator KENNEDY. Let me just ask you a question. You are including the use of false names, including all of these personal questions in connection with Mr. Nader, on the basis that it is a preemployment investigation when in fact it was not? Mr. Nader didn't authorize this.

Mr. GILLEN. When you conduct an investigation under a pretext, you have to carry it out completely, sir. You have to ask all questions normally pertinent to that pretext. If you do anything less or inject extraneous matters, you run the risk of losing the pretext.

Senator KENNEDY. But you were lying. What you mean was that you were conducting an investigation under a lie and that you had to carry the lie out completely.

Mr. GILLEN. Did you ever have that happen while you were the Attorney General?

Senator KENNEDY. No; I did not, but I am asking you the question.

Mr. GILLEN. Did any of the investigators ever do it?

Senator KENNEDY. I want to ask you the question.

Mr. GILLEN. Yes, sir.

Senator KENNEDY. You were conducting it as a lie, were you not? You were conducting the investigation under the category of a lie and thereafter you were carrying it out.

Mr. GILLEN. Well, you get very little investigative material if you conduct it openly on all occasions, sir. You know that.

Senator KENNEDY. I understand that, but what disturbs me—

Mr. GILLEN. If you understand it, why don't you let us do it then?

HARASSMENT OF NADER

Senator KENNEDY. Mr. Gillen, because it disturbs me what you were doing. This was a form of harassment. What disturbs me even more is that you don't seem to have realized it.

Mr. GILLEN. Let me finish the rest of the statement, please.

Senator KENNEDY. You don't have any other comment on that?

Mr. GILLEN. Well, sir, I have heard people on both sides here and up there discuss harassment today. I looked it up in the dictionary of what is harassment.

Everyone apparently has a different interpretation. The general counsel and his associate of GM have a different interpretation. I don't know what is the legal definition. What is harassment? I didn't consider it harassment, no, sir. I said that at the beginning of my statement.

Senator KENNEDY. But my point is, Mr. Gillen, that what you were doing is you were going around to these various individuals and you, yourself, were not telling the truth. You were not in fact conducting a preemployment investigation. You were conducting an investigation of Mr. Nader which was unknown to him, asking personal questions, in a way that would harass him, cause him pain and suffering, which it in fact did.

Mr. GILLEN. Well, sir, you have—

Senator KENNEDY. It disturbs me as you give your testimony before this committee that that didn't seem to have occurred to you at all.

Mr. GILLEN. You continue to say it was harassing him, but I have yet to hear what harassing is.

Senator KENNEDY. All right, you finish and I will have a few more questions.

Mr. GILLEN. Thank you. I said let me put this ridiculous subject to rest by categorically stating that no investigator asked any embarrassing questions or intimated anything lurid.

Furthermore, our investigation uncovered absolutely no indication of any abnormality on the part of Ralph Nader. On the contrary, he obviously is an intelligent, personable young man and I join with him in expressing regret that people have seen fit to misconstrue routine inquiries for their own sensational purposes.

The same thing applies to the questions regarding anti-Semitism. Virtually everyone we talked with in Winsted cautioned us not to attribute to Ralph the attitude and obvious feelings of some members of his family. In fairness to Ralph, we had to ask that question of all those with whom he associated during his adult life. I am happy to state that none of the people we interviewed believes Ralph Nader is anti-Semitic.

CARRYING OUT THE PRETEXT

When you conduct an investigation under a pretext, you have to carry it out completely. You have to ask all questions normally pertinent to that pretext. If you do anything less, or inject extraneous matters, you run the risk of losing the pretext. Hence, we could not ask directly about Mr. Nader's association with attorneys or claimants, in Corvair cases. Such questions would not be germane to the pretext of preemployment. We had to wait for the Corvair matter to develop; it did develop. It did develop. A Boston friend mentioned that Ralph Nader has done much consulting work with several attorneys who happen to represent a number of claimants in Corvair cases. That was a major purpose in our investigation. We achieved that objective. It was accomplished through a routine background type investigation.

I repeat that no one else in my organization knew the real client. Hence, I did not edit from the various investigators reports considerable material, completely irrelevant to the purpose of the investigation. To do so would have indicated the real client to my own staff. I even left in some rather harsh statements about General Motors and some of its officials.

We did talk to his stockbroker, identified through the surveillance, one of the purposes of it, and we did telephone his landlady. Inquiries we made of them are made by the thousands in every community in this country, every day, by credit reporting agencies and investigators. No recordings were made of any interviews. We didn't follow Nader to or from Philadelphia. No harassing phone calls were made to Mr. Nader at his roominghouse. The only other call made there, by our agents was about 11:30 a.m., February 9, to find out if he was there. He was scheduled to be in Albany, N.Y., that day. We had not seen him since about 7 p.m. the night before. The landlady answered, said he was there, and went to get him. Our man hung up.

Midnight calls to a roominghouse obviously will harass all occupants, not just one. Mr. Nader has been quoted as saying he had numerous calls on his private unlisted phone. If he has an unlisted phone, we do not know the number.

We made no calls during the early hours of February 10, while he allegedly was writing a statement to be given here that morning, or made any other night calls.

I established this business at the relatively advanced age of 47. I did not do so to be second-best. The company motto is: "There is no substitute for quality and integrity." I stand on the quality of our reports. I submit my integrity to the scrutiny of all.

Report of Interview With Mr. Gillen*

On Feb. 21, at about 12:30 P.M., I received a telephone call at the office of United Life and Accident Insurance Company at 2 White Street, Concord, New Hampshire (224-7741). The caller introduced himself as "Mr. Warren" and stated that he wished to come to the Home Office that afternoon at 3:00 and speak to me about a friend of mine. He identified this friend as Ralph Nader, and stated that Ralph had written a book which is dedicated to me, and that Mr. Warren has a client who is very much interested in hiring Ralph to do some research and writing and Mr. Warren is doing an investigation into Ralph's background to make sure there aren't any left-wing activities, sexual problems, or that Ralph isn't an odd-ball or anything of that nature. He also stated that they wanted to be sure that Ralph was capable of doing work in other fields, and that they wanted to be sure that he wasn't just stuck on this subject of car design, and intent on pursuing this subject alone to the exclusion of all others. I asked who his client was. He stated: "Well, we never reveal our client's identity." (He later stated to me in the interview that he was working for an organization which was representing another person or organization, and that he didn't know who the real client was, or just exactly what its

* Submitted by Frederick H. Condon, Assistant Counsel, United Life and Accident Insurance Company, Concord, New Hampshire.

interest in Ralph was.) He then said he would be there to see me at 3:00, and started to hang up, when I interrupted and told him I had a meeting at 3:00, and suggested 1:30. This was not suitable for him, as he stated he would be having lunch at this time. He said he could come after 3:00, so I told him to come at 3:30, but I couldn't guarantee I would be free to talk to him at that time, as the meeting I was to attend at 3:00 might well last quite long. He said OK, he didn't mind waiting, and he would be there at 3:30 P.M.

After the conversation, I mentioned to another attorney in the Home Office that I was quite sure that "Mr. Warren" was not after information about Ralph in order to recommend him for any job, but rather that he was investigating Ralph on behalf of one of the auto manufacturers, or a manufacturer's organization, but most likely General Motors. He agreed, although he noted that many other people have reason to want to know all about Ralph.

During my telephone conversation with Mr. Warren, I asked if he was associated with an attorney, and he said yes, a Mr. Gillen of New York City. He gave me to believe that Mr. Gillen's office specialized in investigations, and he also stated that he himself was an attorney. The conversation went something like this:

CONDON: Are you with an attorney?

WARREN: Yes, I am associated with an attorney. Mr. Gillen in New York.

CONDON: And you are an investigator?

WARREN: Why, yes, an investigator (pause) and an attorney. I think it was obvious to him that I was concerned whether he was an attorney or not, and he stated that he was merely to assuage my suspicions.

About 3:40, while I was in the meeting, I saw the receptionist looking for me, and she saw me in one of the vice president's offices, with 4 other officers, and we were quite obviously busy, so she didn't interrupt, but I assumed that Mr. Warren had arrived. The meeting lasted a long time, and about 4:00 the vice president in whose office we were meeting received a telephone call from the receptionist that a Mr. Gillen was waiting for me in the lobby. I told the vice president to tell Mr. Gillen that I was still in the meeting, and he did so, informing her that the meeting would probably not be over until 4:30. The meeting in fact broke up at about 4:20, and I returned to my office to find a note on my desk from the receptionist: "Fred call me when you are free. I have a Mr. Gillen waiting for you in the lobby. Dolly." I called her at once and had her bring Mr. Gillen into my office.

Mr. Gillen was of medium height (5′ 10″), about 45 to 50 yrs. of age, neat, of medium build, but with a peculiar barrel-chested quality. He wore a small pattern sports coat and slacks of neutral tones, brown or gray, with the jacket being light in color in contrast to the dark slacks. He wore a regular shirt, white or light cream in color, with a red wool tie of woven fabric. It was tied in a four-in-hand knot. He wore glasses with heavy black frames. I think his eyes were blue, and his hair was kinky-curly, combed straight back neatly, and steel gray in color. He had a peculiar voice, probably baritone, and a hesitant way of speaking which I cannot put into words, but which I would recognize at once. I was sure from his voice that he was the same person who had spoken to me on the phone, although his name had changed in the interim. Since I was now quite sure he was lying, I didn't bother to question him further in regard to his identity, etc., thinking that I might better be able to draw him out otherwise. This tactic seemed to work. The more questions he asked, the more obvious it was who his client was. He remained seated during the interview, and had a restless way of glancing about him whenever he was going to ask a question which he considered important. He had a tan attache case with him which he held on his lap during the interview, and which was unlatched, but closed the whole while. He drew two pieces of 8½ x 11 blue-lined note paper from the case on which he had already made some notes (illegible) in a peculiar scrawl. These two pieces of paper had come from a pad, as they were joined together at the top. Throughout the interview he made scrawled notations from time to time on these papers, but not enough to make any report from. He was either relying on his memory, or was taping the conversation. The case could easily have held a miniature tape recorder, or a bug with the recorder in his car. Then too, perhaps he learned nothing new, and had nothing to write down.

He did not appear the least disturbed that he had to wait for almost an hour, and I apologized for the wait, but he said it was OK.

One of the first things he did was to establish if I was in sympathy with Ralph's point of view in "Unsafe at Any Speed". I naturally told him that I was in complete agreement with everything Ralph wrote in the book. He asked if I had read the book, and I said I had. He stated that he had read parts of the book, and he "felt like staying in bed" and was afraid to drive a car.

He then asked how long I had known Ralph, after repeating the story about why he was asking about Ralph. I told him I had known Ralph since the fall of 1955, when we both were first year students at HLS, and worked together on the Record. He said: "That's the Record, as distinguished from the Review?" Yes, I said.

I do not remember the things he asked in order, but the following are all of the important points that we talked about.

He asked at least 3 times, or perhaps 4 times, about whether Ralph drove a car or not, and whether he had a driver's license. He asked whether I had ever seen him drive, and I said I thought I had, but couldn't remember, as I hadn't seen him for about three years. He asked: "What kind of car did he have at Harvard?" I said I wasn't aware that Ralph had a car at Harvard. He wanted to know what kind of car Ralph now owned, and I said I had no idea, not having seen him in three years. Then he asked whether I had seen Ralph drive, etc. He asked what state he had a driver's license in, and I answered that when he was at the Law School, he had it in Connecticut.

He asked why Ralph was interested in the subject of unsafe design of cars, and I told him that Ralph's interest stemmed from his senior paper at the Law School, which he wrote to satisfy his senior year written work requirement, and I explained to him what that meant. I told him we each took a seminar, and Ralph took the medico-legal seminar, and I didn't know whether he took that seminar so he could write that paper, or whether he got the idea for the paper after he was in the seminar. I told him that I wrote my paper on unethical and illegal debt collection procedures, and that I pretty much knew I wanted to write a paper on that subject, and chose my seminar accordingly, and that some students did it this way, and others didn't decide on their subject until they had been in the seminar for a while. He stated that Ralph had no technical (engineering) background, and he was wondering why this rather technical subject interested him.

I told him that there were very important sociological implications in the subject, and it was probably that that interested Ralph, and that he did have background in statistics and statistical studies and, as he could see for himself, this was one of Ralph's main approaches to the subject. I also told him that Ralph's an attorney, and has an interest in such subjects, as all attorneys are interested in issues which involve so much human suffering, and have such broad economic implications. It was during this part of the conversation that I became quite sure that he wasn't much of an attorney, as he wasn't aware that lawyers should be interested in anything of this sort, and every lawyer knows about Mr. MacPherson and his Buick.

He asked if there were any reason why Ralph was not married, and I pretended at first not to understand the significance of his question, but then on reflection, I said: "Are you asking me if he's a homosexual?" He said: "Well, we have to inquire about these things. I've seen him on TV, and he certainly doesn't look like . . . but we have to be sure." I told him there was nothing to worry about, and that Ralph had just not found the right girl; that he is serious and intelligent and just not interested in every silly husband-hunter that comes along.

He mentioned that Ralph was of Syrian ancestry, and asked if there were any possibility of anti-Semitism. I told him no, we have several mutual friends who are Jewish, and there was nothing of that sort. There was of course, I told him, the usual bantering between Ralph and his Jewish friends about his ancestry, but certainly nothing whatsoever as far as anti-Semitism is concerned.

He wanted to know if Ralph had any help, financial help, on his book. I told him that I didn't know; that the first I knew of his book was when I read it was being published in an advertisement from my local bookstore. So I had no knowledge of any financial help.

He asked about travel. He said he understood that Ralph had traveled quite a bit. I told him that this was true; that he had been to Mexico, and I thought he had also been back to Lebanon, and perhaps to South America. I mentioned that he spoke Spanish, Lebanese, and perhaps other languages, although I had never heard him speak anything other than English. He said it was a good thing that Ralph liked to travel, and was free (not married) to move around, as his client wanted to offer Ralph a position which would involve a lot of travel. (Later on he said he didn't know what sort of position his client had in mind, but he was sure it would be a good one.)

He wanted to know if Ralph had ever had any auto accidents. I stated that to my knowledge he had not.

I volunteered that Ralph is quite intelligent, capable, modest and very hard working. He asked what Ralph did right after Law School. I told him he went back to Connecticut, took and passed the bar exam and practiced law. I also told him that he also wrote several articles on various subjects, and mentioned the Roscoe Pound article in *Reader's*

Digest, co-authored with Arthur Train. (He thought Pound had been dead for many years, or at least that is what he said. Another reason why I felt he wasn't a lawyer.) He knew the name Arthur Train, as he had heard of Arthur's father. I told him about my Jeep (La Nortena), and how Ralph had met Arthur in Mexico, and that was how I managed to get a Jeep in 1958, by going to Texas to pick it up. He was thinking all the time, as he said at this point: "Arthur Train, I mean the son, he's not a contemporary of yours?" I told him no, Arthur was about 65.

He also asked where Ralph roomed while at the Law School. I told him that dorm space was not available for all at that time, and that he lived in a room off-campus right near the Law School, like many other law students. When he asked if I knew of any left-wing activities, or whether Ralph had belonged to any life-wing organizations at Harvard, which he did early in the interview with the lame joke about "going to Harvard and turning left", I stated that I knew of none, and that in fact I didn't even know Ralph's political affiliation (Republican or Democrat), and that as far as I knew, Ralph had never belonged to any organizations of that sort, either right or left—or middle, for that matter. I said I knew Ralph was on the staff of the Record at Law School, and that he was Phi Beta Kappa at Princeton, but that these were the only things that I knew he had ever "joined".

He didn't seem to know much about me and the reason for my paraplegia. He asked several hesitant questions about it, and I told him it was as a result of an auto accident. He asked if that was what prompted Ralph to write the book, and I said I didn't think so because he had been interested in the subject as early as 1958, as I had explained to him already. He asked if my injury was a result of unsafe design, and I told him that I thought it was, due to the fact that the doors of my car came open and I was therefore thrown out of the car, and I wouldn't have been if the doors had remained closed, or if I had been restrained by a seat belt. He asked the make of car, and I told him. He asked where the accident occurred, and I told him. I told him I had most likely fallen asleep at the wheel, and he said the same thing had almost happened to him the other day, and wasn't I aware that I was sleepy before it happened? I said I couldn't recall any dozing off. I mentioned how I stopped for gas in Chelmsford, and I then turned off the radio, and advised him to keep his radio playing if he felt the least bit tired, as highways have a hypnotic effect on drivers.

He ended the interview after 20 to 30 minutes by standing up and asking a few questions about United Life. Like how we don't do business in New York, and how we'll need more office space soon, etc. Then he said he didn't know what kind of offer his client was going to make to Ralph, but he was sure it would be a good one.

He asked also when Ralph had met Senator Ribicoff. He asked if this was right after Law School when Ralph returned to Connecticut to practice. I said I didn't know that Ralph even knew Senator Ribicoff, although I had supposed that he probably did now, after having testified before his committee. He seemed quite disappointed that I did not know when Ralph had met Senator Ribicoff, and pursued the question from several different angles before dropping it. I got the idea that the circumstances of Ralph's acquaintance with Senator Ribicoff was quite important to him for some reason. His disappointment that I had no knowledge on the subject was written all over his face.

When he stated that Ralph is Syrian, I said I thought this was wrong, that he is Lebanese. He said: "Well, It's about the same thing. We just want to know if there is any anti-Semitic feeling there", or words of that nature. He asked if my accident was the reason that Ralph dedicated the book to me, and I stated that I thought so, *inter alia.*

He mentioned at the end of the interview that at first Mr. Warren was going to come up and see me, but he figured he would come himself, since he was in Cambridge anyway visiting his son. I figured at the time that this was an attempt to explain away the elusive Mr. Warren.

I believe that this covers all the important points.

Testimony of Frank Winchell, Chief Engineer for Research and Development, Chevrolet Motor Division of General Motors Corp., Before the Michigan Senate Committee on Highways, February 21, 1966, Concerning Michigan State Senate Bill 773

Mr. Winchell: In order to assist the Committee in assessing Bill 773, I believe it would be helpful to first describe briefly the essential elements that affect the behavior of a motor vehicle, the design characteristics of the 1960–63 Corvair which have been claimed to be wrong and the evidence we presented in the two trials to refute these claims.

In the most general terms, the CONTROLLABILITY of a vehicle must relate to the degree of difficulty experienced by the driver in putting the vehicle in the required position on the road at the required time—*consistently.*

There are three inseparable and essential elements in the behavior of a car in motion—the car, the driver, and the road. The system is no better than its weakest link. The particulars of the car and path are certainly of utmost importance. The driver, however, is the key link. Vehicle and highway engineers continually seek to maximize the adaptability of the vehicle and highway to the driver. However, until the vehicle can be taken out of his hands, the driver remains the most unpredictable variable in the system; especially when distracted and/or in emergency situations where he has had no training. Likewise, variations of the roadway and general environmental conditions are almost infinite. It is impossible to predict how, where and under what circumstances all the cars will be driven in the course of their lifetime and why, on occasion, the system fails.

Two of the three links—the road and the driver—are essentially indeterminates and outside the influence of the vehicle engineer. Further, the driver is much more of an indeterminate in a personal transportation system than the highly trained operator in commercial air, rail and water systems. The automobile traffic problem is further complicated by a high vehicle density level and inplane relative velocity due to intersections and two-way traffic. However, the evolution of the automobile from the low speed low density horse and buggy days has allowed the engineer to examine the nature or characteristics of vehicles already successful in the hands of the motorists so that even though he cannot know all about how it will be used or where it will be used, he can assume that if it performs as well as or better than the previous model it is satisfactory. Much of our testing, therefore, is comparative; acceptability is based on comparison with successful vehicles in use by the motorist on public road systems.

We also try to measure the vehicle's important characteristics so that we can quantitatively define it. This is a difficult task. In the course of this effort, the layman may be misguided and confused in the interpretation of engineering terms and their significance.

Before proceeding further, let me mention some of the important terms in vehicle control:

> Oversteer/understeer
> Stability/instability
> Response
> Damping

These are control characteristics. They are not control. They are not separable quantities. Individually, they are neither good nor bad. What is important is their relationship to each other; the degree to which they exist and how and where they are manifested.

For example, a very high degree of vehicle understeer may be more or less controllable than an equivalent degree of oversteer. A very high degree of vehicle stability may be more or less controllable than an equivalent degree of instability. Too fast or too slow response may well cause a vehicle to be uncontrollable. The same is true of damping. There are infinite combinations of these characteristics which result in individual behavior of the vehicle.

An oversteering car at the limit of control is inclined to turn sharper than intended and, if unattended, may spin.

An understeering car at the limit of control is inclined to turn wider than intended and cannot be turned in.

A stable car is one that seeks some kind of equilibrium. For example, a pendulum is a stable system. If disturbed, it will eventually seek equilibrium (come to rest). The fact that it may take a long time and that it oscillates in the process does not alter the fact that it is considered stable. An inverted pendulum is unstable. Disturbed, it will fall at an increasing rate until it is restrained by some external force. Stability and controllability are not the same. A bicycle is unstable. A rider and bicycle in motion is a stable system. The unstable bicycle in this system is controllable.

Control engineers generally speak of Stability in two ways:

ATTITUDE STABILITY AND PATH STABILITY

Attitude Stability means that the vehicle (in time) seeks out an equilibrium attitude (angle) with respect to its path. The path may lead anywhere; on or off the road or into oncoming traffic. It may oscillate in yaw, but as long as the oscillations diminish with time, it is considered to be a stable system. Path Stability means that the vehicle (in time) seeks out a prescribed path. Path Stability cannot be achieved without a driver or path seeking control (autopilot, for example).

Camber Angle is the angle of the plane of the wheel with respect to the vertical. Positive camber is when the top of the plane of the wheel is inclined outward. Forces resulting from camber are consequent to the angle of the tire with respect to the road.

Lateral Acceleration is a term used in describing the "severity" of turning. Anybody moving in a curved path will experience side forces. This lateral force is a function of both speed and radius of curvature. The lateral force divided by the weight of the body is called lateral acceleration. Otherwise stated, the lateral acceleration equals the square of the speed (in miles per hour) divided by 15 times the radius of the curvature in feet or $\frac{V^2}{15R}$. This formula simply states mathematically what is common knowledge: that the faster you go in any given turn, the higher the lateral acceleration.

The Corvair differs from other cars only in the arrangement of its components. That arrangement, however, is accepted practice in other independent rear suspension cars, such as Volkswagen, Renault, Fiat, Porsche, etc. Because of the rear engine location, a swing axle rear suspension layout was used, which has and continues to have, great precedent in application to rear engine, independent rear suspension cars. This was the most reliable and widely used independent rear suspension known at the time.

The principal expert used by the plaintiffs in the two trials— Professor Manos—concluded that the 1960–1963 Corvairs are "very well behaved" up to approximately .6g and that above this point, they are essentially uncontrollable. We agree.

However, we disagree strongly as to *the significance of this behavior* and *to what causes it.* The latter is important because we were accused of ignoring elementary mechanisms alleged to eliminate the characteristics.

The significance of this .6g lateral acceleration can be realized only if the following is understood:

(*a*) .6g is the upper limit of control for all American passenger cars of that date.

(*b*) As stated in the American Association of State Highway Officials Publication ("A Policy on Geometric Design of Rural Highways"), the standards by which roads and highways are designed and posted call for not more than approximately 0.3g lateral acceleration at 15 mph and approximately 0.11g at 80 mph.

(c) Highway authorities state that 95% of all drivers' habits are below these standards. The AASHO manual (page 130) states that one criterion in highway design "is the point at which the centrifugal force causes the driver to recognize a *feeling of discomfort and instinctively acts—barring recklessness—to avoid higher speed."* Their instruments indicate "side friction factors (lateral acceleration) .21 for speeds below 20 mph, .18 for speeds of 25 and 30 mph, and .15 for speeds of 35 and higher."

(*d*) Our experience is that in the emergency situation few motorists have the capacity to control any car on public roads at much in excess of .3g at 30 mph and .2g at 60 mph.

The plaintiffs and their experts at the two trials charged that loss of control (at .6g) is caused by so-called "tuck-under" of the outside rear wheel, and that we were negligent in the design of a suspension which allegedly produces this phenomenon.

Our tests prove that up to and including 0.6g the outside rear wheel does not "tuck under." On the contrary, the suspension is compressed. This is demonstrated in a movie of tests made on our skid pad. Color photographs blown up from that movie clearly show that the suspension is still in compression at 0.6g lateral acceleration. Even at 0.75g's lateral acceleration, the suspension has dropped only approximately one degree below its position in a normal straight ahead course. So-called "tuck-under" does not occur until the car is well beyond the limits of control. Tests show that the outside wheel does not go into complete extension until the car is essentially sideways and the lateral acceleration is in excess of .9g.

Photographs of tire distortions with a car sliding sideways will show no significant difference between the proximity of the rim to the pavement of the Corvair and any other automobile. Any car striking a curb, an embankment or similar obstructions with sufficient force and energy will roll over. Any car sideways, on or off the road, is in serious difficulty. Sliding off the pavement sideways will almost certainly result in a collision with an embankment, some other object, or in rollover with any car.

Further, the so-called *"tuck-under"* has no influence on the limit of control of the vehicle. We demonstrated at the trials that oversteer and understeer arise from the inherent characteristics of all tires. The ultimate oversteer characteristics of the car are due to transition from linear to non-linear elastic properties of pneumatic tires at extremely high lateral accelerations.

Tire pressure has also been criticized as contributing to instability of the Corvair. Tire experts would agree that failure to maintain the optimum or recommended tire pressures in any vehicle may result in some degree of oversteer or understeer and some change in stability. However, even reversing the tire pressure differential is unrecognizable at 30 to 40 mph in a Corvair. The effect becomes noticeable as the speed increases, but it does not render the car uncontrollable. The pressures selected for the Corvair were the best choice for satisfaction and value to the customer in control, tread life and ride.

The plaintiffs in the two cases claimed that the so-called *Empi camber compensator,* (sold as an accessory by a west coast company) was effective in reducing the so-called "tuck-under' and oversteer characteristics. Photographic negatives were made of the same car in an identical position with and without the Empi compensator. It is visible in these negatives, when overlaid, that the camber compensator does not alter the camber of the rear wheels of the Corvair. This accessory was tested by Chevrolet and the tests showed that there was no significant effect from this accessory in cornering and, in fact, that the installation resulted in a "measurable" increase in oversteer. Professional drivers operating the Corvair on the skid pad, with and without the camber compensator, recognize no significant results.

The suspension change introduced by Corvair on the 1964 model, while part of it looked like the Empi device, was accompanied by a reduction in rear spring rate, increased front spring rate, and the addition of a front stabilizer bar. These changes did not alter the full rebound control arm angle of the rear wheels. They did transfer more of the roll couple to the front wheels and, thus, transfer more cornering force to the outside front wheel. All of this was in an attempt to extend the limit of control as a step in the normal process of product improvement. This was achieved. The limit of control was increased to approximately 0.7g lateral acceleration with terminal neutral steer. The changes made in the 1965 suspension were for the purpose of improving ride, while at the same time, maintaining the control characteristics and higher limits achieved in 1964. The '64 and '65 changes to the Corvair had no significant effect from 0 to 0.6g's. Engineers have and will continue to increase the range of control as the *practicability* of the art is established. Extending this limit beyond the capability of the drivers cannot and should not be done at the sacrifice of value to the customer. It is desirable that a planned program for the extension of driver capability parallel the development in extended vehicle and highway capability.

The contention made by plaintiffs' experts that the instinctive and natural reaction of the driver to oversteer is *wrong,* and for understeer *right,* is incorrect. In reality, exactly the opposite is true. For example, if an *understeering* car is taken into a right turn at the limit of controllability, the car will tend to generate a larger radius putting the driver left of his intended path. His natural reaction is to turn the steering wheel farther to the right. This action further reduces the cornering power of the front wheels causing the car to generate an even larger radius. A "non-professional" will invariably turn the wheel as far as it will go, while the car continues to slide off to the left. This is why most expert drivers say that an understeering car plowing off the road is the most disconcerting characteristic of all. If he cannot reduce speed fast enough to make the relationship between his velocity and radius compatible with his intended path, he will go off the road, and there is nothing that he can do about it.

The *oversteering car,* on the other hand, taken into the same curve at the same speed, having the same limit of control, will tend to steer to the right or to the inside of the curve. The natural reaction of the driver is to steer left. The car will respond to a left turn. The driver will not be able to stay within the desired path, but if he chooses and if he has the skill, he can steer it off the left side of the road or allow it to spin out. It is true that the driver must be alert and skillful in order to direct the car off on the left. However, no amount of skill will bring the understeering car to the inside in the equivalent situation. Both vehicles can be slowed at the same rate. If the speed is not excessive, a skillful driver can bring either car into the desired path. In brief, the understeering car has more cornering potential in the rear than in the front. The oversteering car has more cornering potential in the front than in the rear. A skillful driver of that car can reduce the cornering of the front tires with the steering wheel. Since the rear wheels are not steerable, the driver of an understeering car does not have the opportunity of reducing the cornering power of the rear wheels.

In summary, plaintiffs' experts conceded that the Corvair behaves well up to 0.6g lateral acceleration. This lateral acceleration is the upper limit of controllability for all passenger cars of the same period. The Corvair's capabilities are greater than the capabilities of their drivers and the highways on which they are driven.

Now with specific reference to Senate Bill 773, I would like to make the following comments:

It should be noted that Section C of the bill imposes a standard of .75g lateral acceleration whereas Section B requires .70g. Since both sections are effective on the same date, the standard proposed in the bill must be assumed to be .75g.

In order for .75g lateral acceleration to have any effect on the safety of vehicles, "directional instability" referred to in the bill must mean controllability. If the bill is truly intended to rule off the roads of Michigan all cars that are not controllable up to .75g's, then after January 1, 1970, the state highways would be bare of all cars built to date because none of the passenger cars made in the world during the sixty-five year history of the motor vehicle business would qualify. All cars except race cars are uncontrollable at some point below .75g's.

If, on the other hand, this statute deals with mathematical instability occurring at less than .75g's, then the bill is intended to deal with theoretical concepts which have no necessary or true relation to automotive safety. A vehicle may be mathematically stable through its entire range of lateral acceleration but, nevertheless, be uncontrollable at a relatively low lateral acceleration of say .3g and not fall within the proscription of this bill. Therefore, the stability characteristics of a vehicle are not sufficient criteria to describe minimum standards of control.

A minimum standard of .75g's would be useless. It can be demonstrated that only the most experienced enthusiast or professional driver has the composure, training, courage and skill to control a vehicle anywhere near .75g's.

A minimum standard for lateral acceleration is not sufficient to define the division between safe and unsafe handling cars. Many additional facts must be considered. A car having a high capability in lateral acceleration may be completely inadequate in the transitional phase of entering or leaving a curve, or in an S maneuver, or in passing, or in turning while braking or accelerating, or on low coefficient pavements.

INDEX

THIS BOOK WAS DESIGNED BY BERNARD SCHLEIFER,

THE TYPE FACE USED IS TIMES ROMAN

AND THE BOOKS WERE COMPOSED BY ELECTRA COMPOSITION CORP.

AND PRINTED AND BOUND BY THE BOOK PRESS, BRATTLEBORO, VERMONT